PEOPLE aNd ME

ROBERT A. CARTER
Coordinator of Social Studies
and Foreign Languages
Midland, Texas

GENE E. ROOZE
Professor of Education
Texas Tech University

ERMA UNDERWOOD
Researcher and Photographer
Midland, Texas

HERMAN F. BENTHUL
Adjunct Professor
East Texas State University

JOAN LOWERY NIXON
Author of Children's Books
Houston, Texas

LOIS G. ROGGE
Coordinator of Elementary
English Language Program
Midland, Texas

CONSULTANTS

Lewis M. Abernathy
Associate Professor of Economics
and Director of Manpower Institute
North Texas State University

Martha Preston
Librarian
Goddard Junior High School
Midland, Texas

BENEFIC PRESS • **Westchester, Illinois**

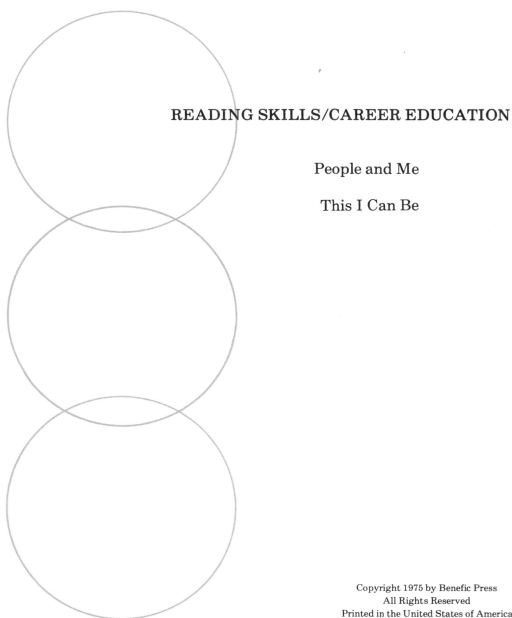

READING SKILLS/CAREER EDUCATION

People and Me

This I Can Be

Copyright 1975 by Benefic Press
All Rights Reserved
Printed in the United States of America
ISBN 0-8175-8740-3
Library of Congress 74-78154

Contents

flight of fancy

As a bird soars from tree to tree, so does the mind of the student fly from idea to idea, always exploring, always finding something new. Interests change, talents develop, and knowledge grows. As these changes take place the question arises: What do I want to be? As you learn about careers, let your imagination ride high—on a flight of fancy.

UNIT 1   FLIGHT OF FANCY

EXPLORING INTERESTS AND CAREERS

THINKING THINGS THROUGH

You are interested in something if you enjoy doing it. For example, swimming is an interest of many persons because they enjoy doing it. Also, many students like to do mathematics because they consider working problems to be fun. Maybe you never thought about your enjoyment of a sport or school subject as being related to a career. Exploring your interests now can help you someday reach a decision about your lifework.

The following article will show you how interests in one area can steer a person toward any number of careers. You will also see that having an interest when you are in your youth does not necessarily mean you will continue this interest when you are an adult.

ABOUT WORDS

Several of the following words are used in the article, "Exploring Interests and Careers."

career	job	vocation
profession	employment	trade
occupation	lifework	position

In what way are all of these words alike in meaning? In what ways do you find them to be different? Use a dictionary to help you find their differences.

9

INVESTIGATE

EXPLORING INTERESTS AND CAREERS

What Is A Career?

What is a career? A career is a chosen pursuit of lifework. Sometimes the word *career* is used in a broad sense to include skilled, professional, semiskilled, paraprofessional (not requiring a college degree), and technical work.

Like most people, you probably are more interested in some school subjects, sports, hobbies, or jobs than you are in others. It is also natural at your age to be interested in one occupation on one day, and on the following day to think that you would like to be in a different occupation. What is important to know is that you should consider all your interests when thinking about choosing a career because most school subjects or jobs will involve a combination of two or more interests.

A necessary thing to recognize about interests is that you may not have had sufficient opportunity to develop interests in all areas. Thus you may not know whether you really like something or dislike it. Consider these three examples:

Greg and Mark's family were not interested in music. They never went to a concert or even owned a record player. Neither boy played any kind of musical instrument. Unlike Mark, however, Greg was an avid reader of biographies of great musicians, and he really enjoyed the musical programs at the senior high school which he attended. He even dreamed of becoming a great symphony conductor one day.

Marcia had played the violin since she was five years old. Now in junior high, she was a member of the school symphony orchestra. For as long as she could remember, she had always been surrounded by music.

10

It should not be difficult to see that Greg and Marcia are both interested in music, but their interests and abilities are different. Mark's musical interest may not yet be developed because he has not had enough experience with music. If a relationship between Greg and Marcia's and Mark's interests to possible musical careers were to be explored, these questions might come to mind:

1. Looking at Greg and Marcia's interests and abilities, which one is the more likely to realize an actual career in a symphony orchestra? Why?

2. Even though Greg and Mark do not play a musical instrument, could they have a career in music?

3. From knowing Marcia, Mark, and Greg's interests, could you tell what their careers will be?

Marcia is the one most likely to have a career in music as a member of a symphony orchestra. Most professional musicians began studying an instrument at an early age. Conductors of orchestras usually know how to play at least one musical instrument. The fact that Greg is in senior high school and has not yet learned to

11

play a musical instrument makes it unlikely that he could ever become the conductor of an orchestra.

Abilities Count

It is not possible to predict accurately the future career of a person from knowing only his interests. A knowledge of your interests can tell you only what you enjoy doing. It will not tell you how well you do these things. How well you do something depends upon your abilities and your experiences.

To point out the pitfall of jumping too quickly from interests to a relationship to

career choices, let's imagine a visit to Greg, Mark, and Marcia ten years after each has finished high school.

Greg is married now with a three-year-old son. Greg works as a carpenter for a construction firm. He likes telling his son all about the great composer, Beethoven. Someday he hopes his son will become a fine musician.

Marcia is a dental technician. She enjoys playing the violin in musical productions at the local theater.

It gives her a change from the dental laboratory and helps broaden her interests in life.

After graduation from college with a degree in journalism, Mark is working for a newspaper in a small city. Since Mark became interested in music when he was in college, his editor had assigned him the job of reviewing local musical events.

The experiences of these three young people indicate another thing to remember about interests. As you grow older and have a variety of experiences, some of your earlier interests may change and later some new ones may develop. Often a person will have several careers during his lifetime because of his changing interests.

Activities And Development Of Interests

Your activities in school and after school are important in the development of your interests. Such activities as debating, selling tickets for a school affair, or selling advertising space for a yearbook or the school paper can lead to the formation of persuasive interests. The opportunity for careers in many areas is available to those people who can convince others of the justice of a cause or a point of view. Salesmen, lawyers, teachers, persons in advertising, personnel managers, and buyers are just a few of the

people who must possess persuasive interests in order to be successful in their chosen fields of work.

So important are school activities to the formation of our personalities that most colleges and many employers ask prospective students and employees what interests they had in school. Of course, there are many opportunities for development of interests outside of school. For example, within the Girl Scouts, Boy Scouts, community centers, some church groups, and civic organizations, young people may find out what they enjoy doing. There are also volunteer opportunities at hospitals and youth camps, and within the community itself to increase one's chances of finding out what is a worthwhile interest. Part-time work such as newspaper delivery, babysitting, or taking care of someone's yard, are ways to explore your interests.

One way of grouping interests and some related careers is as follows:

Outdoor	Recreation, forestry National Park Service
Mechanical	Automobile worker, welder, plumber, carpenter
Computational	Mathematician, computer operator, card-puncher
Scientific	Scientist, underwater archeologist, doctor
Persuasive	Lawyer, salesman minister, teacher
Artistic	Dancer, artist, sculptor
Literary	Writer, poet, proof-reader, newspaperman
Musical	Musician, teacher, singer
Social Service	Social worker, hospital attendant
Clerical	Secretary, salesclerk, accountant

Another way to group interests is according to occupations or jobs, as you can see on the chart. That kind of grouping might be:

Professional and Related
   Occupations
Managerial
Clerical
Sales—Wholesale
   and Retail
Services
Skilled Trades
Agriculture
Mining
Construction
Manufacturing
Transportation, Communication, and Public
   Utilities
Finance, Insurance,
   and Real Estate
Fine Arts
   and Humanities
Government—City,
   State, and National
Unskilled Trades

Where Can You Go For Advice?

Your counselor or teacher can help you discover the relationship of your abilities to your interests. These individuals can help you to decide possible school subjects to take and to choose available useful school activities. They can also suggest part-time work you might consider. The librarian can help you find books appropriate to your interests. Many persons within the community, such as church leaders, leaders of youth organizations, etc., stand ready to assist you in developing your interests. They would welcome the opportunity to help you if you request their assistance with decisions.

The more interested you are in anything you do, the greater chance you will have for success. It is certainly easier and more enjoyable to do things that we like. Sometimes, though, we have to do things we dislike. Exploring your interests will help you direct your activities into channels where you are more likely to achieve satisfaction. By knowing your interests better, you may find out some things that appeal to you even in chores that you have always disliked. Opportunities are everywhere for developing your own personal interests.

CHECKING PROGRESS

Did you discover the main idea of the selection you have just read? If you are not sure, skim through the selection again using the suggestions below.

(1) Skim through the paragraphs one at a time and decide on the main topic of each paragraph.

(2) State the main topic of each paragraph in one word or phrase.

(3) Take a quick look at all the paragraph topics and decide on the one topic which is the same for most of the paragraphs. This is the main topic of the selection.

(4) Decide on the one most important idea these paragraphs are giving you about the topic.

The one most important idea all of the paragraphs together give you about the topic of the selection is the main idea of the selection. After using the suggestions above, state the main idea of "Exploring Interests and Careers" in one sentence using your own words.

CHOOSING NEXT STEPS

Have you ever thought about exploring your interests by taking an interest inventory? An inventory is a detailed list of articles or possessions. Have you ever thought of your interests as being important possessions? Your interests now may determine many of your future choices. Try taking an inventory of your interests and from them predicting how they may affect your future.

THE DREAMER'S INCREASE

THINKING THINGS THROUGH

Sometimes a story or a biography may begin with action. The action invites you into the story or biography. It may also tell you something about the people in the story. This biography has that kind of beginning.

Why would a biography begin with a dream? Why might dreams be very important in the life of the person the biography tells about?

Some people believe that certain dreams foretell the future. Do you think a person may get an idea in a dream that can be turned into a reality if they work to make it come true? As you read the biography, look for ways that dreams affected this man's life. Find ways that his dreams have helped him and ways that dreams may have hurt him. Try to decide why it was given the title, "The Dreamer's Increase."

ABOUT WORDS

The use of *context*, or words and sentences before and after a word, helps you find out the meaning of a word you do not understand. The sentences below are taken from the story you will read. One word in each sentence which may not be familiar to you is shown in italic type. Read the context around the italicized word carefully, then choose the meaning from the list of word meanings.

He was not sure whether he was *haunted* by a dream or a happening.

An *apprentice* worked for and with the master and learned from him.

He arranged court shows and *pageants*.

He showed *mortars* and other engines he invented.

1. A public drama or procession in costume
2. A cannon used to fire shells high into the air
3. A person who works to learn a trade or an art
4. To visit in the form of a ghost

17

The DREAMER'S INCREASE

A long beak pointed down at the boy. Two mighty wings spread out from the big bill. The fan of a tail stirred the air and a shadow hid the sun. It was a dream of a great bird.

This is the way the man remembered it years later. He was not sure whether he was haunted by a dream or a happening. It was a day when dreams were thought of as warnings.

The dream of childhood became the dream of the man thirty years later. The bird of the dream was not the drawing of a mechanical bird. It was an invention.

The wing-flapping flying machine never did work very well. The plan of the machine-bird pointed the way though. It was the basis of the modern airplane.

A man of big dreams and high aims started it all. He was Leonardo da Vinci.

Leonardo was born in the village of Vinci in Italy on April 15, 1452. Little is known of his boyhood. He spent most of the time in the home of his grandparents.

At age fifteen Leonardo went to Florence to study art with a great master, Verocchio. To learn a trade or an art in those days a person would become an *apprentice* to a master. An apprentice worked for and with the master and learned from him.

In his early twenties Leonardo himself became a master. He stayed on with Verrocchio for four more years. They worked much together. The young master soon was doing better painting than the old master. Still Leonardo was not able to get needed support from the wealthy leaders of Florence. At about thirty years of age he left Florence, feeling rejected by the people in his hometown.

He went to Milan. From 1482 to 1499 he was in the service there of the ruler, Ludivoco Sforza, who was called Il Moro, "The Moor."

Leonardo had presented himself as a military engineer who could build bridges and make machines. He showed mortars and other engines that he had invented. He showed the Moor he could paint pictures and do architecture and sculpture.

The Moor employed Leonardo to do much artwork. Here in Milan the growing genius built the clay model for a bronze statue of Il Moro's father on a horse. He was architect for several cathedrals. He did some work as military engineer. He wrote many notes and drew stacks of sketches. Here, too, he painted the great picture, "Last Supper."

Leonardo was never pleased with his art. He studied his subject so much and gained so many ideas and wanted his art to be so perfect that he could hardly finish a project.

In 1499 Il Moro's rule failed. The French army took Milan. Leonardo left.

For a while, the displaced artist was architect and engineer in central Italy. He was in Mantua and Venice.

Now fifty years old, Leonardo returned to Florence. During the twenty years away he had become famous. Now he was to undertake the biggest projects of his career. One was scientific. He would redirect the course of the Arno River so boats could come into Florence. The other was artistic. He would paint a military scene for a great palace, the center of court. He never completed either project, but his drawings for the projects lifted both engineering and painting to new and exciting heights.

In 1506 he went to Milan and won favor with the French rulers. He wrote notes there and painted small pictures.

In 1513 he went to Rome, where Michelangelo and Raphael, other Italian greats, were at the peaks of their careers. Leonardo was growing old and restless. He could not settle down in Rome.

He went to Cloux, France, in 1517. There he continued to write and draw. He also worked on a canal project and arranged court shows and pageants. He died there in 1519.

Leonardo had carried to France one of his great portraits, "Mona Lisa." It was Leonardo's habit to turn from his contracted projects and paint what he wished. "Mona Lisa" was painted this way, probably in Florence. This is a portrait of a friend's wife. The portrait shows how the upper part of a person can be painted to advantage. It now hangs in Paris, in the Louvre Gallery.

Leonardo's major paintings are few. The few are so unusual, however, that they are headliners wherever they are shown. Several of his best known paintings are in the Louvre in Paris. Others are in Florence and Milan. At least one hangs in each of the following cities: Madrid, Spain; London, England; Leningrad, U.S.S.R.; Munich, Germany; Washington, D.C.; and Detroit, Michigan.

Leonardo filled thousands of pages with notes and drawings on art, nature, mathematics, botany, anatomy, engineering, architecture, and related subjects. Included in his notes and drawings are plans for his great paintings and inventions. Many drawings are final pictures in their own right. He especially liked to draw horses, dogs, and people. Most of his notes and drawings are in the Ambrosiana Library in Milan, Italy, and Windsor Castle in England.

See in Leonardo da Vinci's art the closeness of man to all nature. His landscapes were not just backdrops. His people were not just objects on the landscape. The settings and the persons belonged to each other. They blended as one.

Find in his paintings the scientist as artist. He knew the nature of light and shadow and showed new ways to use both in pictures. He knew anatomy and so was able to picture movements of bodies, smiles, hands, and lines of grace with meaning. By knowing the motion of water he brought the swirl of the curl to art. He brought mathematics to art, thus making his spaces exactly right. Because he knew the make-up of atmosphere, he created the mist effect with oils.

He was the searcher, the inquirer. He went straight to first-hand sources to find out. He was a close observer. He had super vision. He carried his sketch pad with him wherever he went and studied every detail of whatever he wished to picture. He made exact plans.

Even as a genius, known now as one of the greatest of all wonder workers for man, he had his problems. He was not from an art family. He had little chance to learn early from others in the arts and sciences he loved. He was a left-handed mirror writer, which was a handicap in his day. His great talent was not rewarded by proper patrons in his hometown. Jealous persons tried to ruin him. He was cramped by the styles of the day.

He had a fancy—a dream. He did something about it. All around us we see the increase as other dreamers and doers build upon his ideas and models.

CHECKING PROGRESS

1. Were dreams important to Leonardo da Vinci? What reasons do you have for your answer?
2. Why did Leonardo leave Milan when Moro's rule failed?
3. Why were the Florence projects important though they were not finished?
4. What were three things about Leonardo that helped him make a contribution?
5. How did Leonardo use his knowledge of many subjects in his art work?
6. What obstacles did da Vinci overcome to achieve success and fame?
7. What message do the happenings of Leonardo's life give to people who live today?
8. Why would the need to do things perfectly take Leonardo da Vinci from one project to another?
9. To what fields of work did Leonardo's work contribute?

CHOOSING NEXT STEPS

You may want to start an individual vocabulary-building program. Many people have a plan for word study. Some learn thousands of new words each year as they study.

A good way to keep track of the words you are learning is to put each new word you learn on a card. You can look the word up in the dictionary and show its pronunciation and a simple definition on the card. Some people like to write a sentence or two using the word on the card, too.

Word cards can be put in a box in alphabetical order. This makes it easy to find the word when you want to review it.

When you study a new subject, you have a good opportunity to add words to your vocabulary. The words you learn will be helpful to you in other areas of study, too.

You may think of other ideas for your own word study plan. Make your plan in the best way to fit your needs.

THE ACTRESS

THINKING THINGS THROUGH

When you read a story about people, do you study each character and try to find out what each person is like? As you read the story, "The Actress," you will find it interesting to learn about the actions, feelings, and thoughts of each of the characters.

Every story has one or more *main characters*. The main character can be identified easily because the story is about something that happened to that person. The other characters in the story are called *minor characters*.

You will learn more about the actions, the feelings, and the thoughts of the characters in a story if you ask yourself questions about them as you read. Ask yourself these questions about one of the characters in this story.

1. Would I like to have this person for a friend? What reason do I have?
2. What would I do if I were in the same situation? How would I feel?
3. Why did this person do or say what he did?

ABOUT WORDS

This story is about a girl who wants to be an actress. The words listed below are some of the special words in the story related to that career. The numbers show the page on which each word first appears.

play 25	actresses 26	line 29
scene 25	stage fright 26	rehearsals 29
part 25	drama 26	props 29
acting 26	curtain 27	footlights 30
stage 26	character 27	audience 30
actors 26	role 28	

INVESTIGATE

THE ACTRESS

Jan Andrews fastened the last button on her youngest sister's blouse. "There you are," she said.

"Jan's going to take me to the park," Debbie said.

"Good," their mother said. "When you do, Jan, take Alice, too." She smiled at Debbie. "Oh, Jan, Debbie really has the good looks in the family, hasn't she?"

Jan had to agree. Little Debbie's blond hair had just the right amount of curl. Her eyes were like their mother's eyes, a clear, perfect blue. Jan threw a quick glance in the wall mirror behind her. Her own eyes sometimes seemed green, sometimes light brown. Her hair, a dull brown color, hung straight on both sides of her small face.

"Before you go, Jan," Mrs. Andrews said, "I'd like to talk to you about those career books you brought home from school yesterday. Your father and I were talking about it last night, and we think you should give some thought to a career in nursing. You have always been such a quiet child. Nursing is a fine job and should suit someone like you."

"Someone like me?" Jan thought. "Maybe Mother sees what kind of a person I am. I wish I did."

Debbie pulled at Jan's hand. "Come on!" she said.

"Don't forget Alice," their mother said.

Jan found Alice in the kitchen, busy with crayons and a coloring book. "Want to go to the park?" asked Jan.

Alice didn't look up. "Wait until I finish this page." Jan turned, Debbie's hand in hers. "We're going to the park *now*. You can either come with us or stay home."

Jan ignored Alice's grumbling as she led the way from the house. She stopped to pick up her English literature book on the way. While her sisters played on the slide and swings,

Jan hoped to find a shady spot under a tree and read the assignment that was due Monday.

It was just a few blocks to the park, and Jan did as she had planned. It was a scene from a play in the book. The play was about a girl Jan understood. The girl named Lily was quiet and shy, like Jan. There were so many things about life she didn't understand, like Jan. And there was a feeling she had deep inside, that she had to find out who she really was, and what she really was like, because something good and happy and right waited for her. She only had to reach out and take it, when she knew what it was.

On Monday, when she came into her sixth period English class, she said to Mrs. Foster: "I liked that play. I guess I liked it because I feel the same way Lily felt..."

The bell rang, and the students hurried to their seats.

"We're going to do something new today," Mrs. Foster told the class. "I want some of you to come up and bring your books with you. We're going to read the scene."

She looked about the room. "I'm going to ask Norman to read the part of Jason and Dotty to read Anne."

She smiled at Jan. "Jan will read the part of Lily."

"But..." Jan began.

Mrs. Foster interrupted her, "You can do it."

Jan took her book and joined the others in front of the class. She was frightened to be here with everyone staring at her. She knew that when she opened her mouth, nothing would come out.

But as she began to read the lines, she forgot about the class and the schoolroom with its smell of chalk and newly scrubbed floor. She spoke as Lily, and she felt as Lily, until the scene was over. For an instant she stood there, surprised to find herself back in the classroom.

Someone in the class said, "Hey, Jan's pretty good!" Mrs. Foster smiled at her. "She is indeed. Jan, I'd like to talk to you for a few minutes after class, if you don't have to leave for home immediately."

After the bell had rung, Mrs. Foster said to Jan, "This year our junior high school is going to enter the district speech and drama festival. I discovered something wonderful this afternoon, Jan. I discovered you have a great deal of acting talent. I'm asking you to memorize the part and act out the scene when we enter the festival."

Jan gasped. "Oh, I'd never be able to act on a stage!"

"You don't know you can't, because you've never tried," Mrs. Foster said. "Most actors and actresses feel moments of fear before they go on stage, even though they've been acting for years. It's called stage fright."

"Then why do they do it?"

"Because they are giving something of themselves when they act a role," Mrs. Foster answered. "They are giving their talents to the people in the audience, to make their lives a little happier, a little more interesting for the time in which they are watching the play."

Mrs. Foster shook her head. "You weren't Jan Andrews a short while ago. You were Lily, and you were giving Lily to the class. Isn't that right?"

26

"Yes," Jan said, "but on stage it would be different."

"Tonight the college drama department is putting on this play," Mrs. Foster said. "I'd like to take you to see it. Would you be able to go, if I picked you up at seven?"

Jan was so excited that her mother gave permission immediately. At dinner Jan couldn't wait to tell her father.

"Is that what all the excitement is about?" he asked.

Jan nodded. "Our school is going to enter the drama tournament," she said. "Mrs. Foster wants us to act a scene from this play. She wants me to play the main part."

"You?" Her mother looked shocked. "I mean, I never quite thought of you as an actress, Jan. Maybe if you could do something with your hair . . ."

"Its just a little school thing," her father said. "You could hardly call Jan an actress for taking part in something like that."

"Jan isn't pretty," Alice said. "Actresses are pretty."

"Not always," Mrs. Andrews said. "But from what I have read, I think that people who act are outgoing people. I've never heard of a shy, quiet actress. I wonder why Mrs. Foster chose Jan for the part."

Jan bent over her dinner plate, picking at her food with her fork, as Alice began talking about something else, and the conversation shifted.

In an hour Mrs. Foster arrived and they drove to the college. They took seats near the front. Jan found it hard to breathe until the lights went out and the curtain rose.

A tall slender girl was seated on a sofa near the center of the stage. She wasn't someone who would stand out in a crowd. She was dressed simply, and her long brown hair was pulled back from her face with a white ribbon.

As another character entered the stage, the tall girl rose gracefully and spoke, and she became Lily.

Jan was startled when the lights in the auditorium were turned on again, and she realized the play was over and the magic was over, too.

"Come and meet her," Mrs. Foster said. "She was one of my students when she was in junior high school."

She led the way backstage, where a group of people stood together laughing and talking. The girl who had played the part of Lily broke from the group when she saw Mrs. Foster and hugged her.

"You were wonderful!" Mrs. Foster said. She pulled Jan forward. "I'd like you to meet another talented young lady—Barbara James, Jan Andrews. Jan is going to be Lily in the district drama festival."

"I like the part of Lily," Barbara said, "because I feel the way she feels. I remember when I was your age, and I was wondering what I could possibly do in life, what direction I should take, and most of all—who I was."

"I feel like that, too," Jan said, "but I couldn't play the part the way you did."

"Of course you couldn't."

Jan looked surprised. Barbara went on, "Each actress gives something of herself to a role, so each one plays it a little differently. Your Lily won't be just like my Lily." She smiled. "If you like, I'd be glad to help you."

"Would you?" Jan asked. "Really? I'd love it!"

"I'm glad you've decided to do it," Mrs. Foster said.

Barbara nodded. "She has to do it, don't you, Jan? If you feel about Lily the way I do, you'll play the part."

A young couple hurried over to tell Barbara how much they had liked the play; so Mrs. Foster and Jan left. Jan couldn't remember ever being so happy.

During the next few weeks rehearsals became frantic, with lines forgotten, props lost, and one of the players out for a week because he had the flu. But Barbara was there, as she had promised. Her good humor made things seem better.

The day of the festival finally arrived.

"You won't get nervous and forget your lines, will you?" her mother asked, pulling at Jan's sleeves to even them.

"I won't get nervous," Jan said. Hearing her mother put into words the fear she herself had felt made Jan feel strange inside. What if she did forget her lines?

"I talked your father into coming to see the play," Mrs. Andrews said. "He wanted to play golf, but I told him it was probably the only time we'd see you in a play."

"I'm going to be in other plays," Jan said quietly. "I'm going to be an actress, Mother."

Mrs. Andrews turned from the mirror and fumbled on the bed for the handbag she had placed there. "Nonsense," she said. "You'll want a steady, sensible job like nursing when you're old enough to know what's really good for you."

Jan tried to make her mother understand. "There are lots of girls who would love to be nurses, but I'm not one of them. I wouldn't be happy doing work I didn't like."

Her mother just patted her shoulder and said, "Hurry, Jan, or you'll be late. And for goodness' sake, try not to be clumsy and trip over your feet on stage."

"Let's go," Jan said, putting down the hairbrush and getting to her feet. She was wishing she could stay home.

Jan left her family at the front door of the auditorium and walked to the stage door, wanting to cry. Suddenly she began to wonder what she was doing there. Her family was right. She had never acted before, and how did she know she could do it now? She was too tall and too clumsy, and not the least bit pretty. And suppose she forgot her lines?

She felt a hand on her shoulder. "Stage fright?" Barbara asked as she put her arm around Jan.

"I'm not an actress," Jan said, looking away. "Maybe I should never have started this."

Barbara turned Jan around, pulled her down to sit beside her on the steps, and gave her a handkerchief. "I thought you might feel the way I once felt, so I brought this handkerchief for you," she said.

"You? But you have acting talent," Jan said.

"So do you," Barbara said. "Do you think for a minute that Mrs. Foster and I would have encouraged you, if we didn't both see a spark within you? You have a real talent, Jan, and that talent can grow until it becomes great."

"But I'm clumsy, Barbara. I'm afraid that I . . ."

"Lily isn't clumsy. Lily is tall and graceful and knows how to move across a stage. Remember, while you are on that stage you are Lily, and you're going to be wonderful! Go on, Jan—they're waiting for you."

Jan took a deep breath and got to her feet. She held tightly to Barbara's hand. "I'll see you after the play!"

The performance from Jan's school was announced as being next on the program. Before she knew it she found herself on the stage. The footlights kept her from seeing the audience, but she could feel them there. The stage was empty, except for herself—Jan.

No, she thought. Not Jan—Lily.

The character named Jason came on stage, and Jan spoke. She was Lily now, and she moved through the scene as Lily.

She spoke the final words and stood silently for a moment, until the other cast members joined her on the stage.

The people in the audience clapped their hands loudly.

"You were great!" someone whispered in her ear. "We're going to win the trophy because of you, I know!"

Jan saw the faces of her parents. They looked a little surprised, a little confused.

"Jan, you were really good," Mr. Andrews said.

30

"And you were beautiful!" her mother said. "Jan, I didn't realize—you actually looked beautiful!"

"I don't think so," Alice said. No one paid attention.

Mrs. Foster greeted the Andrews family. "I hope Jan will go on with her interest in acting," she said.

"We had thought about Jan becoming a nurse someday—" Mr. Andrews said.

"Until we saw her act this afternoon," interrupted Mrs. Andrews. "Now we know that Jan understood something we didn't. She does have talent." Mrs. Andrews sighed. "I just wish that acting wasn't such a difficult life."

"Every career has its moments of joy. Jan has years to decide what she would like to do with her life."

Jan glanced back at the empty stage with happiness. She had found some of the inner self for which she was looking. Someday, after lots of hard work and practice and study, she was going to be an actress. She just knew it.

CHECKING PROGRESS

1. Name the main character and the minor characters in the story you have just read.
2. Explain your reasons for liking or disliking one of the characters in the story.
3. Describe one situation in the story. Tell what you would have done if you had been the character involved.
4. Choose one of the characters and tell how you think that person felt in a certain situation in the story. Example: How do you think Jan felt when this happened?

   "It's just a little school thing," her father said. "You could hardly call Jan an actress for taking part in something like that."

   "Jan isn't pretty," Alice said. "Actresses are pretty."

   "Not always," Mrs. Andrews said. "But from what I have read, I think that people who act are outgoing people. I've never heard of a shy, quiet actress. I wonder why Mrs. Foster chose Jan for the part."
5. Select a character and explain why you think that person said or did something in the story.

CHOOSING NEXT STEPS

If you are interested in learning about acting as a career or more about certain actors or actresses, you could do one or more of the following:

1. Select the biography of an actor or an actress in the library. Find out what this person did as a teenager. Did he or she have the same kind of experiences as those of a character's in the story "The Actress"?
2. Write to an actor or an actress and ask this person several questions about acting. Send a blank cassette tape with your letter and ask the actor or actress to answer your questions on tape.

HOORAY FOR DAN PARKER!

THINKING THINGS THROUGH

Imagination! You'll find Dan Parker has a lot of it. This story allows you to step into the future with Dan Parker as he thinks aloud about career choices.

When a character such as Dan Parker uses his imagination, he often thinks in extremes. On the pages listed you will find expressions such as:

Extreme phrases such as these help you discover that Dan Parker's imagination is at work again.

ABOUT WORDS

Sometimes an author uses *alliteration* in words in a story to build a mood. In alliteration the opening consonants are the same in several words used together. In this story the author uses alliteration in word combinations and in names. Here are some of the places alliteration is used and the page numbers on which it is found. For what reason do you think the author uses alliteration?

INVESTIGATE

HOORAY FOR DAN PARKER!

Danny Parker stared at the blank sheet of paper in front of him and sighed loudly.

Mrs. Jameson, his English teacher, suddenly got up from her desk and walked down the aisle to stand beside him. "What's the trouble?" she asked.

"We're supposed to write about some career we'd like to choose when we're adults, and I can't think of a thing," Danny told her.

Mrs. Jameson smiled. "Think about the subjects you are taking. See if your interests lead to a career."

She walked back to her desk, and Danny slumped in his seat, ready to try her suggestion. His first class was physical education. What would physical education lead to? What did he like best in physical education class? Basketball! What if he were to become a big star in basketball?

He could see the colosseum now. The band playing, the cheerleaders cheering, as the opposing team ran onto the floor. He, Daring Dan, began to rise from the bench on which he was sitting with the other members of his pro team, the Glorietta Good Guys.

"Who is that player on the other team who keeps giving me such angry looks?" Dan asked the coach.

"That's Mean Marvin Mahew," the coach said. "He has a bad reputation. You'll have to watch out for him. He's the star of his team, and he doesn't like anyone else to win."

"I'll be careful," Dan said.

"I have faith in you, Daring Dan," the coach said enthusiastically. "You have a fine sense of how to handle people, along with being the greatest basketball player this country has ever known."

34

The referees hurried out to the center of the court. Then the two coaches waved their players onto the floor.

"Don't think you're going to win this game," Mean Marvin said to Dan as he passed him. "I'm out to get you!"

The centers met and the ball was tipped. Down the court the players charged toward Dan and Marvin.

Dan was everywhere, blocking moves, intercepting passes, confusing the other team. The crowd cheered wildly.

Dan flung his hands up in front of an opposing player who was trying to make a basket. But suddenly a foot was in front of Dan's feet, and he found himself on the floor. Quickly the opposing team had the ball in the basket, with two points scored for their side.

No one had seen what had happened, Danny realized. Everyone had thought he had simply fallen. Everyone, that is, except that Mean Marvin Mahew!

"He won't get away with that again," Dan thought. But Dan, with all his skill and strength, was no match for Marvin's mean mind. Again and again he found himself on the gymnasium floor as the other team gained points.

At the half time the coach put a towel around the shoulders of the tired Dan and said, "This is terrible, Daring Dan! You keep falling over your own feet. Star or no star, I'm going to pull you out of the game!"

"Coach," Danny said anxiously, "let me stay in the game. Whatever has been happening won't happen again."

"Well, all right," the coach said. "The only reason I'm doing this is because your replacement is suffering from a bad case of dandruff. But believe me, Daring Dan, any more playing like you've been doing, and out you go!"

The referee blew the whistle, and Dan got to his feet.

The game began again. Once more the team members thundered down the court toward Dan and Marvin.

This time Dan kept one eye on the ball and one eye on Marvin. It gave him a slight headache, but he did it.

In a split second he intercepted the ball and sidestepped Marvin, who was closing in on him. Dan had the ball down the court and into the basket before Mean Marvin Mahew knew what had happened.

Again and again he scored, and Marvin's face became more and more angry. Without any warning Marvin leaped and grabbed the ball from the air, looking from player to player.

"Here, Marvin!" one of the players yelled. "Here!"

But Marvin said, "No!" and grinned at Dan.

For a moment Dan took one eye from the ball to glance at the clock. Two seconds to go, and the score tied! No wonder Mean Marvin wanted to hang onto the ball.

There was only one thing to do. With lightning speed Dan grabbed Mean Marvin, who was still holding tightly to the ball, and threw both Marvin and the ball into the basket. The scoreboard registered two points as the referee signaled the end of the game. They had won!

"How strong he is!" people were shouting.

"Daring Dan! Dan! Danny!" they cheered.

"Danny!" Mrs. Jameson was calling. "Get busy. You won't have time to write your essay if you keep daydreaming."

36

Danny straightened in his seat, listening to the scratching of pencils on paper, feeling the warmth of the sun as it streamed through the window. Maybe professional basketball wasn't the career for him. Maybe something else...

His next class was science. What if he were a scientist? What if he invented a wonderful, new medicine...maybe...

He entered a room in which fifteen men were seated around a large table. They looked eagerly at him.

"Tell us, Dr. Parker," the man nearest to him said. "You said you had an announcement to make to the press. You said it was about something the world has never known."

Dr. Dan Parker looked around the table at the reporters from the top newspapers and television networks in the United States. He said, "Gentlemen, once again I have done what no other scientist has been able to do."

"You've invented so many things," one of the reporters said. "Last year you gave us a formula that banned baldness, cured cuts, and kept people from topsy-turvy tummy."

"I've gone even farther this time," Dan said. He noticed the shifty eyes of the reporter sitting next to him. He was staring at Dan in a very strange way. He was also sitting on the edge of his chair as though ready to jump to his feet. Clearly there was something wrong here.

Dan reached into a case and brought out a bottle of clear liquid that was still bubbling hot. "One dose of this vaccine," he said, "will prevent all diseases known to man! With this medication there will be no more illness in the world!"

There was silence in the room as all the newsmen sat with their mouths open, trying to understand the importance of what Dr. Dan Parker had just said. But one of them jumped to his feet and pulled out a gun.

"I am not a news reporter," he cried. "I am Sneaky Samuel Sippy, secret spy!"

"I thought there was something suspicious about you," Dan said, as the others fell back in fear. "You have shifty eyes!"

"I know," he said. "I try to make them look shifty. A spy should have shifty eyes. Now, hand over that bottle."

"Why?" Dan asked.

"Because spies do not want everyone in the world to be healthy. When people are healthy they feel happy. When they're happy they don't want to fight with each other. When they don't want to fight—then they don't need spies, and we don't want spies to go without jobs."

Dan coolly held out the steaming bottle. No one had noticed that he had taken out the stopper.

Shifty Samuel reached for the bottle. Dan, in one quick movement, splashed the hot liquid on Shifty Samuel's finger.

"Ouch!" the spy said, and put his finger in his mouth.

"It was hot enough to burn him, gentlemen," Dan said, "but soon you will see a change come over our spy friend."

The spy took his finger out of his mouth and looked surprised. "That cavity in my left molar—I don't feel it there any more!" He looked at his hands. "And my rare skin disease has been cured! I feel so happy!"

Dan said, "Your eyes aren't shifty any more."

"Give me the gun, Samuel Sippy, ex-spy," Dr. Dan Parker said. "We'll find you a new job—one that will make the world a better place, and you a better person."

"Hooray for Dr. Dan Parker!" the reporters cheered.

Dan raised his head to see Mrs. Jameson standing next to him. "The papers have been collected, the bell has rung, the class has left, and still you sit here," she said.

"I'm sorry," Danny said. "I tried and tried to think of what I might want to do when I grow up, and I don't know. First, I thought of being a basketball star, and I won the game for my team. Then I was a doctor who invented a cure-all medicine and was able to save it from being stolen by a spy. But I never did think of a career to write about."

Mrs. Jameson said, "You have a good imagination, Danny, and you write well—when you do get busy writing. Why don't you think about becoming a professional writer?"

"You mean write books?" Danny was surprised.

"Professional writers can work in many ways," she said. "They write books for adults and for children. They write magazine stories and articles. They write the plays you see in the theater and on television and in the movies. They write the newspapers you read each day. There are many, many ways in which a writer can work."

"I might like that," Danny said. "I think I could do it!"

"When you get home," Mrs. Jameson said, "write an essay about being a writer. It will be due tomorrow."

"Thanks!" Danny said. He grabbed his books, hurried out the door, and was soon on his way home.

A writer? That might be fun! Maybe. . .

Dan Parker straightened his tie and moved to the center of the stage. The audience cheered.

Finally the man at the microphone was able to quiet them and turned to Dan Parker.

"We are glad to give you this award for the best novel of the year! You are the finest writer in the world today!"

"Thank you," Dan said. "Ladies and gentlemen, I would like to say a few words about. . ."

Dan Parker began to hurry. Before he wrote his prize winning novel, he knew he had better write his essay!

CHECKING PROGRESS

1. Of the three imaginary career situations, which did you like best for Dan? Why?
2. How did Dan see himself in each future situation? Was he a success, a failure, a hero? Explain your answer.
3. Do you consider the title, "Hooray for Dan Parker!", a good title for this story? Why?
4. Did you find the names of the characters in the story interesting? These names were intended to give you clues to the personalities of the characters. Using their names and other information you learned about them in the story, list several personality traits of the characters named below. Instead of writing personality traits, you may draw cartoons of the characters if you like.

Daring Dan   Glorietta Good Guys
Mean Marvin Mahew   Sneaky Samuel Sippy

CHOOSING NEXT STEPS

1. Can you use your imagination? Listed below are two suggestions of how you might share your thoughts about your own career.
   (a) Pretend you are established in a career. Write a letter to one of your classmates explaining how you feel about your work and tell some of the things that you are doing.
   (b) Pretend you are established in a successful career. Record on tape some of the things you are doing and things you plan to do in the future. Share this tape with a classmate or your teacher.
2. Interview one of your parents, a friend, or a teacher and ask this person such questions as:
   (a) What were you interested in as a career when you were my age?
   (b) Why did you decide to do the kind of work you do?
   (c) Have you always done the same kind of work?

SCHOOL! WHO NEEDS IT?
THINKING THINGS THROUGH

Questions, questions, questions! Problems, problems, problems! Yes, you are right. It is the school counselor's office. As you follow Mrs. Perkins, a junior high school counselor, through a school morning, you will see how she helps students think through their problems and plan for the future.

As you read this selection, give special attention to the following words and phrases which Mrs. Perkins uses as she talks with the students who come to her for help with their questions and problems.

study habits	ability
self-discipline	desire
time schedule	job opportunity
college	

ABOUT WORDS

Sometimes when we are reading, we may come across words that we are not sure how to pronounce. We may not be sure which syllable has the accent or stress. It may be that more than one syllable is accented. Equal stress is not placed on both syllables, however. The primary accent has greater stress than the secondary accent.

Read these words which are used in the story. Divide them into syllables and mark where you think the primary and secondary accents should be. Then look in your dictionary to see if you were right.

estimate	telephone
opportunity	graduation
difficult	satisfy
understand	education

41

INVESTIGATE

SCHOOL!
Who Needs It?

Mrs. Doris Perkins is a counselor for Westwood Junior High School. She has to look after the interests of about eight hundred students in the seventh and eighth grades. She likes working with students at the junior high level.

After checking her mail Mrs. Perkins goes to her office. There are already three students waiting to see her. All of them want to see her about the same thing—low grades in Mr. Gates' social studies class.

"Come in, Tammy, Bill, and Marsha. Let's see what I can do to help you."

"Oh Mrs. Perkins, it's just awful! My parents have taken away my telephone privileges. And Mr. Gates was so unfair in the first place," exclaims Marsha as the group settles down into the chair in Mrs. Perkins' office.

"Marsha, why do you say Mr. Gates is unfair?" asks Mrs. Perkins. She knows that most of the students think Mr. Gates is a fair teacher.

Before Marsha can reply, Bill blurts out, "Who needs to take a dumb old history course anyway?"

Mrs. Perkins realizes that she has a difficult task before her. How can she help each student realize the importance of social studies, answer the questions about the fairness of Mr. Gates' grading, and still not sound as if she were preaching? She will have to find out why each student feels the way that he or she does.

She repeats her question. "Marsha, why do you say that Mr. Gates was unfair?"

"He said we were going to have a short test, probably twenty to thirty minutes," answers Marsha. "It lasted a whole hour. And I only studied for a short test."

"Bill, did you and Tammy understand the same instructions about the length of the test?" asks Mrs. Perkins.

"We sure did!" replies Tammy.

"Did any of the students finish in thirty minutes?"

"Well, most of them did," says Bill.

"What do each of you think you might do to improve your grades in social studies?"

"I don't know," says Bill. "Just get me out of the class!"

"Maybe I should have studied more," says Tammy.

"If I were interested in school, perhaps I could do better," Marsha adds.

"Tammy, you're a bright girl," says Mrs. Perkins. "It could be that your study habits could stand some improving. Self-discipline can mean a lot in helping get better grades. Read this booklet on how to study. Tomorrow I want to hear

a brief report on what you've read. Also, I'll talk to Mr. Gates. Between the three of us, maybe we'll find out what the source of your problem is.

"Bill, I can't change your schedule now. But I'm going to give you a pamphlet to read called *Job Opportunities in the Social Sciences*. Perhaps it will partially answer your question about who needs social studies. In the meantime, I'll talk with Mr. Gates about seeing if you can do an assignment connected with your interests. Come back to see me when you finish with the pamphlet."

Mrs. Perkins dismisses Bill and Tammy. But she asks Marsha to remain behind for a few minutes.

"Marsha, how do you feel about being in school?"

"It's okay, I guess. But I'd rather be somewhere else."

"Tell me what your interests are outside of school."

"Sports, mainly. I like softball and swimming. I also like to talk with friends on the phone," Marsha answers.

"Could it be that you misjudged your study time? With talking on the telephone and swimming, you may not have allowed enough time to study for your test. That may be why it took you longer than your classmates to do the test. If this is true, could you possibly be blaming Mr. Gates and your parents for something you failed to do? Why don't you keep a schedule of the time you spend on each activity this week, and then come to see me to discuss it?" suggests Mrs. Perkins.

"O.K. I don't see what good it'll do," replies Marsha, "but I'll do anything you ask if you'll call my parents to get them to let me use the telephone again."

"I'll call your parents to discuss the time schedule, Marsha, but not to ask them to give you back your phone privileges," states Mrs. Perkins. "You'll need to show you can manage all your activities and still make passing grades. Now, go to your first class."

Mrs. Perkins' next visitor of the morning is Tommy O'Shane. He has a question about going to college. Tommy isn't sure whether he wants to go to college or go directly to

44

work after graduation. He thinks Mrs. Perkins might be able to help him reach a decision.

"Tommy, going to college requires looking at a number of things," says Mrs. Perkins. "Lets see if we can list some of them and comment on each.

"First comes ability. You need to have passing grades.

"Second is desire. You have to want to stay in school for several years, at least three, to get a degree. It isn't easy to stay in school if you don't like to study or don't like to be confined.

"Third, what about job opportunities? Going to college can provide them. But not going to college can, too. In fact, by 1980 it is estimated that only about 20 per cent of the jobs available will require a college degree. There will be many demands, however, for people with technical training which can be obtained at a two-year community college.

"Fourth is interests. You may have interests which can be satisfied without going to college.

"You need to ask yourself these questions," continues Mrs. Perkins. "What are your interests? What will be your chances of obtaining a particular job when you finish high school? What kinds and how much education and training will be needed for the particular job? Would a two-year community college program meet your needs? So you can see, Tommy, there really are a lot of things to be considered about a career. But you don't have to decide all in one day," she concludes.

"I'll think about what you've just told me," says Tommy. "May I take some of these career pamphlets with me?"

"Of course," says Mrs. Perkins. "You may have them."

"Thanks," says Tommy as he goes out the door.

Mrs. Perkins sighs. It has been a busy morning. She still has a dozen student class schedules to change by four o'clock. She finally gets started on the scheduling task around noon. But now she looks up to see Mr. Gates pass by her door. She gets up to stop him. Maybe they could discuss his students' grade problems during lunch.

45

CHECKING PROGRESS

In her suggestions to students who came to her with questions and problems, Mrs. Perkins used the words which were called to your attention before you read the story. Review the meaning of these words by forming a discussion group with several of your classmates and discussing your ideas with them.

1. Name the student who was talking with Mrs. Perkins at the time she used each word or phrase.
2. Discuss how each word or phrase related to the question, answer, or problem involved.

As your discussion group works together, one member might chart your ideas on the chalkboard, a poster board, or a large sheet of paper. The form below will help you to start the chart.

Word or Phrase	Student	How Word or Phrase Relates to the Problem

CHOOSING NEXT STEPS

Think of a question or a problem concerning school that you would like to have help with at this time. Write it down for yourself. Look over the list of words and phrases used by Mrs. Perkins and see if any of them give you an idea for answering your own question. If they do not, make an appointment and discuss the question or problem with your counselor at school.

LIFE: A DRAG RACE

THINKING THINGS THROUGH

Have you ever done any "wheel spinning"? Maybe you are not really sure.

The author has written a selection based on something a young man said to him while they were having a conversation about youth. After thinking about the youth's very wise observation in likening life to a dragster, the author decided to use it as a way to show how important the use of time can be in furthering a career choice.

As you read this selection, find out what the author means by "wheel spinning," and decide if you have done any.

ABOUT WORDS

The author of "Life: A Drag Race" used some words that were probably unfamiliar to you. Sometimes the meaning of the word or words could be understood when more of the story was read even though the exact meaning was not known. In the following sentences which are taken from the story, the exact meaning of the word is noted in the parentheses. Study the sentences. Then reread the story for a clearer meaning or to include these words in your planned vocabulary list.

(1) Do your part-time jobs help you gain experience for your future career? Or do these jobs simply lead to *dead ends* (leading nowhere or no outlets)?

(2) The *impending* (about to occur) danger was first noticed by the boys.

(3) Just then they heard the jet *revving* (to operate at an increased speed) its engines as it taxied toward the end of the field for takeoff.

(4) *Invest your time* (to make use of for future benefits or advantages) in doing useful and valuable tasks, even when the jobs seem long and time-consuming.

(5) One day this time and effort will *pay off* (will benefit you in some way).

47

INVESTIGATE

life: a drag race

"Life is like a dragster after it gets the green light. It would get goin' faster if we could do away with the wheel spinnin'."

This was how the young man ended his talk with me about youth. How wise his observations were!

How much "wheel spinning" have you done? Some say, "Time is money." Actually, time is more important to us than money.

Do your part-time jobs help you gain experience for your future career? Or do these jobs simply lead to dead ends?

Has someone's ability to solve problems quickly surprised you? The solution was probably the result of both knowledge and experience. This took time either doing a job, or watching or reading about experts performing a job. Perhaps an illustration will help you to understand how this idea works.

The Baker family share many flying hours together. The boys help their dad with many of the jobs he does flying a small aircraft.

This afternoon they were out in search of some gliders. Twelve-year-old Mark wanted to take a ride. As they landed at the small Texas airport where gliders were kept, Vernon, not quite eleven, yelled, "Hey, look at that big jet!" On the field was a twin-engine jet getting ready for takeoff.

In the terminal building an old radio sat on the small counter. Voices came from the box asking for landing instructions or providing information to other aircraft that the airport was near.

Two pilots standing nearby said that all gliders had been moved to another airport. Mark and Vernon were disappointed. Just then they heard the jet revving its engines as it taxied toward the

end of the field for takeoff. The impending danger was first noticed by the boys.

Vernon jumped to his feet and shouted, "They've left their baggage door open!" He dashed to the radio and began sending this message: "November 5 0 8 3 Whiskey, your baggage door is open!" The jet slid to a halt. The pilot stepped from the plane, closed the open door, and waved his thanks to Vernon.

Hours spent watching and listening when his dad was working had taught Vernon radio operations and terms.

Using time to advantage builds experience. Should Vernon decide to become a pilot or control tower operator, his experience could be very helpful. It may also influence his choice of a job in the future.

Invest your time in doing useful and valuable tasks, even when the jobs seem very time-consuming to you. One day this time and effort will pay off. Many careers begin as hobbies in childhood. Young people must often wait to obtain the jobs which they really want. This waiting can be "wheel spinning." It can also be time spent learning.

Experience in a summer part-time job can often help you make a career choice. If after working at a summer camp a person decides that he doesn't like to work with children, then he knows that it would be foolish to spend time at college, training to become a teacher. On the other hand, if he likes this work, then he has some idea about which direction to follow for a career. A lot of time is spent "wheel spinning" in search of careers for which we have too little previous knowledge and information. You can begin gathering the knowledge you need about your future career today.

49

CHECKING PROGRESS

1. What did you decide that the author meant when he talked about "wheel spinning"?
2. After reading this story, what do you think was the main idea for this selection?
3. Why didn't Vernon wait for one of the adults to send the warning message to the jet?
4. Why do you think a person should be selective about which part-time jobs to take?
5. How can our childhood interests and hobbies be of value to us when we are grown?

CHOOSING NEXT STEPS

1. Think of several things that you have done or had to do that you consider "wheel spinning" for you. Make a list for yourself or discuss them with your classmates or with your teacher.
2. Learning the meaning, spelling, and pronunciation of words related to a career or hobby that you are interested in is a good way to become a better conversationalist, reader, and writer. This story told about one family's hobby, flying airplanes. On a separate paper, list all the terms you know or can think of that pertain to airplanes. When you have finished, select five and give the meaning of each. You may use an encyclopedia and dictionary to help you do this.

THE WAITRESS OF 1984
THINKING THINGS THROUGH

Some information can be made simpler and clearer when it is organized into the form of a graph. Graphs present facts so that it is easy for you to make comparisons. Look at the graph below. The title above the graph tells you what information the graph presents. The sample here shows the population of four cities. Answer the following questions as you study the graph.

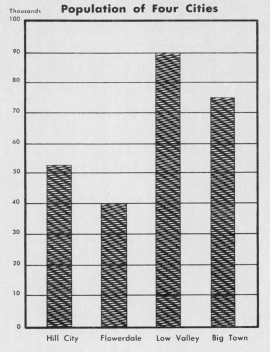

Population of Four Cities

1. Which city has the largest population? Which has the smallest?
2. Which city has a population of about 75,000?
3. About how many people live in Hill City?

In the article you're about to read, you will find three graphs. Study them carefully. Check the information on the graphs with the information stated in words.

ABOUT WORDS

A prefix is something joined to the beginning of a word to change its meaning. *Un* is a prefix meaning not, *dis* means the opposite of, and *re* means again. Copy the following words on a sheet of paper. Connect each prefix to a word with which it may be used.

re-	satisfied
un-	placement
dis-	skilled
	ceive

INVESTIGATE

THE WAITRESS OF 1984

The young woman smiled as she approached. "Good morning. How are you?"

"Fine. I'll have an egg, radiated; poached soy cereal, warm; banana-orange juice; and hot jello to drink."

Except for the rather odd order, this conversation is not unusual. We could find similar ones in any restaurant today. The difference is in the waitress. She has a new life style.

Andrea is trained for her job. After high school she spent a year in food service school. This school was operated by the company that now employs her. Both the state education agency and the company helped develop and fund her course of study. Andrea received pay for attending the school.

Then she took a job in a hotel restaurant. She has worked a year and is happy. She realizes that a waitress is only one of several occu-

pations she will hold in her lifetime. There are many types of jobs within Foods Incorporated, the company for which Andrea works. In fact, she is training to become a dietitian.

Foods Incorporated is a rather new idea, too. It manages several top restaurants, public cafeterias, a hospital dietary kitchen, and a farm.

Since the early seventies, good labor had been difficult to obtain. Many companies began to develop special services to attract quality employees. They began to offer recreation, camps, and private clubs to their employees. Also, they provided further education.

Andrea has taken part in the educational program of her company. She also has some opportunity for recreation. Each year she spends her vacation in a camp for company employees. At the camp are such activities as boating, golfing, swimming, flying, riding, and camping. It is located in a forest preserve near the city in which Andrea works. There are also weekend programs offered during the year.

Foods Incorporated offers household and child care specialists. The company can purchase large quantities of food at cheaper costs. If Andrea wishes, the household service will clean her house once a week and buy groceries. Child care is provided by a man and woman team.

Andrea's husband Gill is a carpenter. He could work for the company, but he prefers to be his own boss. However,

he can still take part in the services offered by the company, such as the camp.

The working situation described above may seem a bit strange to us today. But now many such programs are actually being planned.

In the past such jobs as waiting on tables, child care, and house cleaning have all been looked upon as low status occupations. Yet, these service industries are rapidly growing and will continue to grow, according to *futurologists*, or people who predict the future by studying present day trends. This prediction is based upon data such as the graph below.

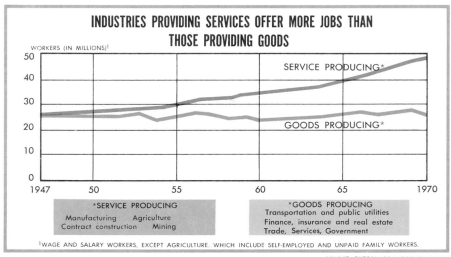

INDUSTRIES PROVIDING SERVICES OFFER MORE JOBS THAN THOSE PROVIDING GOODS

WORKERS (IN MILLIONS)[1]

SERVICE PRODUCING*

GOODS PRODUCING*

*SERVICE PRODUCING
Manufacturing   Agriculture
Contract construction   Mining

*GOODS PRODUCING
Transportation and public utilities
Finance, insurance and real estate
Trade, Services, Government

[1]WAGE AND SALARY WORKERS, EXCEPT AGRICULTURE, WHICH INCLUDE SELF-EMPLOYED AND UNPAID FAMILY WORKERS.

SOURCE: BUREAU OF LABOR STATISTICS

Industries which provide services offer many jobs. What kinds of employment does this involve? According to the 1972-73 edition of the United States government publication entitled *Occupational Outlook Handbook,* these jobs include:

law enforcement
barbers and beauticians
food services
household services
child care services
nursing assistants

According to the graph below, people entering into occupations will cause job growth to vary. During the next few years, more people will probably become pro-fessional and technical work-ers. This includes teachers, engineers, dentists, accountants and clergymen. The second largest amount of job growth will be shown by service workers. The graph also shows that there will be more clerical workers. These are the people who help us communicate in today's business world. They operate office machines and computers, record accounts, type letters, and take dictation. Also the graph shows there will be more sales workers. These jobs are found in retail stores, wholesale firms, insurance companies, and door-to-door sales of products.

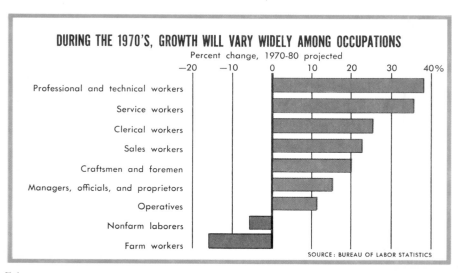

DURING THE 1970'S, GROWTH WILL VARY WIDELY AMONG OCCUPATIONS

Percent change, 1970-80 projected

—20   —10   0   10   20   30   40%

Professional and technical workers
Service workers
Clerical workers
Sales workers
Craftsmen and foremen
Managers, officials, and proprietors
Operatives
Nonfarm laborers
Farm workers

SOURCE: BUREAU OF LABOR STATISTICS

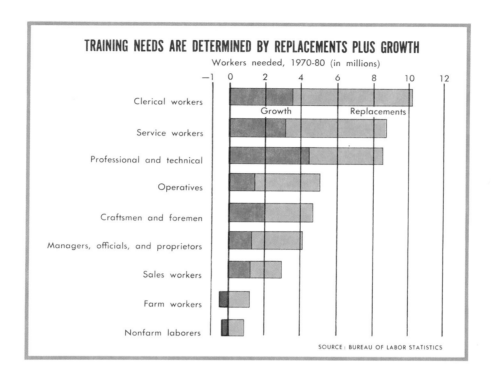

TRAINING NEEDS ARE DETERMINED BY REPLACEMENTS PLUS GROWTH

Workers needed, 1970-80 (in millions)

| | −1 | 0 | 2 | 4 | 6 | 8 | 10 | 12 |

Clerical workers

Growth   Replacements

Service workers

Professional and technical

Operatives

Craftsmen and foremen

Managers, officials, and proprietors

Sales workers

Farm workers

Nonfarm laborers

SOURCE: BUREAU OF LABOR STATISTICS

Careers which fall under some of the slower growing occupational groupings include electricians, bus and truck drivers, store managers, carpenters, machinists, and assembly workers. Yet these careers should not be overlooked. The graph above shows that often the number of people entering a particular occupation are too few to fill the number of replacements needed. For example, the need for clerical workers is greater than the need for professional and technical workers.

Our choices of careers are based on values. But our values are changing as rapidly as our world. Today company benefits are becoming as important as wages. Many companies reward their employees with benefits. Remember the waitress of 1984. In making your job choice, would you prefer having better wages or benefits?

CHECKING PROGRESS

1. What information did the first graph show?
2. Tell in your own words what the second graph means.
3. How could you use the information on the third graph to help you choose a career for yourself?
4. What kinds of jobs are included in the service occupations? Would you like to do any of these jobs?

CHOOSING NEXT STEPS

1. The first graph you used is a line graph. The second and third graphs are bar graphs. Besides these, there are several other kinds of graphs such as the circle or pie graph, and the pictograph or symbol graph. Look for illustrations of these in encyclopedias, dictionaries, and other textbooks.
2. It would be interesting to make a graph showing information about you and your classmates. You might use the idea below.
   (a) Ask each of your classmates to tell you the career or occupation he is interested in at this time.
   (b) Organize this information into four or five broad areas, such as those shown in the third graph.
   (c) Put this information in graph form. Remember to include the title and explanation words at the side and bottom (or top).
3. Foods Incorporated offered many benefits to its employees such as recreation, private clubs, camps, and education. What other benefits do you think would be good to offer to employees? Tell why.

WHATEVER HAPPENED TO MAN ON EARTH?

THINKING THINGS THROUGH

"Whatever Happened To Man On Earth" is a play. You may be asking yourself such questions as:

1. Is a play like any other story?

Yes. They are alike in many ways. Both a story and a play have characters, a setting, and a plot.

2. How is a play different from a story?

A story is written to be read. A play is written to be spoken aloud by the characters on a stage. A play is written in a form that describes the setting and lists the characters at the beginning before the action starts. The plot of the play is developed through the conversation and action of the characters. In a story that is to be read, the author tells you things about the characters, setting, and plot throughout the story.

3. How is reading a play different from reading a story? As you read a play you must visualize the characters in the setting that is described. It is best to try to see them on the stage in costume.

ABOUT WORDS

Take a close look at the following groups of words which have been divided into syllables. Think of a rule for each group explaining why the words are divided in that particular way.

what-ever	set-ting	mem-o-ry
some-where	but-ton	heav-en-ly

Now, on a separate sheet of paper, correctly divide the following words. Check your work with a dictionary.

anything	happened	planet
tolerate	spaceship	intelligent
economics	correct	downhill

57

WHATEVER HAPPENED TO MAN ON EARTH?

ACT I

Setting: Mars
Time: 3,000 A.D.
Action: Two Martians are speaking together somewhere in space. They are checking out the dials on their new updated memory banks.

Martian One: What is a man? I seem to be getting an impulse from my memory bank about such a creature.

Martian Two: He is a being who lives on Earth. He once had a future as bright as the North Star.

Martian One: Why didn't he realize this potential you have just indicated? (He continues to dial for a memory tone.)

Martian Two: First, we have to go back in time to see what happened to him. Let me check my memory bank. (He dials a button on the front of him. Lights flash.) Yes, I get a faint impulse from the time of the ancient Greeks. In those days man knew who he was and what he wanted from life. He was a real prince of a fellow.

Martian One: I'll bet he was as intelligent as life in Outer Space in that day. How did he lose such a royal position?

Martian Two: It all began so slowly and over such a span of hundreds of years that Man wasn't aware of what was happening to him. Things began to go downhill when

Galileo said the sun was the center of the Universe, not Earth. It was a terrible blow to man's sense of worth.

Martian One: Did he ever recover from such a shock?

Martian Two: No, things just kept going from bad to worse. At first Man was told he was something special—then someone came along and told him he was the same as an animal. Man's confusion increased.

Martian One: Great Nova Sea! Man must have felt like he had been hit by a meteor. Surely, Man used his mind to solve his dilemma.

Martian Two: Yes, Man did have a mind once. However, a psychiatrist came along and told him about his id, ego, and superego fighting inside his head and Man lost his mind over that bit of information.

Martian One: But man still had a free will!

Martian Two: Wrong again! Someone else came along with an idea about human behavioral control. He said Man was beyond using a free will. Man gave in to this and . . .

Martian One: . . . lost his will. What a waste of potential! But tell me. What did finally become of man?

Martian Two: Oh, he's still down there on Earth. At present he is trying to figure out who he is. Poor creature!

Exit: The two Martians exit still trying to find the correct memory dial tone on their new memory banks.

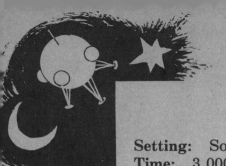

ACT II

Setting: Somewhere in Outer Space—Galaxy 300
Time: 3,000,000 A.D.
Action: Enter two Angevids "talking" by electronic pulse sensation. Over 1,000,000 years ago, they had improved on the dial tone memory banks of the Martians.

Angevid One: I had crossed electrode sensation just now and pulsed you were trying to tell me about a distant species named Homo. Whatever happened to them?

Angevid Two: I was pulsing to you. Genus Homo, or "Man," as he was called, died out in the year 9,000 A.D. He once occupied the now-empty planet Earth.

Angevid One: From what did he die?

Angevid Two: Institutional disease, or faulty governments, economics, and schools, was the beginning symptom. But finally a knowledge crisis developed which led to Man's extinction. He never learned that knowledge is like a tree with the separate subjects as its branches. He made the mistake of thinking the branches were the tree. You

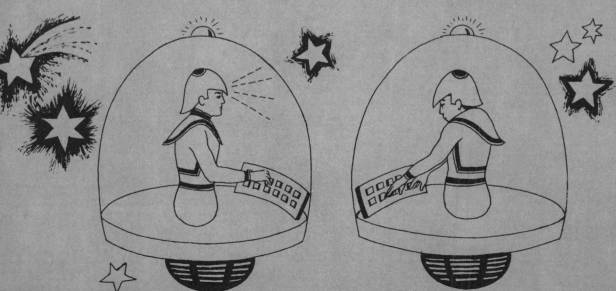

might also say man died from becoming too specialized. *The Dictionary of Occupational Titles* finally grew so large it weighed a ton! There were not enough counselors available to help young people select a career. Too many occupations to choose and too many people.

Angevid One: Please explain further.

Angevid Two: Institutions collapsed when Earthlings no longer practiced what they preached. Overpopulation, lack of career planning, crime, war, disease, hunger, pollution, and an "I don't care" attitude killed all but a few. These few knew the end was coming. They got together and built a spaceship and left Earth forever. They landed on Galaxy 300 and were our ancient ancestors.

Angevid One: Didn't the Earthlings have any outstanding wisdom-seekers like our old men to guide their thinking?

Angevid Two: Yes, they had wise men who advised them on right from wrong ideas. But these wise men became so engrossed in their own words that they studied the meaning of the meaning's meaning. Finally, the meaning became meaningless. No one knew right from wrong.

Angevid One: Surely their scientists had the answers!

Angevid Two: You must have another crossed electrode sensation. Their scientists' experiments dealt with such things as hairless mice, courtship practices of bees, and electrode pleasure sensors in birds.

Angevid One: Absurd! How did they last until 9,000 A.D.?

(The Angevids exit, excitedly pulsing about a new system for speeding up interstellar transmission of light waves.)

61

CHECKING PROGRESS

1. As you observed the characters in the play, how did you find them different from the people of earth today?
2. Did you understand the descriptive expressions that were used? Form a discussion group with several of your classmates and discuss the meaning of the following:

    "prince of a fellow"

    "as intelligent as life in Outer Space"

    "felt like he had been hit by a meteor"

    "what a waste of potential"

    "practiced what they preached"

    "outstanding wisdom-seekers"

    "the meaning of the meaning's meaning"
3. How do you suppose the Earthlings got to Galaxy 300?

CHOOSING NEXT STEPS

1. Plan with some of your classmates to present the play in costume on a stage.
2. Try writing another act for "Whatever Happened to Man on Earth?"
3. Make a list of the types of occupations that a society of Angevids might be engaged in.

He leaned toward Garn. "This is a great chance for all of us! You and your grandson would share in the profits, too! Times are changing. We have heard that other city-structures have found-things they are not sharing with us. Why can't we do the same?"

"Because it is not right!" Garn's voice was angry. "If it is true that the others are not sharing thoughts and found-things which will help us all, then I am sorry. But we cannot join them in these actions. If we do, we will soon have the same type of situation on earth that once before caused the Great Explosion. Is this what you want?"

A buzzer sounded, and the three of them silently opened the boxes and ate their share of capsules.

The light in the bubble was dimmed as the men felt the need for rest. But Deid lay on his stomach on the cushion, looking into the darkness until he fell asleep.

He thought he would be the first to awake in the morning, but Garn and Firtt were already up. They were folding the air cushions and preparing to take apart the camp-structure.

It took only a few minutes to load the equipment into the surface-craft. Garn started the motor.

The canyon was wider than Deid thought, and they were able to drive into it, following the turns and twists. They moved carefully and slowly over the rocky ground.

Then Garn brought the craft to a stop. "We'll have to go the rest of the way on foot."

Firtt looked at the scanner. "The canyon narrows here," he said, "and widens again up ahead. If there is something living in that canyon, it will have trouble getting out."

Garn led the way with Deid following. Firtt walked behind. They climbed over a few rocks until they came to a bend in the canyon, and there they stopped in surprise.

The high walls of the canyon spread outward to enclose a valley about two miles wide and four or five miles long. High grasses covered the floor of the valley, and a natural spring had formed a lake under the cliffs to the west.

"Beautiful!" Garn whispered. He took a pair of binoculars from a case that was fastened to his belt and looked through them, adjusting them slightly. Then he handed the binoculars to Deid. "If you look ahead about a mile, a little to your right, I think you'll see what we've come for," Garn said.

Eagerly Deid raised the binoculars and turned to the spot Garn had pointed out. Before, it had been a dark shadow in the meadow. Now he could see the animals there.

They were large animals, broad of shoulder and lean and strong. From their heads spread the long, pointed horns he had seen in the film. "Texas Longhorns!" he shouted.

He turned to Firtt. The man was already studying the animals through his own binoculars.

"Grandfather! I can't believe it!" Deid said. "Could they be descendents of the first Spanish Longhorns?"

"How many are in that group?" Firtt interrupted.

"Maybe seventy-five...or a hundred," Garn said slowly.

Deid thought of the great Longhorns he had seen through the binoculars. A thought struck him, and he turned to Garn. "There's one thing the film and books didn't tell me," he said. "What did they do with the cattle after they rounded them up and drove them into the city?"

Firtt laughed and said, "They were killed and eaten."

"No!" Deid shouted. "Even those ancient men wouldn't do a thing like that to a great animal!"

"What Firtt said is true," said Garn, shaking his head sadly. "These men didn't have food capsules. In order to stay alive they had to eat plant life and animal flesh."

"I'd like to get a closer look at them," Firtt said.

"We must be careful," Garn said. "They'll be dangerous. They have come from generations of Longhorn cattle that turned wild to survive. They will be frightened of us."

As they came within range of the cattle, Garn put out a hand to stop Deid. "We must come upon them very carefully, very quietly," he said. "If they should charge us, we can run to the safety of the rocks. He turned to Firtt. "The cattle cannot climb the rocks," he explained.

Quietly they moved ahead a few yards. They were close to the cattle now. Some of them raised their heads and examined the strangers. One cow nervously pawed the ground as she watched them, her calf moving around her feet.

"Stand very still," Garn whispered.

"Listen, Garn," Firtt said, "we don't have to turn these animals in to the government office. We can bring them back with the help of some men I know who share our ideas. And we can sell the cattle for a great profit."

69

"I told you," Garn said, "that wouldn't be honorable!"

"Honorable? After you spoke in the meeting about your hope of finding cattle in the canyon, members at the meeting began to talk. Many of the wealthy citizens have heard of this exploration trip and have let us know that they would like to try the taste of the food that was once prized by men. They will pay a great deal to eat these cattle."

"The captain would not permit this!" Garn said.

"The captain has already made arrangements with some of them," Firtt said.

"No!" Garn said.

Firtt pulled out a paper. "Here is a note the captain gave me. You will recognize the handwriting. It is a list of those who will pay well to own one of the cattle."

Garn took the list from Firtt and studied it.

"Grandfather!" Deid said. "We can't let them do it! If we take them back to the city-structure, soon they will all be dead! We can't let that happen."

Suddenly Firtt backed away from them, moving out into the meadow. He reached into a pocket, pulling out a weapon.

"Firtt!" Garn said. "Men do not use these on each other."

The small calf that had been nuzzling its mother became excited and bounded toward the men. The cow looked up and bellowed in fear, seeing her calf among the strange figures. Again she pawed the earth.

"Be careful!" Garn said to Firtt. "They are ready to be spooked. We must get to the shelter of the rocks."

"What do you mean by 'spooked'?" Firtt asked, frowning.

"I mean anything can frighten them into panic. When they are frightened they will run together, not knowing where they are running. They can kill us if we are in their path."

"I don't believe you!" Firtt said. "You are trying to keep me from my plan!" He raised the weapon, pointing it at Garn.

Deid remembered something else about that film. He remembered that when the cattle in the film heard a loud noise, it caused them to panic. There was no time to waste.

70

Directories, indexes, dictionaries, encyclopedias, and other organized data may be arranged in alphabetical order either letter by letter or word by word.

1. In *letter by letter* alphabetizing, all letters across a line are arranged in alphabetical order regardless of where the words break. The separate words are alphabetized as if they were run together. The space is not considered.

Example: newborn
New Brunswick
newcomer
New Hampshire
newspaper
New Testament
Newton
New York

2. In *word by word* alphabetizing, the letters within each word are alphabetized letter by letter to the end of the word. The break between words is alphabetized as coming before the letter "a". The first word is considered, then the space, then the second word if there is one.

Example: New Brunswick
New Hampshire
New Testament
New York
newborn
newcomer
newspaper
Newton

On a separate sheet of paper, arrange the following list of words letter by letter and then word by word.

atomic clock	atomy
atom	atom smasher
attack	atomic
atoll	atoms
atomic theory	atomic age
atomize	atop
assure	awe
atom bomb	atomic energy
atomic weight	atone
attic	attire

7   USING ALPHABETICAL ORDER IN THE ENCYCLOPEDIA

The following lists are subjects which might be found in volume "P" of an encyclopedia. The subjects in the left column are listed in the order they would appear in the encyclopedia. The subjects in the right column should also appear in the same volume. Choose the two subjects in the left column which each of the subjects in the right column would be listed between in the encyclopedia. Write them on another piece of paper.

Pacific Ocean	Phoenicia
Pakistan	Petrified Forest
Palsy	Peru
Papoose	Priest
Parent	Pollution
Parrot	Panama Canal
Pasteur, Louis	Park
Pecan	Parliament
Pecos Bill	Plants
Petersburg	
Petroleum	
Photography	
Planet	
Police	
Portugal	
Prehistoric Animals	
Prince Edward Island	

8   USING ALPHABETICAL ORDER IN A DIRECTORY

On a separate piece of paper, arrange these names in alphabetical order leter by letter, then word by word. Which method would be best for a directory listing people's names? Why?

Summer, Betty	Smallwood, Vera
Small, Yvonne	Summers, Ann
Summer, Ted	Southerd, Don
South, Jack	Smithers, Howell
Spear, Tom	Southland, Claude
Smithen, Andy	Smith, Margaret
Speers, Flora	Speer, Van

patterns and designs

Patches of color...patches of interest...they slide, they change, they grow, they fade, then reappear. Like the colors of a kaleidoscope merge into one another, so do our interests merge into careers of the future. What are your interests now? Will they expand into your choice of a career?

UNIT 2　　PATTERNS AND DESIGNS

78

Her grandmother said, "I really came out here to invite you girls for cookies and lemonade, but if you're too busy . . ."

"No!" Judy and I said together. "We're not too busy." But we were really too excited to eat.

All afternoon we worked until our fingers were stiff from holding the brushes. At the end of the day we had about a dozen stones with small designs on them.

I kept painting birds. I took one of my stones home to show my parents.

"It's really beautiful," my mother said. "Where are you going to sell your stones?"

"Judy and I are going to have a store of our own someday."

"But I mean now," my mother said. "You won't get customers if they can't see your merchandise."

"We haven't thought about that," I said.

"Well . . ." my mother said, "what about a garage sale?"

"Garage sale? But that's what women have when they want to get rid of stuff around the house they don't need."

"It doesn't have to be like that. You could put an ad in the newspaper and tell what you've got for sale."

So we had a garage sale, and it turned out to be a great success. Besides our painted stones, we also sold some little baskets that Judy had painted with delightful designs. It was so exciting to collect money for our work!

We were ready to end the sale when a woman came up.

"I was here earlier," she said. "I bought one of the stones with the little birds painted on them. I'd like to carry your stones in my gift shop. We'd raise your price a little, and I would take a percentage. Would you be interested?"

Would we be interested! Judy's parents and her grandmother sat down with us, and my parents came over; and by the time we were through talking with the lady, it was agreed that we'd give her some of the stones and paint some more. She would try selling the stones for a month and if they sold well, Judy and I would paint some more for her.

Judy and I couldn't believe our ears!

For a whole month we worked at Judy's house. Then the woman called and asked for more stones. She had sold most of the stones she had—especially the ones with the little birds.

"You have real talent," she told me. "Have you thought of studying art? I know a woman who is a fine teacher, and I'd be glad to tell your mother about her, if you're interested."

I was interested, all right. I had found a real joy in what I was doing. I had begun painting the little sand crabs and the noisy seagulls; and the small sunfish boats, with their red-striped sails, which dotted the bay in the afternoons.

Everything was going as Judy and I hoped it would.

"Someday we'll have our own store!" Judy said.

"We'll have it down by the beach and run it together."

"Just the way real sisters would. Promise?"

"Promise!"

But one night, as I was finishing one of my art lessons, Judy phoned me. "My father has been transferred to another state," she said in a tearful voice. "We have to move."

"Judy..." I said, "you can't go! What about our store?"

We didn't have a choice. Judy left, and I went on with my life...schoolwork and new friends, art lessons, art exhibits, and eventually an art scholarship to a university in Houston. Judy? I almost forgot about her. That is, until I heard she was coming back to Corpus Christi again...

It's summer again, as I sit on the seawall. A tall young woman gets out of a car...walks down the steps toward me. An angry gull scolds her, flapping its wings over her head, then heads out to the sea.

I stand up to greet her. I would know her anywhere—Judy, who still looks so much like me!

"Hi," she says, with a big grin.

"Hi," I say. We stand there looking at each other, searching for words until Judy laughs.

"Sit down," she says, "and tell me what you are doing. My aunt said you've won an art scholarship! I always knew you had it in you!"

84

"Tell me about yourself!" I say. "Are you in college?"

"I'm in college," Judy says. "I'm going to be a nurse."

"You? Why...you used to scream at the sight of blood!"

She laughs. "Kathy, my grandmother was ill a long time before she died. I had to take care of her. I found out that helping someone ill gave me a feeling of peace." She looks out to sea. "I guess I was discovering what I wanted to do with my life in the same way you decided to be an artist."

A sailboat comes in close to shore. The children on it wave to us. We wave back.

"Remember the stones we painted?" I ask her.

"And the store we were going to have down by the beach? What nice dreams we had when we were young."

"I thought we were so much alike," I say. "It surprises me to find our interests turned out to be so different."

"Kathy, we are still alike in so many ways," Judy says. "We are alike, and yet we are different. Do you understand?"

"I guess so," I say.

"We are still sisters."

Together we sit on the steps of the seawall with the sun on our backs. Judy is right, of course. We are still alike—in the ways that really count.

CHECKING PROGRESS

1. In what ways were Judy and Kathy alike when they were seventh graders? In what ways did they find that they were different when they were college students?
2. In what ways were Judy and Kathy still alike at college age even though they were different? What do you think the last sentence of the story means? "We are still alike—in the ways that really count."
3. Both Judy and Kathy made discoveries of abilities and interests while they were in school, which later helped them choose a career. At what point in the story did Kathy discover her interest in painting? What did she think, do, or say that indicated her discovery? When did Judy discover her interest in becoming a nurse? What did she think, do, or say that indicated her discovery?
4. Find as many examples of personification as you can in the story. Tell what things are being personified and why the personification is effective.

CHOOSING NEXT STEPS

1. Choose a classmate for your partner that you think is like you in some way. Discuss the following:
   A. Ways you are alike and different
   B. Interests you both have
   C. Careers that could develop from present interests
2. Make a "ME" poster. Find pictures of things you like, things you are interested in, and careers that could grow out of the interests you now have.
3. Make several cartoons which illustrate personification.
   Example: The gull scolding Judy
   The bay that curls toward the gleaming white building of the city

A WHIRL WITH MECHANICAL INTERESTS

THINKING THINGS THROUGH

What is a mechanic? Is it someone who works on your car? Is it someone who builds airplanes? Is it the person who repairs your TV? What if someone told you it was a cook, a baker, or a paperhanger? The following story may shed some light on the many careers in the area of mechanical interests.

ABOUT WORDS

Many words can be changed from verbs to adjectives, verbs to nouns, nouns to adjectives, or adjectives to nouns by adding a suffix to the base word. For example, in the sentence "The mechanic worked late," *mechanic* is a noun. When the suffix *-al* is added, as in "His mechanical ability was outstanding," the word becomes an adjective.

A word is underlined in the first sentence in each of the pairs below. On a separate paper, write the second sentence in each pair using the underlined word with an added suffix to fill the blank space.

1. Will you please *explain* the chart again?
   Your _____ was not clear.
2. These jobs require different kinds of *education*.
   The _____ requirements for these jobs vary.
3. An *excellent* pilot cannot necessarily repair his engine.
   His _____ as a pilot does not mean he can do repairs.

The following are some suffixes characteristic of nouns, adjectives, and verbs.

Nouns		Adjectives		Verbs	
-tion	-ian	-al	-ous	-ate	-fy
-ance	-ment	-ly	-ary	-ize	-en
-age	-ship	-ish	-ful		

87

A Whirl with Mechanical Interests

"I'm really interested in mechanical things," Danny told his counselor.

"What do you mean by that?" asked the man.

Danny's neck turned red. He began to feel angry, but realizing that getting mad would not help, the youngster replied, "Well, I like to work with radios and televisions. Many of my friends think I'm pretty good. I've repaired some of their black and white TV sets," Danny went on.

"I noticed you became a little upset when I asked you to explain what you meant by mechanical things," said the man. "Let's explore that for a minute. You may be surprised at all the careers involved in the area of mechanical interests.

"I have a small chart here (see chart 1) that lists some mechanical careers. What do you notice about careers in the field of mechanics?"

"Well, it looks like a lot of the careers don't have very much to do with repair," Danny replied.

"Why do you think that architects, physicists, and engineers are included?" the counselor continued.

"Well, these guys might work with the machines, but usually they design them," answered the boy.

"So what does this tell you about the mechanical career cluster?"

"I guess it covers people who repair machines, work with machines, and... even those people who design or make machines."

Selected Mechanical Careers	
Engineer	Radio/TV Service
Physicist	Technician
Architect	Carpenter
Contractor	Maintenance Man
Pilot	Paperhanger
Mechanic	Painter
Cook, Baker	Butcher
Electrician	Laborer

We will leave Danny and his counselor now. They may have helped us clarify some ideas about mechanical interests and abilities.

Mechanical ability helps one to see how things go together. It allows one to fit together all the parts of a puzzle, just as a baker mixes ingredients to make a loaf of bread.

Mechanical means having to do with machines or tools. Different kinds of interests and education are required in this career area, which includes designing, repairing, and operating machines and tools.

All mechanical skills require some special training.

Some skills are acquired through training on the job, while others are learned in school.

A degree from a university or college is required for some of the mechanical careers listed on the chart on the facing page. Other jobs mentioned there, such as a carpenter, require a high school education plus a period as an apprentice. An apprentice begins his career as a helper. He receives training from experienced people in his trade.

With the increased use of machines, we can expect an even stronger demand for people who design, operate, or repair machines.

CHECKING PROGRESS

1. What three types of work did Danny discover could be included in the mechanical career cluster?
2. Form a discussion group with several of your classmates.
   (1) Add as many occupations as you can to the list of mechanical careers found in the chart on page 88.
   (2) Divide the occupations on your list, as well as those in the chart, into the three types of work in the mechanical career cluster.
   (3) Indicate the amount and type of training that would be necessary for each occupation.

Use the library, card catalog, and encyclopedias to help you with this activity.

CHOOSING NEXT STEPS

1. Do you know someone who is working at a mechanical occupation? If so, ask this person such questions as:
   (1) When did you decide to become a _____?
   (2) What kind of training did you have?
   (3) What advantages does this work offer?
2. Choose books to read which are related to a mechanical career that you seem most interested in.
   (1) Biographies
   (2) Informational books
   (3) Fictional stories
3. Locate magazines in the library on mechanics and read an article which interests you.

THE SCIENTIFIC PUZZLE
THINKING THINGS THROUGH

Science is a way of thinking about the world. People with scientific interests tend to think in this special way. If you skim through the next article, you will find the following statement: "The greatest difference between the sciences and the nonsciences is that sciences use the scientific method to arrive at an answer." If you know what the scientific method is, you can better understand how a scientist thinks. The scientific method has five steps:

1. The scientist states the problem of situation.
2. He forms a hypothesis or statement of explanation.
3. He observes and experiments to test his hypothesis.
4. He tries to understand the results.
5. He draws a conclusion.

ABOUT WORDS

You may notice that many scientific words end with the suffix *-logy*. This suffix means the study of. As new fields of science were invented, this suffix was often used to create a word that would name the science. For example, *psycho* means mind. *Psycho* was combined with *logy* to form *psychology* meaning the study of the mind. Listed below are some other scientific words and what they mean.

anthropology	the study of humans
geology	the study of the earth
meteorology	the study of weather and atmosphere
paleontology	the study of prehistoric plants and animals
sociology	the study of society
zoology	the study of animals

99

INVESTIGATE

the scientific puzzle

What does a scientist look like? What does he do? How does he behave? Some people think a scientist has white hair, bushy eyebrows, and wears glasses. They think that he is terribly busy using microscopes, finding cures for diseases, and performing strange experiments that he has no time for his family. Also, they think he is very forgetful about things other than work.

This idea of a scientist is a *stereotype*, a general idea you may have in your mind about what a particular person is like. A stereotype is not always true. The picture of the scientist presented above is not always true.

A scientist is a person who uses scientific methods to obtain his knowledge. The scientist observes an event or situation and forms a *hypothesis,* a statement which is general enough to explain the event. Then using special methods, he finds information, or *data*, to prove or to disprove the hypothesis. After trying to understand the data, the scientist arrives at a final answer.

The means of forming and testing a hypothesis is the basis of all science. The answer must then be tested by other scientists before it can possibly be considered true, or valid.

The greatest difference between the sciences and the nonsciences is that sciences use the scientific method to arrive at an answer.

Three branches of science are the physical sciences, the biological sciences, and the social sciences. Physical scientists try to solve problems in the physical world. They study the earth and happenings that take place in it. Biological scientists experiment with origins, physical traits, and habits of plants

and animals. Social scientists study man and society. Sometimes social scientists have difficult times with the acceptance of their experiments. When humans are used as subjects, experiments cannot be as carefully controlled as they can be with nonhuman subjects.

Let's look at selected careers in science:

anthropologist
astronomer
botanist
chemist
dietitian
economist
nurse
oceanographer
pharmacist
physician
psychologist
technician
veterinarian

Many of the occupations shown here, especially those related to health, have great potential in terms of growth of jobs. Many of these jobs do not fit the stereotype of a scientist. Any person in the supermarket, dime store, or bank may be a scientist. Perhaps you even know several scientists yourself.

CHECKING PROGRESS

1. What are three branches of science? How do they differ? See if you can name two types of jobs in each branch.
2. Why do social scientists sometimes have difficulty with the acceptance of their experiments?
3. Name the scientific field in which each of the following persons serves:

	Person	Field
Example:	psychologist	psychology
	botanist	
	astronomer	
	physicist	
	oceanographer	
	anthropologist	
	chemist	
	economist	
	optometrist	
	pharmacist	
	biologist	
	veterinarian	

4. What suffixes are most commonly added to indicate the person who works in a scientific field?

CHOOSING NEXT STEPS

1. Draw a cartoon representing the scientist as he is often stereotyped. Draw cartoons of other people in careers that have also been stereotyped:
   (a) a farmer
   (b) a teacher
   (c) a librarian
   (d) a banker
2. Find information in the library about some scientific careers, such as those of an oceanographer or an anthropologist, about which you know very little. Make a chart showing the daily work of each career.

ZOE CHINN—MOUNTAINTOP GIRL

THINKING THINGS THROUGH

Sometimes certain jobs require a person to be more courageous than other jobs. This story is about one of those jobs, a
mountaintop lookout forester. This is a job that means being
alone, meeting wild animals, being in danger of fire, and
climbing a tower about sixty feet high. This story is also
about a city girl who accepts a job as a mountain lookout forester. As you read the story of Zoe Chinn, try to think about
what fears you would have to overcome if you were in her place.

ABOUT WORDS

Use the meanings of the following suffixes to help you build
words which are found in the story.

Suffixes	Meanings
-ion	act of or condition
-less	without
-er	that does
-ous	full of
-ness	state of

Word Definition	Word in Story
without speech	speechless
act of inspecting	
full of danger	
without care	
act of instructing	
state of being alone	
act of applying	
one that does camping	
state of being without care	
one that does traveling	

103

ZOE CHINN— MOUNTAINTOP GIRL

The tower is not there any more. The lookout is done by helicopter and other devices. Zoe Chinn is gone from the lonely spot in the mountains.

Maybe the helicopter is better. It allows greater range and closer inspection than the tower watch does. Maybe a space eye, or something else, will be even better still some day. But the tower way, with Zoe Chinn doing the lookout, will always suggest the way of a woman's will.

Come, then, to the mountaintop tower.

Meet Zoe Chinn, the mountaintop girl.

Zoe was twenty years old when she applied for the job. She had had two years of college. She was hoping to be a mountain lookout forester for the summer. Her parents had driven her over from her home in Chicago to the Shoshone National Forest in Wyoming's big mountains. They had managed the four miles of road from the bottom to the top of Warm Springs Mountain only after putting mud chains on the tires. Then they came to a dead end, several thousand feet up. They looked up at the tower top sixty feet higher still.

"You must climb to the top if you want the job," the ranger in charge told the would-be forester.

"Now?" Zoe exclaimed. She was surprised to have to be taking so sudden a test.

"Yes, now," the ranger said firmly.

She looked at the metal ladder. It stuck straight up to the cab (watcher's box) at the top of the tower. Layers of ice covered the rungs. Her head started swimming at the very prospect of it all, for she was inclined to be afraid of heights even ten feet off the ground. Where were the towers that had staircases? Not here.

She smiled at her speechless parents, then went briskly to the ladder. She started to climb it strongly, but carefully. About half way up she paused to rest. Then she noticed slats were missing from a wire basket put around the ladder as an intended safety device. "I'll just have to be sure not to fall," she thought and moved slowly on up.

Finally at the top she had to pull herself up onto a slick platform, about two feet wide and three feet long. It had no railing or guard of any kind. She stood sixty feet up in the air, the freezing drizzle of rain icing her eyebrows. Here she would have to stand every trip up, hold to a tower post with one hand, and try to open a trap door to the cab with the other. If she could get it open, she could hoist herself into the cab to do her lookout duties.

The ranger let her find this all out for herself. Then he followed to explain, "Your timing must be just right on that door. Sometimes there are strong gusts of wind and you can't open it against them!"

In the cab, which was only about a four- by five-foot box, Zoe observed a shortwave radio, a telephone, binoculars, a canebottom chair, and a stool. The seats of the "furniture" were covered with rubber pads, and there were glass coasters under the legs of the chairs.

"That's insulation," the ranger told her. "Lightning is fierce up here in the mountains." Then he showed her a pulley outside the cab. It was attached to a telephone below and would be used to ground the telephone for safety.

Here in the cab she took a minute to view the nearby cabin which she had admired before coming to the tower. Now she noticed the pile of logs behind the cabin. She would have to cut her own wood. She would have to do everything that was to be done on the mountaintop. She would be living alone.

The ranger had become silent. He wanted to let her look and think. She was thinking about what she wrote in her application: "I'm not afraid to live alone. I can do the job." She had been told, "It isn't for rewards, but it pays well—time and a half for weekends and one-third more as hazard pay."

She was looking at the river that was crawling between a sheer, deep cliff and a great forest. "People could walk off of that cliff," she noted aloud.

The ranger nipped that concern quickly. "But people aren't allowed up here!" he said.

Zoe turned to him and asked a question, part jest, part protest. "What is the hazard pay for up here?" she said.

The ranger answered back. "Wood chopping is dangerous. If you cut off a toe, you'd get fired for carelessness."

They climbed back to the ground.

"You're hired if you want the job," the ranger told her.

"I want it," she said quickly before her parents objected.

"You're on the lookout from sunrise to sunset," the ranger explained. "Each day report the temperature, wind speed, and other weather facts. Look for smoke and other trouble signs fifteen minutes every hour. Do as you please the rest of the time. Just be sure to watch from the tower." Then he told her, "The first day you'll learn your instructions. Then it's up to you. If you make the first two weeks, you'll stay."

After her parents left, Zoe went into the cabin and began to make it hers. She noted again that there weren't curtains. Then she laughed at herself, "You don't need curtains up here or in an airplane rest room. Nobody will be looking in!"

The next day she learned about the mountain area and the fire fighting methods. She even learned to pack mules for fire fighting. She also would be the relay person for messages between rangers, ranchers, campers, and villagers. The ranger told her, "In case of a fire near you, stay in the tower until we give you permission to leave. When you get permission, head for the meadow. We'll try to reach you there." The tower had already burned down once.

On duty, Zoe began to find out what being alone meant. She rarely saw anyone except the ranger who delivered her water and mail twice a week. She stayed in the tower from sunrise until lunch and then after lunch until sunset. Within a few days she had read all the books from the village library and had finished a correspondence course.

Zoe's notes tell what it was like to be alone as a mountain lookout forester. Some of her comments are about the small details of living: "There is no electricity in the cabin, nor piped-in fuel or water. I cut wood for cooking and heating. I wash my jeans and bathe in a galvanized wash tub."

Alone in the pitch dark of night on a mountaintop, with no help nearer than a camp ten miles away over rugged roads, she lived with a noise in the attic of her cabin. It was first a rattling rasping sound, then a gnawing, scratching noise. "I got used to it. I decided it must be pack rats at work."

Then there was a much louder noise. "There was a bump and a scratch and a bang outside. I opened the door slightly. I had no gun. I wasn't allowed to have one up there. But I looked. There was a big brown bear helping himself to my lunch meat, which I had put in a box outside that I use as an ice box. I locked the door. The bear took my meat and left.

"Another time," she wrote, "I met a mountain lion on the way to the tower. It had a rabbit clutched in its mouth. I stopped. The lion stopped. I eased back. He went down the mountainside after passing within three feet of me. He wasn't interested in me. He had his breakfast."

She wrote about taming chipmunks by getting them to eat out of her hands and of friendships with other animals. "One group of female deer I named the 'sewing circle'. The group of does was always together. Never was there a fawn nor a buck with them. I wondered what they gossiped about."

In the tower, too, there were special moments to note. "Today I left most of my clothing at the bottom of the tower, for I wanted to sunbathe on the tower. I looked down later and saw a whiskered man. It turned out all right. He brought my clothing and pitched it into the cab for me. He was a geology student who was lost and just wanted to get his bearings..."

Another time she wrote, "...the wind was blowing about seventy miles an hour. The tower was swaying so that my chair was first on one side and then on the other."

When she was asked what benefits come from mountaintop experiences like this, Zoe answered, "In this aloneness you

108

learn whether you like yourself. You'd better like what you are if you want to be alone very long . . . You learn to overcome your fears. I was afraid of heights until I worked on this tower. My first climb took seventeen minutes, my later ones only seventeen seconds. I was afraid of bears until I saw one . . . You learn whether you are a cheat. I could have made my reports from the cabin. Usually it would have been as well, for there were few fires and none serious. But what if a fire had started, and I had not discovered it? How much damage would there have been? How many men might have lost their lives? I couldn't do it!

"In time I quit listening for the noises of the city and learned to listen for sounds of the forest. I got to where I could sit in the tower and just look, drink nature in, review poems and songs I knew, or just sit blankly at will. I learned to look and listen, to read the beauty of the Tetons in the distance at sunset, to find the wonder of changing snows, to explore inside myself."

But along with the dreaming and the daring, there were hazards and hurts. Lightning struck the cab! Zoe Chinn fell to the cab floor.

The village operator tried to call the tower during the storm. The telephone had melted to a glob. There was no answer, of course. The operator decided to notify the ranger station. An hour or so later a ranger was at the cab telling Zoe, "I will carry you to Riverton for treatment."

"No," she insisted. "I was knocked out, but I will be all right. I was numb, but feeling is coming back."

After eighty-eight days alone as mountaintop girl for the United States Forest Service, she returned to college.

She advised, "I wouldn't take anything for my forestry experience. Yet, I wouldn't suggest it for anyone else. It is a matter of personal preference. What I do suggest is that any person, somehow, should have the test of self that I had—the aloneness, the challenge, or whatever is needed to discover what the self is made of—what really matters in life."

CHECKING PROGRESS

1. You learned many things about Zoe Chinn as you read the story of her adventure as a mountain lookout forester. What feelings and thoughts do you think she might have had at each of these times?
    (1) when the ranger said, "You must climb to the top if you want the job."
    (2) when she was inside the cab for the first time
    (3) when the ranger said, "You're hired if you want it."
    (4) when Zoe went into the cabin and began to make it hers
    (5) when the wind was blowing about seventy miles an hour and the tower was swaying so much that Zoe's chair was first on one side and then on the other.

2. What were some of the things Zoe learned to do when she was alone that she hadn't done before?

3. Reread the last paragraph in the story. In your own words tell what you think Zoe meant when she said, "...any person, somehow, should have the test of self that I had..."

CHOOSING NEXT STEPS

1. Read an informative book about forest rangers or about a national forest.
2. Read a fiction book or a biography about a ranger or someone who lived in a forest area.
3. View a filmstrip or 16mm film about forests, forest fires, or forest animals.
4. If you live in the area of a forest, plan to take a trip to visit the ranger station.

OUTDOOR CAST

THINKING THINGS THROUGH

Camping, hiking, picnicking, boating, fishing, or skiing are activities which might make you think of a fun happening you have had. Close your eyes and recall for a moment an exciting outdoor experience that you have enjoyed. What do you see? What do you hear and feel? Can you almost smell or taste something? As you read "Outdoor Cast," make some comparisons to your own experiences of a fun happening.

ABOUT WORDS

Adding a suffix to a base word changes the meaning of the word. The meaning of the base word and the meaning of the suffix work together to give meaning to the whole word. If you know the meaning of both the base word and the suffix, you will be likely to know the meaning of the whole word. Listed below are several words which end in the suffixes *-or, -eer, -al, -tion, -ion, -ment*. Use the meanings of these suffixes to help you get the meaning of the whole word which appears in the story.

Suffixes	Meanings
-al	pertaining to
-or, -eer	person who
-ment	act of
-ion	act of or condition
-tion	result of or condition

Using the guide above, complete the meanings for the following words on a separate piece of paper.

counselor	conservation
engineer	concession
survival	sanitation
revival	management
agricultural	entertainment

Example:	Word	Meaning
	inspector	one who inspects

111

INVESTIGATE

OUTDOOR CAST

There were seven boys, (that is, there were seven including Mr. George) on a survival hike in the back hills as a science experiment. Mr. George was their adviser. He was also an expert in survival techniques.

The boys were sprawled in a half-circle. They sat across from the log wall they had built as a heat reflector oven. It would bake the air plant roots which were gathered for food from a nearby lake.

Talk had turned from living outdoors to making a living out-of-doors. JK had made a statement that there was no other way.

When Mr. George heard JK's remark, he said, "Maybe you are like my old friend who works out-of-doors."

"Who?" JK asked. "What does he do?"

"My friend Barney," Mr. George continued, "stayed at the boarding house where I lived one summer. He was

chief of the crew there in search of peach tree diseases in the orchards. He would always say, 'Th' outa doors for me! Can't work inside much at all.'

"Barney walked over hot rocks in peach orchards all day with other men. In the evening he sat on the front porch and whittled monkey figures from peach seeds and just talked. 'Th' outa doors for me,' he would say every time we talked about work.

"Barney studied science in college and knew everything about the diseases of plants. Now he works as a U.S. government inspector. He inspects plants that might be shipped making sure that no diseases are present.

"Barney was always saying, 'Th' outa doors for me! I just can't work inside.' When someone would ask him why he didn't become a doctor like his buddy, he would just smile and after a short pause, say, 'Th' outa doors for me! I had thought about medicine but decided at camp one summer, it was outa doors for me.' "

Then Mr. George turned to JK and said, "Just like Barney, camping out fixes you on the out-of-doors."

"Maybe so, maybe not," JK replied. "Not this survival hike alone," he said as he took a baked root from the trail oven. "I have an idea I'd like a job that keeps me out-of-doors."

After tasting the baked root, he said, "Mmm-mm, all right!" Then the others tasted theirs, too.

After a while, JK asked Mr. George, "Do you think I should be a mining engineer like you?"

"No," Mr. George quickly said. "I wouldn't say that. Study yourself. Find out all about different kinds of outdoor work. Then decide what fits you best. What would you like to do?"
"I am trying to find out. I think I like the study of our minerals, or mineralogy, best of all."

"Have you talked to your teachers or counselor?"

"Yes, I talked to some of them last spring."

On the hike JK could not take notes nor jot down his thoughts. He marked only with a grass brush and juice from poke berries on a stump here and there. The hikers carried very little. They even made flint rock axes to cut the oven logs. Much of what was experienced was committed to memory, and JK's was packed full.

Back at school the survival hike was the main topic. Soon Mr. Taylor, the science teacher, asked the team to report on their hike. Each member was to include at least one highlight.

JK named his report, "A Night Like Barney's." Reviewing the campfire talk with Mr. George, he told about "outa-doors Barney." Also, he gave his ideas about working out-of-doors.

"I guess I had a camp-out like Barney's," he said. "I looked at stars through tree tops all night and thought about being a king of all those diamonds."

JK told of all his talks with his teachers, counselor, librarian, and jeweler about his interest in mineralogy. He even included addresses of letters he had written to mining and oil companies for information about different outdoor jobs.

JK also included a sheet with notes on some subjects which he found useful for studying out-of-door careers. On the sheet JK listed all the different outdoor jobs which could be considered under special subjects.

For Art, JK listed: landscaping, sculpturing, scene painting, pottery-making, sign painting, gem cutting,

114

gem polishing, carving, and rock crafting.

Listed under Parks were: gardening, landscaping, botany (plant science), tour service, camp and resort management, ornithology (bird science), fish culturing, concession operations, conservation services, and zoology (animal study).

Under Agriculture, he listed: farming, ranching, forestry, horticulture (tree science), entomology (insect science), operation of hatcheries, and research.

Other subjects which include outdoor jobs were <u>Rural Services</u> such as mail, utilities, health, recreation, sanitation, mining, drilling, lumbering, logging, fishing, hunting, marina operations, distributing farm implements and other goods, outdoor sports and sports entertainment, and road safety and beautification.

JK said, "I found occupations in these fields and many others listed in books in the library. One book I found was the *Dictionary of Occupational Titles.*

"Here are some questions my counselor said we should ask about any career we explore: What is the work like? What do I need to know or do to perform duties well? How do I prepare for this work? How much does it pay? What are the advancement possibilities? Will the job last? Will I be away from home much? Is the job for men, women, or both? How do I get started?"

"Well," Mr. Taylor noted, "it seems you had a revival hike as well as a survival hike. That helps all of us."

JK explained that if any of the students wanted to use the information on his sheet of outdoor careers they could copy it any time. He added that the librarian would be glad to find information on any of the jobs that were listed.

Several class members wrote down subjects that interested them from the list. Cathy had a question:

"Why isn't water ballet on the list?"

"That might be under sports entertainment or resort operations," said JK. Then he teased, "Isn't there enough on the list for girls, Karen?"

"Everything on the list is for girls!" Karen shot back. Everybody laughed. The girls clapped, and JK bowed. Karen wrote down OUTDOOR SPORTS ENTERTAINMENT on her list and added water ballet.

Together the class would explore many outdoor careers. You can, too.

CHECKING PROGRESS

Sometimes the author helps you to understand words in the story by giving you their meanings immediately following the words. The following words were defined by the author in the story you have just read. As you read each word, try to remember its meaning. Check back into the story to see if you have remembered correctly.

mineralogy	zoology
ornithology	botany
entomology	horticulture

CHOOSING NEXT STEPS

Select an outdoor work category that represents a preference you may have for a career. Make lists of work titles suggested by the category. Use the card catalog in the library and indexes of books to find where you can get information about the work related to each title.

Example: **Category**   **Work Titles**
Conservation   Soil Conservation Specialist
Water Conservation Specialist
Environmental Control Agent
Game Warden
Naturalist
Fishery Biologist
Forester
Game Biologist or Manager
Ranger

THE ART OF PERSUASION

THINKING THINGS THROUGH

Whenever we convince others to believe in a certain cause or to respond in a certain way, we are using *persuasion*. We use some form of persuasion every day. In order for us to be most effective it is helpful to know and use the five steps of persuasion.

1. Get your listener's attention.
2. State the problem and tell how the listener is involved.
3. Offer a solution or a way the problem can be solved.
4. Describe how the situation would be if your solution was used.
5. Push your listener into accepting your solution and acting immediately.

See if you use these steps when you are trying to persuade someone. In the next story of a used car salesman, these same steps are followed. First, the salesman greets the customers and introduces himself. Second, he lets the customers state the problem of needing a car. Third, he offers them the solution of a certain car. Fourth, he shows them the good aspects of the car. Fifth, he tells them about the honesty of his company and lets them make the final decision.

ABOUT WORDS

Which of the following statements do you think are persuasive? Tell why.

1. "You should wear your seatbelt because seatbelts save lives."
2. "If I clean my bedroom, may I go to the movies?"
3. "Come to my house, and I'll give you some cookies."
4. "Please pass the potatoes."
5. "Uncle Bill is wondering where you are."
6. "With every gallon of milk you purchase, our store will give you a dozen eggs free."
7. "Your shoe is untied."

117

INVESTIGATE

the art of
PERSUASION

"I'll take it!"

"The jury finds the defendant—not guilty."

"Yes, you may go to the movie if you wish."

Do these expressions sound familiar? They should. They are part of the everyday world. And they have one thing in common. In each expression, someone has persuaded someone else to do something.

Persuasion can be defined as the act of convincing others to believe in a certain cause or to respond in a certain way. There always is some control of behavior in the art of persuasion.

Persuasion is important for meeting and dealing with people. Most salesmen, personnel managers, and buyers have high persuasive ability. Lawyers, ministers, people in public offices, teachers, and advertisers also use persuasion.

The following short story is an example of using the art of persuasion.

The Automobile Salesman

Tom Haney is a salesman for a used-car dealer. He has been working for almost six months and has learned how to convince people that they are making a wise decision. He sees a young couple looking at a sports car and hopes to persuade them that this car is the one for them.

"Hello. I'm Tom Haney. Can I help you?"

"We're looking for a car which is in good condition," says the man.

"You've come to the right place," says Mr. Haney. "This car had only one owner and was carefully taken care of. Please get inside and see

118

how it feels." Tom Haney knows that he will get a better response if he tells them instead of asking them. He has learned that one part of the art of persuasion is telling people what to do in terms of their own needs and interests.

"You make a fine couple, sitting there together. You won't go wrong with this particular car," he adds.

"Are you sure this car had only one owner?" asks the woman, looking at Tom.

Mr. Haney knows that a successful sale depends upon the persuasion in his facial expression, eyes, and voice. He looks directly at them and replies, "I am positive. Here is the name of the owner whom you can contact if you wish. We are an honest dealership. We want you to come back again for your next car."

In this way, Tom Haney has become a top salesman. He knows how to use the art of persuasion.

119

CHECKING PROGRESS

1. What is persuasion? Do you think that persuading someone is the same as controlling their thoughts?
2. What careers mentioned in the article use persuasion? Can you think of other careers that use persuasion?
3. How did Tom Haney use persuasion? Do you think the people will buy the automobile?
4. If you are interested in developing persuasive ability, what school activities could help you? What activities outside of school could also help you?
5. Review the definitions of persuasion and science before answering the following question. Why is persuasion referred to in this article as an art instead of a science?

CHOOSING NEXT STEPS

Try out your persuasive art; prepare one of the following activities on your own. Then present it to the class.

1. Pretend you are selling a car to a customer. Use spoken language only.
2. Sell a floor wax product. Either use movement and gestures to act it out, or use pictures to communicate the message. Do not use spoken words.
3. Persuade someone to help you with the dishes. Use gestures only. Do not use spoken words.
4. Persuade someone of an idea which you think is important, such as wearing seat belts, fighting pollution, or giving up smoking.
5. Sell a new kind of breakfast cereal. Use written words only. Then read your words out loud to the class.

ART IN BLUE, RED, AND YELLOW

THINKING THINGS THROUGH

Have you ever thought about classifying careers by color? The author has prepared a chart at the end of the story selection classifying different art careers by color. After reading the story, study the chart. You may decide that there are other careers related to art which are not now on the chart.

On the first page of the selection the author writes, "Along with the creative gift there must be a determination to develop this talent, and a persistence to pursue an artistic career." What do you think this sentence means?

ABOUT WORDS

The author of "Art in Blue, Red, and Yellow," has used some words which may not be familiar to you. The following is a list of these words. Use your dictionary to find the correct meaning as the author has used the word in the story.

artistic   masterpieces
art-related   acrylic
commercial   bas-reliefs
artifacts   composer
determination   compositions
persistence   instrumentalist
pursue   continual
impact   overemphasized
techniques   curators

After you have learned the meanings of the words in the list above, select five of the words with a root form and write the root on a separate sheet of paper.

121

ART IN BLUE, RED, AND YELLOW

Fortunate are those who can earn a living doing the thing they most want to do.

Persons with talent in art or who work in art-related fields are in this position. But before you decide to make a living as an artist, let's talk about the different careers in the artistic field.

There are many different ways that one may work as an artist. There are also many different types of work in each kind of art. Let's think of them in terms of color—blue for the fine arts, red for the commercial arts, and yellow for the applied arts or crafts. On page 125 you will find a chart. Since no two people would classify these careers in the same way, you may rearrange them if you wish.

The importance of art cannot be measured in terms of money or time. The most primitive cave dwellers scratched pictures on their

122

walls. Much of the history of early mankind is discovered through the art and artifacts which have been preserved until the present time.

Several qualities are necessary to be successful in any artistic work. At the top of the list is talent, which is a combination of imagination and the ability to express it to others. Along with the creative gift there must be a determination to develop this talent, and a persistance to pursue an artistic career.

Most artists study with experienced artists to build techniques. A few have developed their talent through their own efforts. Until the artist becomes better known, he may have difficulty making a living, and often goes for long periods without selling any of his works.

Many fine artists work in the field of commercial art to make a living and paint their

masterpieces after working hours. Teaching art is a useful way to meet the need for money. There are many other ways the artist can use his or her talent to make a living in either the red area of commercial art or the yellow area of applied art.

Each person must make his decision about which type of artwork to do.

The Painter

The fine art painter usually works with oil, watercolor, or acrylic paints. His works are found in museums and galleries. Some painters will also work in the commercial art field, such as drawing, illustrating, advertising, or making prints. Other painters teach, work as directors or curators of museums, or own art galleries. Still others may prefer the quiet satisfaction of making a living in the applied art and crafts field, using their talents and skills to make decorative things.

The Sculptor

The sculptor may work in marble, bronze, wood, metal or clay. For steady income, the sculptor may make statuettes, carve bas-reliefs, design furniture, or teach. Pottery-making is another way he may earn income. Both in the red and yellow areas, the sculptor is using his imagination and his skill to create something useable and salable as well as artistically valuable.

The Musician

In the blue area we can place the composer, performer, and director. The composer uses creative imagination, muscial talent, and knowledge of the mechanics of music to create songs, orchestral pieces, solos, operas, and other types of compositions. The performer may be a singer, an instrumentalist, or a director. He or she uses creative imagination, talent, and the knowledge of music to perform the composition as the composer meant it to be performed.

Many musicians earn extra money by arranging, teaching, or writing music for commercials.

The Dancer

Dancing requires special talents, long and hard training, and continual practice. Though not every dancer is in the blue class, we must include the choreographer who plans the dances and the star dancer. Other dancers are classified under red—teachers, show business producers, or performers. In the yellow area are TV and night club acts.

The Actor

The competition in the theatre is fierce, but some people become top-notch actors, directors, and playwrights. Directing a community theatre group is a good goal for someone who does not want the uncertainties of the theatre.

The Architect

The architect who designs a superb building can be considered a fine artist. The truly great architect has fewer money problems than other artists. The architect in the red column plans and supervises the construction of buildings and homes. The

124

architect in the yellow list might be the draftsman, builder, or nurseryman.

The Photographer

Many beautiful things are done with cameras which require creative imagination, knowledge of the camera, the film, and the quality of light. A select few are listed in the fine arts column. Most photographers fit in the other two lists. Craftsmen with an interest in photography might find satisfaction working in a processing laboratory or the newspaper and TV photography field.

The Designer

Great fashion designers could be classified as blue because of the impact they have on our culture. The other designers can be found on the red and yellow list.

The importance of the teacher of art cannot be overemphasized. He or she passes the knowledge, skills, enthusiasm, and the inspiration from one generation to the next.

FINE ART	COMMERCIAL ART	APPLIED ARTS
Art done for personal satisfaction without expectation of immediate cash returns	Art for a purpose (like making money) but still creative	Art primarily done to make money, but done skillfully
PAINTING		

Painter
  Oils
  Watercolor
  Acrylic
	Graphic artist, print maker, curator, teacher,	Decorative articles sold in stores.

SCULPTURE		

Sculptor
  Marble
  Bronze
  Wood
	Statuettes, work with precious metal, fine furniture, bas-reliefs, pottery.	Decorative items sold in stores. Rock polishing, teacher.

MUSIC		
Composer Performer Director	Musical show producer, performer in opera, orchestra and shows, amateur performer.	TV, movie, and radio personality, music publisher, technician.
DANCE		
Choreographer Ballet dancer	Musical show producer and star dancer,	Chorus line, ice revue skaters, teacher.
THEATRE		
Dramatist Actor	Author, actor, director, teacher, community theatre director.	TV, movie, radio, night club entertainer, others.
ARCHITECTURE		
Architect with different or new ideas.	Architect, landscaper.	Draftsman, builder, nurseryman.
PHOTOGRAPHY		
Photographer for art books, salon photographer	Documentary photographer, advertising	TV and newspaper, laboratory processor, repairman.
DESIGN		
Leaders in design field of fashion or industry.	Interior decorator, fashion designer,	Dressmaker, decal or stencil designer

CHECKING PROGRESS

1. This selection begins with the statement, "Fortunate are those who can earn a living doing the thing they most want to do." Explain what you think this statement means in terms of art and the artist.
2. Read the chart on page 125 for help in answering the following questions.
   (1) Work with precious metal is classified as:
   fine art   commercial art   applied art/crafts
   (2) Rock polishing is considered to be:
   sculpture   architecture   design
   (3) A dressmaker is included in the field of:
   photography   sculpture   design
   (4) A person interested in TV might find a career in the field of:
   photography   music   theatre
   (5) The music composer falls into the classification of:
   fine art   commercial art   applied art/crafts
3. Think of someone you know who is an artist. What type of art does this person do? In what field of art does he work?

CHOOSING NEXT STEPS

1. Read a biography of a person who is successful in one of the arts in the list.
2. Which of the arts interests you most? Find another classmate who is also interested in that field. Discuss the following:
   (1) When did you first become interested in this field of art and why?
   (2) In what ways do you find this art rewarding to you?
   (3) What careers could grow out of your interest in this field of art?
3. Ask an artist who lives in your community to visit your classroom and tell about his work in art.
4. Make a bulletin board display of clippings pertaining to art and artists from the daily newspaper.

THE DANCER AND DANCING

THINKING THINGS THROUGH

Most of you have probably never even considered the possibility that being a dancer requires many of the same qualifications as being an athlete. Both a dancer and an athlete must be in top physical condition. Both must train and practice long and hard. Both must have good coordination and be very agile. Both must be very good at what they are doing in order to become a success. This selection about Jack Tygett will give you a better idea of what the career of a professional dancer would be like.

ABOUT WORDS

Synonyms are words that have similar meanings and *antonyms* are words that have opposite meanings. One word in each of the following pairs has been taken from this selection. Decide which of the word pairs are synonyms and which ones are antonyms. Use the dictionary if you think you need help with the word meanings.

intricate - simple
feats - achievements
agile - nimble
audition - tryout
scarce - abundant
diligently - industriously
mastery - command
devoted - undedicated
disillusioned - disenchanted
counsels - advises

BEFORE YOU READ

127

INVESTIGATE

The Dancer
and Dancing

Look! It was a sight you probably never thought you would see. A football player was ballet dancing.

Look again! He was perspiring furiously. Dancing was hard work! The muscles in his legs were as hard as rocks. Good dancers have to be as well trained as athletes in order to be successful. Indeed, this young man was working out as an athlete through ballet dancing. He was waiting for his eligibility to play college football at the University of Illinois. He was keeping in physical condition by dancing.

He liked the feeling of power and control which accompanied the mastery of intricate combinations of difficult dance feats. But, he was thirty-five pounds overweight for a dancer. The others laughed as he threw his weight around.

No one was laughing seven months after he began his lessons. He auditioned for the Chicago Opera Ballet—and won his first performing role. At twenty-one he was on his way to becoming a graceful, agile dancer with a bright future.

Who was this young man? He was John P. Tygett, known as "Jack." He is now head of the Musical Theatre Department at the San Diego Campus of the United States International University, School of Visual and Performing Arts. He has been a choreographer for the Dinah Shore and Doris Day television shows, among others. He has danced on most of the major television programs, such as the Andy Williams, Johnny Carson, and Walt Disney shows. He has danced in many movies, including *Mary Poppins* and *My Fair Lady*.

Jack was born in Valier, Illinois, on February 5, 1926. In 1933 his family moved to Chicago. When he was older, he went to San Francisco and Los Angeles to perform in night clubs. It is important for a dancer to be where the jobs are.

This usually means living in or near Hollywood, Las Vegas, New York, or some other large metropolitan area.

When Jack was in Los Angeles, a Hollywood choreographer saw him perform and asked him to work in a movie, the first of many movies in which Jack would perform.

Later, while performing in his first live musical in 1952, he met Marjorie Ayers, who was to later become his wife. They worked in numerous movies, musicals, and night clubs.

In 1959 the Tygetts moved to Van Nuys, California. They opened a dance school in their home. Work was very scarce at this point in their lives. Jack was still taking dance lessons around Hollywood and trying to become a choreographer. He had to drive a cab to meet expenses. Disillusioned by the lack of artistry a choreographer was allowed in commercial shows, he returned to the performing side of dance.

In 1961 they moved to Canoga Park, California, and enlarged their dance school. Through the 1960's Jack developed a name as a dancer, teacher, and choreographer. He taught dance classes at the University of Southern California. He became known to most choreographers of movies and television. Through these contacts he received many job offers.

He has been devoted to his career these past few years, working ten to twelve hours a day. He counsels young dancers, teaches, and does choreography. Jack thinks hard work is needed if one is to obtain professional excellence.

Look! The dancers are dancing. They are perspiring furiously. And Jack Tygett is working as hard as any of them. The art of dancing must be mastered.

CHECKING PROGRESS

1. Discuss the life style of a dancer.
    (1) What did you learn about the life style of a professional dancer that you did not know before you read this story about Jack Tygett?
    (2) What do you feel is most rewarding about this career?
    (3) What do you feel are the greatest problems that a professional dancer might have to face?
2. In what ways would a career in dancing be similar to a career in athletics? Consider interests, skills, job opportunities, and working conditions.
3. What are some important things to remember if you want to have a career in dancing?
4. Skim through the story and find what you consider to be the most important happenings in the life of John P. Tygett. List them in the order they occurred and choose the one you consider most important of all.

CHOOSING NEXT STEPS

1. Mr. Tygett has had some disappointments in his career. Have you already had some disappointing experiences? How did you feel? Did the disappointments you had help you in any way? How?
2. If you are interested in dancing as a career or as a hobby, select books and films from your library about:
    (1) kinds of dancing careers.
    (2) biographies of dancers in the United States and in other countries throughout the world.
    (3) kinds of dances in various countries.

LITERARY CAREERS

THINKING THINGS THROUGH

When you study you will often find it helpful to make an outline of the selection you are reading. An *outline* is a brief summary of main points, and it is written in a special way. It helps you recall the details of an article. In making an outline, you will first need to choose the two or three main topics of the selection.

Choosing main topics:

(1) Read the title of the selection and think of a question that you expect the material to answer.

(2) Read the entire selection and find the answer to your question.

(3) List your answer in the form of two or three main topics. You will be able to do this if you have chosen a good question.

Choosing subtopics:

(1) After choosing the main topics, think of questions that you expect the material to answer about each main topic.

(2) Read the selection and find answers to your questions and other important information relating to each main topic.

(3) These topics which relate to the main topics are called *subtopics*. They are listed in the outline underneath the main topics.

The title of this selection is "Literary Careers." Before you read, ask yourself this question: What are some kinds of literary careers? Then as you read the selection, find two main topics about literary careers.

ABOUT WORDS

Watch for these words as you read:

salary	an amount of money paid regularly for work done
free-lance	one who works on his own without committing himself to any one employer
manuscript	a handwritten or typed article

131

INVESTIGATE

LITERARY CAREERS

"I want to be a writer."

"What kind of a writer?"

"Why, uh...a writer. What do you mean, what kind?"

Many students do not know what various types of work come under the title of being a writer. Most writers are paid a salary for what they write. Other writers work on their own and then try to sell their work to book publishing companies and

magazines. These are called *free-lance writers*.

A salaried writer usually reports to a place of business to write each day. He may work as a newspaper reporter interviewing people and gathering information for a story. He may work as an editor for a book publisher preparing manuscripts for publication. He can also work as an editor for a magazine. He can write commercials, news reports, public service programs, and dramatic programs for radio or television. He can write movie scripts. He can work for the government writing books, pamphlets, and reports. He can work for a university writing scholarly books and literary magazines. He can work for a company as a technical writer, taking the facts in science or engineering and turning them into understandable reading. He can work for a company with an employee newsletter.

A free-lance writer need not go to a special office. He can set up an office anywhere. He needs a typewriter because everything sent to editors must be typed and double-spaced on the paper. He will want to keep a copy of everything he mails to editors. A freelance writer has no definite hours. His time is his own. He can work at writing every evening, or he can write one day a week. The amount of time he puts into his work often determines the number of manuscript sales he makes. A free-lance writer usually does literary work in writing poetry, plays, novels, essays, short stories, and book reviews. Many also write magazine articles and scripts for movies and television programs. Sometimes people ask a free-lance writer, "When do you find the time to write?" The answer is that he does not find the time. He makes the time. He wants to write more than anything else, so he puts other activities aside. This takes discipline.

Whether salaried or freelance, a writer should be a person who likes people. For the most part, he is writing about people or to people. The writer can take facts and make them so interesting that people want to read what he has written. He can use his imagination to create pleasure for readers. He should enjoy turning his ideas into words and be willing to practice as his talent grows. Writing is an exciting career open to anyone who shows interest, talent, and willingness to work at it.

133

CHECKING PROGRESS

1. What main topics did you choose? Probably you chose: (1) salaried writers and (2) free-lance writers. Most of the selection explains these two types of careers for writers.

2. What subtopics did you choose? Probably you chose the specific jobs a person can have either as a salaried or as a free-lance writer. Your outline should look something like this:

Literary Careers

I. Salaried writers
   A. Newspaper reporter
   B. Book editor
   C. Magazine editor
   D. Radio or television writer
II. Free-lance writers
   A. Poet
   B. Writer of plays
   C. Writer of novels
   D. Writer of essays

Continue writing down all the possible jobs for each. This outline answers the question "What are some kinds of literary careers?"

CHOOSING NEXT STEPS

1. Keep a journal for yourself of things you do, see, or think about. Try to write something each day.
2. Write a poem expressing a thoughtful idea.
3. Write a silly jingle or rhyme that could be used for a television commercial.
4. Write a newspaper article about an event that happened at school or at home.

WRITING A STORY FOR PUBLICATION

THINKING THINGS THROUGH

Are you interested in writing a story or an article for publication? Many teen-agers have their stories, poems, or other writings published every year.

In the following selection the author has written some guidelines for successful writing. Read the story to find out how to go about writing a successful story for publication.

ABOUT WORDS

1. After reading the selection on writing a story for publication, make up a list of descriptive adjective phrases suitable for main characters in a story.

   For example: The *leathery-faced* ranger

   The *wispy gray-haired* grandmother

   How many were you able to think of? Now, set your imagination to work again by making up a list of action verbs which will paint a picture, tell you how a character feels, or set a mood for a story. You may use complete sentences this time.

   For example: Johnny *stomped* out of the room.

   He *dashed* for the train.

   Fires *raged* all around them.

   Use your dictionary to find out the meaning of *sensory perception*. Then write some descriptive words which invite your sensory perception.

   For example: The *pungent* flavor of the spices

   The *stale* air

   Mother's *spicy, moist* cake

2. The author has used the word *empathy* in this selection. In your own words, explain what you think empathy means. You may use your dictionary to help you find the exact meaning of this word.

INVESTIGATE

BEFORE YOU READ

Writing A Story For Publication

Writing a story for publication means that the author writes with the purpose of sharing his idea with other people. An editor buys the story from the author, but his readers pay to receive the magazine and read the story. This means that before the author can reach his readers, he must please an editor first.

An author keeps in mind the kind of story the editor wants to publish. Then when the author has an idea for a story and knows to which editor he will send it, he is ready to write.

What is the most important part of any story? The answer to this question is: the main character.

The author must get acquainted with his main character before he ever begins to write about him. He must be sure he likes him, because if he doesn't, this feeling will be sensed by his readers, and they won't like him either. A person with terrible faults is not always popular, although a small fault or two makes the character seem more human and likable.

A reader decides whether he likes the main character or not, soon after beginning the story. If he does not like him, often he does not want to finish the story. If he does like him, he becomes interested in what will happen to him.

In order to show how his character thinks and feels the writer must assume his role. While he is writing, the author must actually be the character for a little while. This is called *empathy*.

How do we understand the feelings of others? How do we get inside them to figure them out? Imagination is the answer. Empathy is needed to write convincingly about the character.

136

The main character should come alive to the reader.

There are three ways in which an author makes this happen. First, he gives the reader just a little description of the character.

Second, the author shows what the character is like through his actions.

Third, the author shows what a character is like through his dialogue or speech. Dialogue should be easy and natural. Each person has his own pattern of speech, and often it fits the type of work he does, his age, his education, and the part of the country in which he lives. As the characters speak, they are discussing what is going on in the story. Any conversation they might have which has nothing to do with the *plot*, or the action, of the story does not belong in the story.

The story begins with the plot. What is plot? Simply, it is what happens to the main character. At the beginning of the story he is given a problem, and he must solve that problem.

Sometimes the problem can be with another person, with nature, with an idea, and even with himself. However, there it stands in the way of what he wants or where he is going, and he must do something about it. That is plot.

When you are turning the pages of a magazine looking for a story to read, what makes you stop and choose one? It is usually the beginning sentence of a story — something that sounds so interesting that you want to read the rest to find out what happened.

An author, writing for publication, is very careful

137

of the opening of his story. Often he writes it over and over again, working for a beginning that will catch and hold readers' interests.

He is also very much aware of description. Description is important to a story, making it come alive for the reader. Long ago writers would stop the telling of their stories to write pages of description. But readers in our modern times are impatient. They want to see what will happen next. They do not want to stop the story to find out what a house or a room or a sunset looks like. So the author today puts description into his story in small doses—two or three sentences here, two or three words there—and he is careful to make good use of each word.

If you were to be asked, "Give me the name of a part of speech that describes," you would probably answer, an adjective. You would be right; but the author has found a part of speech that is even more descriptive than an adjective—*an action verb*.

One action verb can *paint a picture*. One action verb can *tell you how a character is feeling*. One action verb can *set the mood of a story*.

Another tool of description is called *sensory perception*. It is simply making use of the five senses to make the story more real to the reader.

Not many people think about their five senses in their reactions to things about them. How about you? When is the last time you really looked at the many colors in the leaves on a tree? Have you ever run your fingers back and forth against a piece of velvet, trying to put into words the contrast between the roughness and the smoothness of the material? You are used to listening to your favorite records, but have you ever taken time to listen to the quiet, familiar sounds in the house when the records have finished playing?

A writer learns to do these things because his awareness is important to his writing. It makes the difference between "black and white" and "glorious living color" as the ads for television used to say. The author presents his "living color" to his readers, helping them to see it with the same excitement as he sees it. A reader is drawn into the story when he "feels" it happening.

Often an author is asked the same question: "Where do you get ideas?" Ideas aren't really hard to get. Sometimes an author has to work a little for one, but most of the time he almost has to beat them off, because they crowd in like moths around a porch light and refuse to come in one at a time when needed.

The more a writer explores ideas, the more aware he is of what is going on around him, the more ideas he will have. They may come from conversations with friends, from newspaper articles, or from things he sees. The author takes the idea, changes it, adds to it, and turns it into a story he has invented.

He develops the idea of asking himself, "What if...?" See that man at the airport walking up and

down, up and down. Why is he impatient? What if...? Here the author's imagination takes over. In this way an author finds story ideas he can use. However, ideas, just like the moths that flit away, can be gone if they are not caught. So the author keeps a file of ideas. He uses a large envelope, a box, or a desk drawer. He collects newspaper clippings or cards with ideas written on them. When he needs an idea about which to write, he looks through his file. There, suddenly, is exactly what he wants. One of the ideas he had thought about before stands out and suggests a new story.

Editors care only about what is written on the pages mailed to them. If they read a story they like, and they think their readers will like it, they buy it.

There is great enjoyment in writing, and a special thrill for the author when his story is published. Under the title is his name and the story he himself has created for people all over the world to see and read.

139

CHECKING PROGRESS

Make an outline for the selection, "Writing a Story for Publication," listing main topics and subtopics. Reread the selection to help you with the assignment. The first main topic is shown below.

Writing a Story for Publication

I. Author must please the editor.

CHOOSING NEXT STEPS

Using the selection, "Writing a Story for Publication," develop a checklist which includes the important points an author must remember in writing. This checklist may be used for evaluating stories which you write or which you read in books in the library.

Checklist for Evaluating a Story for Publication

Important Points	Good	Needs Improvement	Author
1. _____	_____	_____	_____
2. _____	_____	_____	_____
3. _____	_____	_____	_____
4. _____	_____	_____	_____
5. _____	_____	_____	_____

Work with several of your classmates to gather, evaluate, and compile stories, poems, riddles, and other original writing done by members of your class. You could share this work in one of several ways:

(1) Make an interesting display on a hall or classroom bulletin board.

(2) Arrange material in an interesting way in a large loose-leaf notebook. Decorate the cover and give the collection an interesting title, such as "Tells and Tales."

I KNOW WHAT I WANT TO BE

THINKING THINGS THROUGH

Some people find it difficult to decide just exactly what kind of work they want to do when it is time to choose a career. For many, this decision is made easier by the use of counseling and educational tests. These tests can be done at any time in your life. They show your likes and dislikes and may be used to predict the fields in which you would have a good chance for success. In this story, a junior high school class is taking such a test. One of the pupils seems to know her own mind and rebels against the test. Read to find out if Terri really knew what she wanted to be.

ABOUT WORDS

Some words are defined in the dictionary as having a particular meaning similar to other words. We call such words synonyms. However, synonyms often have their own particular *connotation*, or distinct special quality that makes them more correct in one context than in another. For example, *childish* and *childlike* are defined similarly in the dictionary. But do the following two sentences leave you with the same impression or feelings?

1. Jody had a childlike attitude about religion.
2. Jody had a childish attitude about religion.

The following sentences are from the story. When you read the story, decide which of the synonyms shown under each sentence presents the correct connotation of the italicized word.

"I'm sorry," she said,"but this is such a *dumb* test."

    silent   foolish   stupid

"One, count the people crossing the street! That's *crazy*."

    insane   flawed   impractical

. . . she was quiet with the exception of a few quick *explosions*.

    outbursts   blasts   upheavals

141

INVESTIGATE

I KNOW WHAT I WANT TO BE

Miss Whitebush, the school counselor, held up a folder before Terri's class. "This test might help you choose a career someday," she said. "It will bring out your talents and show you where your interests lie."

"Then I don't have to take the test because I know what I'm going to be," Terry said. "I'll give my folder back."

"Everyone must take the test," the counselor said. "Now, inside your folders are test questions. The questions are multiple choice. Each section has four answers, so pick the one you like best and mark the right number for it on the sheet. Look first at the sample question."

She read aloud: "Which do you like best? One, I like to grow vegetables; two, I like to sell vegetables to people; three, I like to paint pictures of vegetables; and four, I like to see displays of vegetables at the county fair."

Terri raised her hand. "I can't put anything down because I hate vegetables. I'm glad they didn't say, 'I like to eat vegetables,' because that would make me sick. And how can I check number four if I've never been to a county fair?"

"Terri, you are missing the point of the test," Miss Whitebush said. "The questions may seem strange but when all the answers are added together they give a good picture of what you might like to be when you are grown."

"I told you, I know what I'd like to be," Terri said. "I want to be the captain of a submarine."

"There aren't any women in a job like that."

"There isn't a woman president either. But...."

"All right, Terri! We must start this test!"

Terri bent over her paper and for a few minutes she was quiet. Then she muttered, "Oh, my gosh!"

"What is it now, Terri?" the counselor asked sternly.

"This one says, 'I like German shepherds'! Blah! I don't like German shepherds!"

"You have to check something in each section! For goodness' sake, do your best!"

"What if I flunk this test?" Terri asked.

"You can't flunk a test like this," the counselor answered. "Now get busy!"

Terri obediently went back to her paper, but she was soon laughing. "I'm sorry," she said, "but this is such a dumb test! Listen to this: 'What would I like to do best? One, count the people crossing the street'! That's crazy. Who wants to do that?"

"Terri, I'm not going to warn you again!"

But in a moment Terri spoke up again. "I have to ask you something. I like everything in this one. What do I do? 'I like to make popcorn; I like to sell candy; I like to sail boats on the lake; I like to tell stories to children.' "

The counselor said, "When you come to a section in which you like everything, try to find the thing you like best."

Terri began to work, and for a while she was quiet with the exception of a few quick explosions:

"Raise turkeys? Did you ever try raising a turkey? Ugh! Collect garbage? Yecccch!"

The bell rang. Terri gave her paper to the counselor.

"That test wasn't any good," she said. "It won't tell me what I ought to be when I grow up."

"We'll know the results tomorrow," the counselor said.

The next day the counselor was waiting anxiously for Terri.

"The test showed that you have a definite interest in the sea and machinery. You could be a captain of a submarine!"

Terri sighed.

The counselor was puzzled. "Aren't you happy about it?"

"Why should I be happy?" Terri said. "I told you I was going to be a captain of a submarine. So think of all the time I wasted taking that dumb test!"

CHECKING PROGRESS

1. Did Terri know what she wanted to be? How did she prove it to Miss Whitebush?
2. Do you feel as though you know Terri? How did the author introduce you to Terri with descriptive language, word images, dialogue, and actions?
3. Write down five of Terri's statements which give you clues to her personality.
4. Do you know anyone who reminds you of Terri? In what ways?

CHOOSING NEXT STEPS

Ask yourself the following questions and be prepared to give the answers if necessary.

1. Did you like Terri? Why or why not?
2. Why do you think Terri had problems answering the test questions?
3. Describe Terri. How does she look? What are some of her personality traits? Does she get along well with other people? Does she have a sense of humor?
4. Do you think Terri will ever become captain of a submarine? Why or why not?
5. With the results of Terri's test in mind, try to list several other occupations in which she might be happy. Besides an interest in the sea and machinery, what other aptitudes might a person need to captain a ship?

A PEEK AROUND OUR BLINDERS

THINKING THINGS THROUGH

After a day of educational testing, you might hear someone exclaim, "Boy, I really messed them up on that test! I answered every question opposite of the way I felt."

This incident happens often in junior highs across the country. Teachers and students play the "testing game." Teachers believe they are providing a good guidance program. Students think they are beating the system. We are defeating each other. All of us are losing in the game of life careers.

We need to remember that an educational test is merely a tool that allows us to gain information quickly and systematically about the individual. These tests tell us about a person's abilities, interests, knowledge, and skills. They tell us things about ourselves of which we may not be aware. Most of us see ourselves through a set of blinders. These blinders are our needs to belong, to be loved, to feel self-worth, and to feel in control of our own lives. These needs often prevent us from looking clearly at ourselves. We are afraid of choosing a career because it might make us look too bright and ambitious, or because it might make us look dull and worthless. We think of many reasons why we should or should not do something.

In order to look at ourselves clearly, we need truthful information. Educational tests help give us that information.

ABOUT WORDS

Watch for these words as you read:

guidance	the process of giving advice on careers and school problems to students
blinders	flaps put over the eyes so that a person cannot see everything in sight
standardized	a test given to many people so that one can compare his results with the rest of the group

BEFORE YOU READ

145

INVESTIGATE

A PEEK
AROUND
OUR BLINDERS

People in the guidance department of our school need information about us in order to help us make decisions. To get information, they give us educational tests. Tests help us to take a peek around our blinders. They help us to look clearly at ourselves.

Three types of tests are important to us in terms of career guidance. These are achievement tests, interest tests, and aptitude tests.

Achievement Tests

The *achievement test* measures a person's present knowledge and skills in a particular area or field. It is usually *standardized*, which means that a person can compare his performance against a group of similar students. A counselor who uses this test can tell the person's strongest and weakest subjects compared to students across the country.

Interest Tests

The *interest test* measures our tendency to like or dislike certain activities. There are many things that attract our interest and there are other things that do not interest us at all. Although we could simply ask a person what he likes and dislikes, we know that people put on their blinders and tell us what they think we want to hear. On an interest test, a student is told to mark "A" if the activity represents something he likes to do. He marks "C" if he dislikes the activity, and he marks "B" if he is undecided. Below is a sample.

If you were on a trip to a large city you would:	
26. Visit an art gallery	A B C
27. Browse in a library	A B C
28. Visit a museum	A B C
You usually like to:	
29. Collect autographs	A B C
30. Collect coins	A B C
31. Collect butterflies	A B C

The special aptitude test is designed to make predictions in any career area. One important point to remember is that aptitude scores can be changed with experience. If a person gets more education or on-the-job training, he may be able to score higher than before.

Many people dislike tests, but tests are here to stay. They are a means of assessing our achievements, interests, and aptitudes. We should use the data tests give us. We need all the information we can get so that our blinders don't block us from seeing our path.

The danger of interest tests is that we often misinterpret what the tests tell us. Interest in an area does not necessarily indicate ability.

Aptitude Tests

The *aptitude test* predicts future success based on the person's knowledge and skills when he takes the test. Two types of such tests are the scholastic aptitude test and the special aptitude test. The scholastic aptitude test allows us to predict a person's likely success in school. It helps students make decisions about attending college or not.

CHECKING PROGRESS

1. The title of this selection is "A Peek Around Our Blinders." What are blinders? Find the definition in *About Words*. What does the author mean by blinders? Find his meaning in *Thinking Things Through*.
2. Three types of tests are discussed in this article—achievement, interest, and aptitude tests.
   (a) Which type of test measures a person's tendency to like or dislike certain activities?
   (b) Which type predicts a person's future success in school or a career?
   (c) Which type measures a person's present knowledge and skill in a particular area?
3. What do you think about such tests? Did this article help change your feelings?

CHOOSING NEXT STEPS

1. Ask your counselor if you can examine samples of achievement, interest, and aptitude tests. Ask the counselor to explain them to you and to tell you how they can help you know more about yourself.
2. See how much you know about your own achievement, interests and aptitudes.
   (a) In which academic areas do you achieve the highest? Lowest? How do you account for these differences?
   (b) In what school subjects and other activities are you most interested? Why do you like these best?
   (c) In what future areas do you feel you will do well? Why do you think so?

USING THE DICTIONARY

The dictionary is an important tool. It is useful for spelling and for the study of word meanings and pronunciations. This reference book is immensely helpful as you write and study. It helps you to clarify the meanings of words used by others, and to use words more effectively in your own writing.

ENTRY WORDS IN THE DICTIONARY

Entry words are all the words that are listed in the dictionary and arranged in alphabetical order. Each entry word is followed by its pronunciation and definition. Use a dictionary to find the following information about entry words for yourself.

1. When you open the dictionary in the middle, what letter or letters do the entry words begin with?
2. Suppose you open the dictionary halfway between the middle and the beginning, what letter or letters do the entry words begin with on these pages?
3. Now open the dictionary halfway between the middle and the end; what letter or letters do the entry begin with here?
4. Is there a difference between the type used for the entry words and the type used for other words on the page? Explain how you think this type differs.
5. Locate each of the following entry words in a dictionary. Before looking for them, decide where you will open the dictionary:
   (1) near the beginning
   (2) near the middle
   (3) near the end

classify	yam	sanitation
tangent	oxide	entertainment
liquid	ascot	counselor
military	joist	commercial
vacancy	clamor	pursue
knell	survival	techniques
brier	revival	valve
numerical	agricultural	computer

Excerpts used in dictionary skills taken from THORNDIKE-BARNHART INTERMEDIATE DICTIONARY by E. L. Thorndike and Clarence L. Barnhart. Copyright © 1971 by Scott, Foresman and Company. Reprinted by permission of the publisher.

Dictionaries have guide words that help you to find entry words without reading all the words on the page. Guide words are located at the top of each page. They are usually in darker print and larger than the print used for the entry words. Guide words may be arranged in more than one way at the top of the page.

1. A guide word may appear directly above each column on a page. Example:

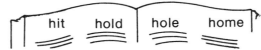

2. Both guide words for the page may appear on the right or left side of the page. Example:

3. Only one guide word may appear for each page. The word on the far left of the two facing pages indicates the first word on that page. The word on the far right indicates the last word on that page. Example:

You may find other ways that guide words are arranged, but in every case the first word listed on the two facing pages will be located at the far left and the last word on the two pages will be on the far right.

1. Look in three different dictionaries and see how the guide words are arranged.
2. Find the page in a dictionary that each of the following entry words will be found. On a separate sheet of paper write the entry word. Next to the entry word write the page number and the guide word or words which appear at the top of the page.

ground	buffet	taffy	monogram
angry	gullet	relation	purse
cobalt	guarantee	impulsive	gymnastics
clutch	tempest	regality	tentative

A dictionary gives you help in pronouncing words by providing a respelling of each entry word. This respelling immediately follows the entry word and is usually enclosed with slant marks. In some dictionaries, however, parentheses are used to enclose the respelling. In every dictionary you will find a pronunciation key to the respelling code that is used in that dictionary. This pronunciation key is found on one of the first several pages of the dictionary and is usually repeated in brief form on every two facing pages, at the top or bottom.

Pronunciation Key—a brief form appearing at the top of one of two facing pages.

hat, āge, fär; let, ēqual, tėrm;
it, īce: hot, ōpen, ôrder;
oil, out; cup, pùt, rüle; ch, child;   e represents a in about,
ng, long; sh, she; th, thin;   e in taken, i in pencil,
ŦH, then; zh, measure: o in lemon, u in circus.

1. Look in three different dictionaries and find the pronunciation key in each. Compare the three keys for likenesses and differences. Notice the following:
   (1) diacritical markings—the marks used in the key to identify a certain sound are called diacritical markings.
   (2) accent marks—the mark or marks (ˈ) in a word to indicate where the stress on a word should be placed are called accent marks. A heavier mark is called a primary stress and indicates a stronger stress on the syllable. A lighter mark is called a secondary stress and indicates a lesser stress on a syllable. These marks may appear before or after a syllable.

2. Using the pronunciation key above, pronounce the following words.

   (ka shir')   (nēl)
   (dis klōz')   (man' yü əl)
   (fē' bəl)   (pėr' pən dik' yə lər)
   (här' nis)   (skwēz)

A dictionary gives the meaning of each entry word. When you cannot determine a word's meaning by the context or other words around it, a dictionary can be helpful. The definition of each entry word is given after the respelling of the word for pronunciation. If a word has more than one meaning, it may have two or more entries, or one entry with several meanings listed by number.

Entry Word Example:

wedge (wej), 1 piece of wood or metal in the form of an inclined plane, thick at one end and tapering to a thin edge at the other, used in splitting logs, etc. It is a simple machine. 2 something shaped like a wedge or used like a wedge: *Wild geese fly in a wedge. Her grand party was an entering wedge into society.* 3 split or separate with a wedge. 4 fasten or tighten with a wedge. 5 thrust or pack in tightly; squeeze: *He wedged himself through the narrow window. The man's foot was wedged between the rocks.* 1,2 *n.,* 3-5 *v.,* wedged, wedging.

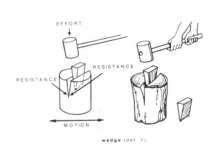

wedge (def. 1)

1. Read the definitions of the word *wedge*, and then decide which definition is used in the sentences below.
   (1) He could hardly *wedge* himself between the box and the wall.
   (2) He drove the *wedge* into the ice.
   (3) He ate the huge *wedge* of pie.
2. The word *bunting* has two entries in the dictionary. Find the word and decide the correct meaning for the sentences below.
   (1) The little *bunting* was almost hidden by the big leaf.
   (2) The red and white *bunting* waved in the spring breeze.
3. The italicized words in the sentences below have more than one meaning. Find the correct meaning for each word.
   (1) The *court* heard his case.
   (2) He followed the *course* of the river.
   (3) The girl handed a *flier* to the man.
   (4) Our fishing *gear* was left in the tent.
   (5) We could hear the *lap* of waves against the wall.

journey toward goals

Off on a journey! But there are things we must take on any journey: tickets, money, a road map, maybe even a passport.

A journey toward a goal is no different. We have to be sure we are on the right road before we start. We have to be sure we have the skills to achieve those goals.

Which direction will your journey take you? Get ready . . . and go!

UNIT 3   JOURNEY TOWARD GOALS

BUT WHAT SHOULD I BE?

THINKING THINGS THROUGH

It is good practice to preview or survey any piece of material you are planning to read for a specific purpose. A quick look at the material will help you to:

1. See how the material is organized
2. Formulate questions about the topic that the material will answer.
3. Decide which part or parts of the selection to read.

According to the difficulty and length of the material, you might look at each paragraph, or you might read both the beginning and ending sentences of the paragraphs. Follow the suggestions below as you preview this selection.

1. Looking at the title, what is this selection about?
2. What subtitles do you find? Think of a question that you expect to be answered in the first section.
3. Do you see any changes in writing format?
   (a) Is there conversation?
   (b) Do you find words that are called to your attention by being underlined, italicized, capitalized, or printed in boldface type?
4. Read the entire introduction of the selection down to the first subtitle. Read the last paragraph.
5. Read the selection.

ABOUT WORDS

As you read the selection, "But What Should I Be?" you may encounter several words that you possibly did not have in your vocabulary. Choose the best meaning for each word below according to how it is used in this selection.

(1) frustrations - disappointments - confusions or baffling situations
(2) surge   - swelling - a sudden rise in activity
(3) alternatives - choices - courses - propositions
(4) technique   - method of accomplishment - movements

155

INVESTIGATE

BUT WHAT SHOULD I BE?

Mark sat with his legs crossed in the middle of his bed. "Dad, I've just got to find out what kind of job I'm going to choose!"

"What do you mean?" his father questioned.

"Well, I'd like to be a deep sea diver, but I really like horses, too. Maybe I could be a rancher."

"Why do you feel that you must be in such a hurry to decide?" his dad asked.

The seventh grader went on, "Well, lots of the kids know what they're going to do, but I don't. Many of my friends know what colleges they are going to attend."

"Don't you think some of them will change their minds?" asked his dad.

This question seemed to puzzle Mark. There was a moment of silence. "I don't know. But shouldn't I know soon what I want to do?"

"Not necessarily," replied Mark's father.

"But I'm interested in so many things. I know I'd like to be an oceanographer. I know you'd like me to be an airplane pilot."

"How'd you ever get that idea? Have I ever said that you should go into flying?"

"No," Mark replied, "but I know you like it."

"Yes, I enjoy flying," his father mused. "Many of the things we like are unrelated to the kinds of jobs we actually choose to do. Riding is an example. You could select oceanography as a career and still own a ranch. Many people choose to do things they enjoy in their leisure time, but they do something entirely different to make a living. Interests are not the only things we use as guides in choosing our professions. You shouldn't choose a job you think *I'd* like as your life's occupation. You should choose a job which *you would like* to do."

good advice in terms of their own backgrounds, interests and training in their own career field.

A Place To Begin

There are really two types of interests—*expressed interests* and *measured interests*. Expressed interests are less permanent than measured interests. For example, you may be a proficient athlete and may think that a career in football would be great fun. Next season, you may decide that a career in basketball would be the field to be in. Measured interests are discovered by taking an interest test. This tells you more accurately what your likes and dislikes are. For example, the test might show that you seem to show a high interest in subjects related to science. You might show a definite dislike for a subject pertaining to social studies. Obtaining and using information is our most important task as we begin studying different careers.

Let's assume that Mark had taken an interest test and received high scores in the mechanical career area. What would this mean to him in junior high or high school? He may want to take a shop course which would let him explore the mechanical area more fully. This information might help him decide what kind of further training was needed.

If Mark showed high interest in math or science, he might want to select an academic high school. Such a choice would give him a good basic education and the advantage of continuing into a college program. The disadvantage of such a choice would be that he could not go directly into repairing machinery. A vocational high school would be a better choice. To expand his knowledge Mark should begin to read publications in his interest area.

Most people can choose any of several careers and be happy as well as successful. Many career fields overlap or are related. The purpose of career guidance is to offer you *alternatives*, or choices, based upon your interests, skills, and abilities.

CHECKING PROGRESS

1. Recall the questions you formulated before you read the selection. Can you answer them now? Share your answers with some of your classmates.
2. Give some examples of expressed interests and measured interests as explained in this selection.
3. How do we depend on the experiences of others to help us get firsthand information about a particular career?
4. Is it possible to write to authors of magazine articles? Where do you send the letters?
5. What are the specific purposes of career guidance?
6. Why did Mark's father advise him to choose a career that he would like rather than one which he thought his father would like?
7. How can interests in childhood help build toward a future career when we are grown up?

CHOOSING NEXT STEPS

1. Review the steps for previewing a selection. During this week use this method as you study social studies, science, and other subjects. In your preview or survey be sure to include the following:
   (1) Titles and illustrations
   (2) Subtitles or any type of paragraph or section headings
   (3) Changes in writing format such as: conversational parts, underlined words, italicized words, words written in boldface type
   (4) The first paragraph or two of the selection
   (5) The last two or three paragraphs of the selection
   (6) The beginning sentence of each paragraph
2. Talk over what you think you "want to do" as your future occupation with one of your parents. Write a brief report on this discussion.

AN INTEREST PROFILE

THINKING THINGS THROUGH

The preceding article, "But What Should I Be?" was about *measured interests*. If you remember, these are interests that are discovered through taking an interest test. After a student takes an interest test, his scores are plotted on a graph. This graph is called an *interest profile*. In the following article we are going to look at the interest profile of a real student. We will read the information and try to interpret the results.

ABOUT WORDS

The following article tells about a test that shows our interests in ten different areas. Each of these areas is explained below. Also listed are sample jobs in each area.

OUTDOOR means you like to work outside with plants and animals. Jobs include fishermen, foresters, farmers.

MECHANICAL means you like working with machines and tools. Jobs include engineers, plumbers, toolmakers.

COMPUTATIONAL means you like to work with numbers. Jobs include accountants, bank tellers, bookkeepers.

SCIENTIFIC deals with finding solutions to problems in the physical world. Jobs include chemists, doctors.

PERSUASIVE means you like dealing with people and selling things. Jobs include salesmen, personnel managers.

ARTISTIC shows you like to do creative work with your hands. Jobs include painters, sculptors, dress designers.

LITERARY is an interest in reading and writing. Jobs include news reporters, novelists, poets, librarians.

MUSICAL shows an interest in singing or playing an instrument. Jobs include musicians, teachers, music critics.

SOCIAL SERVICE involves helping people. Jobs include nurses, counselors, social workers, religious people.

CLERICAL means you like to do clearly-defined work that is accurate. Jobs include secretaries, file clerks, salesclerks.

161

AN INTEREST PROFILE

Do you remember what an *interest test* does? It measures our tendency to like or dislike certain activities. It does not measure our ability to do something. It only shows where our interests are. The *Kuder General Interest Survey* is a well-known interest test. A student who takes this test can find out his strongest and weakest interests in ten different areas.

A boy in seventh grade, who we will call Gene Martin, took the Kuder interest test. When he got his scores back, they looked like this:

Outdoor	*22*
Mechanical	*52*
Computational	*28*
Scientific	*46*
Persuasive	*54*
Artistic	*29*
Literary	*39*
Musical	*24*
Social Service	*33*
Clerical	*30*

Gene did not understand

162

these scores. They were merely numbers which had no meaning for him. He still did not know the areas in which he was most interested.

To help him understand his scores, Gene's teacher gave him a *profile form* or graph. This profile is shown on the next page. Gene was told to follow certain steps:

1. For each section, he wrote down his score in the boxes at the top of the profile chart.

2. In each column, he found the number that is the same as his score in the top of that column. He drew a line through the number from one side of the column to the other side.

3. He colored in the entire space between the bottom of the column and the line he had drawn.

Since Gene has followed these steps, his interests are ready to be analyzed.

Look at the graph. There is a dotted line at the 75 percent mark. Any scores appearing above this line indicate high interest. Gene shows high interest in literary and musical areas. This means that Gene prefers these activities more often than most other people in his age group.

There is another dotted line at the 25 percent mark. Any scores below this line indicate low interest. Gene shows low interest in social service and clerical areas. This means that Gene does not seem to have preference for these activities.

Scores falling between these two dotted lines indicate average interests. The rest of Gene's interests are about average.

Remember that high interests are not better than low interests. And that one kind of interest is not better than another. What counts is that you know your own interests, both high and low. Then you can more easily make choices concerning further education and a future career.

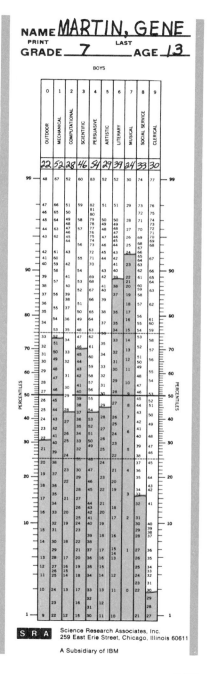

163

CHECKING PROGRESS

1. What is an interest profile?
2. What are some jobs in the Computational area? Literary area? Social Service area?
3. Which interest area do you think you would like the most? the least? Tell why.
4. What does an interest test do? What is something that it does not do?
5. At what mark on the graph does a score have to appear in order to show high interest? low interest?

CHOOSING NEXT STEPS

1. Did you ever take an interest test? If so, what were your areas of high interest? low interest? If not, which areas do you think would be of high and low interest? Tell why.
2. Do you think that every person has at least one high interest? Explain why.
3. Why do you think it is important to know your own interests, both high and low?
4. Suppose you took the Kuder test and your scores showed high interest in the Musical area. What kind of job would you most like to have? What kinds of hobbies would you like to do in your spare time?
5. The Kuder test is often given to junior high and high school students in order to give them some ideas about their future careers. Do you think it would be helpful to give the Kuder test to adults who are unhappy in their jobs? Explain why.
6. Read an autobiography from the library of an athlete, a musician, an actor, or a statesman. Imagine that this person took an interest test. Try to make an imaginary interest profile for this person based on the facts you have learned about the person's life.

AND IF I'M ELECTED ...

THINKING THINGS THROUGH

Have you ever thought about running for a class office or an office in a club or some other organization to which you belong? If so, you may have had some of the same feelings that Burnell Jefferson has in the story, "And If I'm Elected...." Read the selection and decide if you have had a similar experience when running for an office.

ABOUT WORDS

In the selection, "And If I'm Elected..." the author has used the expression "fired up." In your own words explain what you think this expression means.

Look up the meanings of the words below in your dictionary. On a separate sheet of paper, write the word, the diacritical respelling, and the meanings. Then write a sentence using each of these words.

legislative	councilman
civic	candidate

Other words which are often used in politics are listed below. Find out what they mean and how to pronounce them.

caucas	projections
propaganda	ethics
electoral college	ballots
incumbent	landslide

165

INVESTIGATE

And If I'm ELECTED...

The final school bell clanged loudly. Burnell Jefferson went nervously up the aisle to Mr. Collin's desk as the other students hurried from the classroom. He wasn't sure why the teacher had asked him to stay after school. His grades in government class had been constant A's and he hadn't caused any problems.

"Have a chair, Burnell," said the teacher, pointing to a chair kept for visitors. "Pull it over to the desk."

Burnell did, facing the teacher across a stack of papers the students had written that day about Congress. He said, "That's interesting stuff, Mr. Collins. I like learning about our government."

"You're interested in politics, aren't you?" the teacher asked, with a smile. "I've been talking with the district chairman in your area, and he told me that you volunteered to help at the last election."

"I liked the man who was running for councilman," Burnell said. "Leroy Hutchins." He smiled. "He won, too!"

"It takes work to get elected—not just the work of the candidate but the work his helpers put in."

"I liked it," Burnell said excitedly. "Someday I want to go into politics myself. Ever since I started finding out how the government works and how anyone can get involved in it— well, I just wanted to be a part of it all." He stopped, looking embarrassed. "I didn't mean to get so fired up about it, Mr. Collins."

The teacher laughed. "If you're going to get anywhere in politics, you've got to get fired up about it. That's what I want to talk to you about. We could use someone with your abilities to run for seventh-grade class president."

"Oh, no!" Burnell said, shaking his head. "I couldn't do that—get up and talk in front of everybody! I'd be too scared to say a word."

"That's part of politics," Mr. Collins said. "You'd get used to it. You've answered questions in my class."

"That's because I get so interested in what this government is about that I forget about the people around me and just speak up," Burnell said.

The teacher leaned back in his chair. "Well, think over what I suggested. You might change your mind."

Burnell left the classroom, hoping that the teacher wouldn't be angry with him. This was his favorite class, and he didn't want to spoil it. The man was right—a candidate had to talk with the people. Burnell would have to forget about politics if he couldn't stand up and talk.

In class the next day Mr. Collins called Burnell and three other students to the front of the room. "We're going to try something new," he said. "We're going to ask these students questions about the assignment, and if they get stuck for an answer they can throw the question back to the person who asked it, and he has to provide the answer."

Burnell was the last one to get his question. It was an easy one about the powers of legislature, and he knew the answer. But when he opened his mouth to speak he suddenly saw all the faces staring at him.

"Come on, Burnell," Mr. Collins said.

Burnell just shook his head and made a dash for his seat. He slumped down as far as he could, expecting Mr. Collins to scold him. But the teacher just said: "We'll throw the question back to the one who asked it."

Burnell avoided seeing the teacher when the class was over. He felt he had ruined everything. It was an easy question, he told himself, and he couldn't even answer that.

That evening Mr. Collins phoned Burnell's house, and for a moment Burnell was afraid to come to the phone. He was sure now the teacher would scold him.

"Burnell," Mr. Collins said, "I'm going to a civic meeting tonight to hear Mr. Hutchins speak. If it's all right with your mother, you might want to come along."

"I would!" Burnell said. "I know it will be all right!"

It was a short ride to the auditorium, and Burnell had another surprise coming when he arrived there with Mr. Collins. "I want you to meet Mr. Hutchins," Mr. Collins told him.

Mr. Hutchins was standing over in one corner with a few important-looking women. He greeted the teacher warmly.

"This is one of my prize students," Mr. Collins said to the councilman. "This is Burnell Jefferson."

"I know Burnell," Mr. Hutchins said, smiling. "He worked for me in my campaign."

Burnell's eyes opened wide. "You remember me?"

"Of course," Mr. Hutchins said. "Running for office takes a lot of hard work on the part of a lot of people. I may not have been elected if it weren't for you!"

Mr. Hutchins laughed and held out his hand. Burnell shook hands excitedly, then suddenly realized that the man's hand felt damp. The surprise must have shown in his eyes, because

168

the councilman said, "I'm sorry, Burnell. It's just that I get scared before I have to speak."

"You get scared?" Burnell asked.

"You bet I do! It's always been hard for me to stand up and face a big group of people."

"I run away," Burnell said quietly.

"Well, maybe next time you won't," the man said. "If you want something badly enough, you have to go after it."

"Even if I'm scared?" Burnell asked.

"Even if you're scared."

Burnell listened intently to what the councilman had to say at the meeting—thinking of what he had said to him.

The next day before class, Burnell went up to Mr. Collins and said, "If you're going to do that thing you did yesterday of calling people to answer questions—I hope you'll give me another chance."

"Fine, Burnell," Mr. Collins said.

Burnell sat down nervously in his chair and waited for the teacher to call his name. When he did, Burnell took a deep breath and walked to the front of the class, taking one step at a time. Then it was his turn to answer a question again. It was another easy one and he knew the answer as well as he knew his own name. He began talking. . . .

To his own surprise, Burnell found himself answering the question, and then another and another. . . . Before he knew it the school bell rang and without thinking he said, "Is the class over already?" Some of the students laughed.

"Those were good answers, Burnell," Mr. Collins said.

"I was scared," Burnell said, "but I didn't run away this time. I'll think about working to be class president. It was hard enough standing up just before the class. I don't know yet if I could do it before the whole school."

"You can try, Burnell," Mr. Collins said.

"I guess I have to try," Burnell said, smiling. "I have to start somewhere, don't I—if I'm going to be President of the United States someday?"

CHECKING PROGRESS

Study the following questions and answer them. Give reasons for your answers.

  A. What kind of person was Burnell?
  B. What kind of person was Mr. Collins?
  C. Why do you think Burnell asked to be on the student answer panel on the second day?
  D. What do you think Burnell's classmates thought when he went to the front for the panel on the second day?
  E. If Burnell decided to choose a career in politics, how do you think his experiences as related in this story could have helped him? What other careers could Burnell have besides politics?

CHOOSING NEXT STEPS

1. Plan with some other members of your class to attend a meeting of your city council.
2. Make arrangements for an interview with the mayor of your city, a city councilman, or other city officer. Ask them such questions as:
   A. Why are you interested in serving in a public office?
   B. What are some of the things you like about serving? What do you like least?
3. Write a congressman or congresswoman who serves your area. Send a cassette tape and ask this person to answer questions such as the following:
   A. How old were you when you decided you wanted to run for public office?
   B. What are some of the courses that you took in high school that have helped you most in your profession?
   C. What are some of the rewards a person may achieve by serving in public office?
   Play the tape for your classmates.

SKYLINE HIGH SCHOOL

THINKING THINGS THROUGH

What kinds of subjects do you study in school? If your school is like most schools, you probably study science, mathematics, language arts, and history. If you are fortunate, you may even get to study music, art, and physical education. These are the usual school subjects.

How would you like to study some unusual subjects in school? Instead of learning from a textbook, how would you like to learn something practical that you can actually do with your own hands? There is a special school in Dallas, Texas, for learning unusual subjects. At this school students can learn how to repair airplanes, how to cut and style hair, how to perform on television, or how to operate computers. They can also learn how to lay carpets, how to nurse patients, how to operate cameras, how to make sculptures, or how to do architectural drawings. The name of this school is Skyline High School. The following article will tell you more about it.

ABOUT WORDS

There are two words which apply to the subjects taught in schools. Most schools have subjects which are *traditional*. These are the usual subjects (such as history, reading, science, and mathematics) which have always been taught in schools. Other schools, such as Skyline High School, have *vocational* subjects. These are subjects which give training in a skill or trade (such as metal work, wood work, and photography) which may later become a person's career. Some schools have both traditional and vocational subjects.

Make a list of the subjects taught in your school. Tell whether each subject is traditional or vocational.

171

INVESTIGATE

SKYLINE HIGH SCHOOL

Many people are interested in your career. These include teachers, parents, school board members, and people in business, industry, and the professions. These people have come to depend more and more upon the talents, skills, and knowledge of one another. They are especially interested in careers for young people because they know that the young people of today will be the leaders of tomorrow. As a result, more and more attention is being given to careers in school programs today.

One fine example of the emphasis on careers in public schools is the famous Skyline High School in Dallas, Texas. This unusual school was developed by school planners, the entire city of Dallas, and big businesses all over the United States.

At Skyline the *campus*, or school grounds, covers

eighty-one acres. There are several buildings grouped together on the campus. The buildings themselves cover fourteen acres and cost over $21 million to build.

You may wonder how the school got its name. It is named after the *skyline*, or outline of tall buildings against the sky, in the city of Dallas. This scene gives the school its name.

There are three parts to the Skyline center: a regular high school for a section of the city; a community center, or evening school, for adults and high school students; and a career development center for high school students from all over the city. It is this center which makes Skyline special.

Students call it the CDC, for Career Development Center. They come to the CDC from over twenty other schools within the city. Here

172

they can learn things which are not taught in their regular high schools. They spend one-half of each day in their home high schools, and then come by bus to spend a half day at Skyline.

By bringing students together from all over the city, teachers and equipment can be provided for just about anything the students want to learn. Here students can learn how to make a sculpture, repair airplanes, air-condition a building, cut and style hair, operate computers, speak languages, perform on television, or do just about anything they want to do. Some will get certificates here and go on to jobs. Others will go to college for further study in their chosen fields.

Skyline resulted from much planning and work by many people. The idea for a career development center came from the superintendent of schools, his staff, and the school board. A committee was formed for planning. Clubs and other groups in the city were asked to suggest ideas for

courses. The Chamber of Commerce was asked to study occupational needs in the present and future. Presidents of companies in business and industry were asked to provide help in planning areas of study and career development. State agencies, such as the Texas Education Agency, were called upon for advice. Local school administrators traveled to outstanding schools across the nation and gathered more information about buildings, equipment, and the nature of educational needs. Big companies helped to establish plans for the studies and to test ways of learning for job requirements. Many teachers, parents, and students have also helped to develop Skyline.

At Skyline there are twenty-seven groupings, or *clusters*, of program studies. These include mathematics, science, agriculture, business education, electronics, health occupations, clothing manufacturing, plastics, music, air conditioning, wood industry, eye lenses, television, world languages, homemaking, advanced English, and others.

Within each cluster there are several subject areas. For example, in world language, a student can study such languages as German, French, Chinese, or Spanish. Different students may study these different subjects in the same room at the same time. One student may be studying Spanish while another is studying Chinese. One may be a beginner and the other may be advanced. With tapes and tutors they study individually, even though one teacher may be helping all of them to learn.

The method used at Skyline is for a student to work directly in a subject area. He learns by experience. Each cluster is open to any student who shows a record of interest, achievement, and self-discipline. Each cluster is open to both boys and girls.

Skyline High School provides its students with an opportunity to try many different careers. Students can find careers in which they will be happy and useful. Skyline shows that people really are interested in your career and your happiness.

CHECKING PROGRESS

1. Why are people especially interested in the careers of young people today?
2. What is a campus? Do you think that Skyline High School has a large campus?
3. How did Skyline High School get its name?
4. What are the three parts of the Skyline center? What people use each part?
5. How do students from other schools get to Skyline? How much time do they spend there?
6. What kinds of things can students learn at Skyline?
7. Who helped in the planning of Skyline?
8. Name several clusters of program studies which are taught at Skyline. Which of these clusters seem especially unusual or interesting to you?

CHOOSING NEXT STEPS

1. If you were a student at Skyline High School, in which career cluster would you most like to participate? Give your reasons why.
2. Can you think of any more unusual subjects that could be taught at Skyline? Name some.
3. What are some other subjects you would like to learn in your own school?
4. Skyline gives students an opportunity to try many different careers. Why is this a good idea?
5. Take a field trip to a vocational high school in your area. What subjects are taught there?
6. Choose one of the occupational skills listed below. Try to find information in the library about that skill.
   carpet laying
   photography
   beauty culture
   airplane repair
   computer programming
   sculpture

DEAR BARNEY

THINKING THINGS THROUGH

Do you have a "best" friend who writes to you? Barney does. Read the letters Hank writes and find out all you can about Barney's best friend.

As you read the letters you will find out many things about Hank's feelings and personality. Be prepared to support your answers as you decide whether the statements listed below are true or false.

1) Hank had a poor relationship with his family.

2) Hank was lazy.

3) Hank was eager to try out new ideas.

4) Hank did not accept advice from other people.

Decide if you like Hank and why. Decide whether you would like a "writing" friendship like this one, to help you with your problems.

ABOUT WORDS

Hank used some interesting words and phrases in his letters to Barney. As you read along, watch for the word or phrase that is listed below and decide what it means from the way it is used in Hank's letter.

"throw the book at me"

"late grower"

"shrimp"

"golden opportunity"

"as though the Martians had landed and no one told her."

INVESTIGATE

DEAR BARNEY

Dear Barney,

I wish you could have been here Tuesday when everyone started jumping on me. I could have really used a good friend. I still think it's terrible that your dad had to get transferred so far away just before school started.

Oh, well, that's not what I was going to write about. I read this book about a guy on a football team who discovered some kidnappers and missing jewels and stuff, so I thought I'd like to be a pro football player some day when I grow up.

Then I thought I had better get started in football now, since I'm in the seventh grade and the school has a pretty good team. So I went to the try-outs. The coach told us to line up, and that was a crazy feeling, Barney, because all of the guys on each side of me were almost as tall as my dad.

The coach came down the line and stopped when he got to me. "You sure you want to try out?" he asked.

The guy on my right started to laugh, and the one on my left looked me up and down, and said, "How could we win a game with a shrimp like that on our team?"

"Football is a rough sport," the coach said. "The rules about who can play are worked out by age, but some boys—well, they're a lot bigger than others at the same age."

"I run fast," I told him.

"Then why don't you try out for track?" he asked me.

I looked around again and saw what he meant. I thought about having some of those big guys tackle me, and I really didn't like the idea any more than he did.

"Well," I said, giving a shrug, "maybe I'm a late grower. Maybe next year I'll be tall."

The coach stuck his pencil behind his ear and said, "Then come back and see me next year."

I was pretty discouraged as I walked home. I knew I really wouldn't be a late grower. Everybody in my family is short. So I'd have to think about something else. I guess going around with a football team and solving mysteries and stuff would be a lot of fun, but that other part—

178

the part where somebody tackles you or steps on your face—wouldn't be so good, would it, Barney?

Well, my dad saw I was feeling bad, so he took us all out for pizza that night. Do you know, Barney, if you measure the size of two small pizzas, and one giant pizza, the giant-sized pizza is still bigger? I tried to tell my sister that but she said I was a math nut and two small pizzas look bigger than one giant pizza, so she ordered two small pizzas. When you come back for a visit, Barney, we'll get some pizzas—giant size.

> Your best friend,
> Hank

Dear Barney,

A dog bit me in the leg and hit me in the head. It was kind of crazy how he did it, and as soon as I get out of bed I'll write and tell you all about it.

> Your best friend,
> Hank

Dear Barney,

After I got over wanting to be a professional football player, I was sitting in the kitchen with my mom, going over the bank statement with her. My father doesn't know how to add straight and always gets things mixed up, so I fixed it up for him. But I don't want to write about how dumb my father is at math, so I'll tell you now what happened about the dog.

Well—while I was sitting at the kitchen window, this cutiest little mutt walked by. I told my mom how nice it would be to have a dog like that, and she said, "You know how your father feels about dogs. I'd forget about it."

Then an idea hit me. "I could be a veterinarian some day," I said. "Then I could work with lots of animals."

Mom put the check book away and brought out some cookies. "Maybe you could get a job taking care of someone's pet," she said. "Then you'd know if you'd like to be a veterinarian."

I thought that was a great idea. So I got the newspapers and looked in the ads and found just what I wanted. Someone wanted a kid to walk her dog. (Can you imagine getting paid just to take a dog for a walk?) I dashed to the telephone and called the number, and the lady told me to come right over.

I guess I was remembering that cute little dog that went by our house, Barney, so I wasn't prepared at all for the lady's dog. It was the

179

biggest Great Dane I ever saw. The lady was kind of old and needed the big dog to protect her from burglars. But she wasn't strong enough to walk him.

"Hi, Amos," I said, when she told me his name.

Amos just sniffed at me as though I was his next dinner and he wasn't sure it was good enough to eat.

"Are you sure you can manage?" the lady asked, handing me the leash. "You're not a very big boy."

"I'm very strong," I told her, smiling. "Some day I'm going to be a veterinarian."

"Very well," she said. "Be a good boy, Amos."

Amos and I got as far as the front sidewalk when I found out that the job wasn't going to be as easy as I had thought. "Come on, Amos," I called out, turning right. But Amos turned left, and I didn't have much choice. Well, I pretended that I had wanted to turn left all along, just in case the old lady was looking out her windows. For a while it was all right, as long as I walked real fast to keep up with Amos.

Then Mrs. Priddy's big yellow cat came strutting down the sidewalk as though she owned it. Amos stopped and looked at her, then made a funny noise in the back of his throat.

"No, Amos!" I shouted. The cat looked at Amos as though the Martians had landed and no one had told her about it.

She ran. So did Amos. And so did I, because I was holding the leash. The cat didn't have enough sense to climb a tree. She streaked into Mrs. Priddy's garage instead.

Amos was right on her trail, and so was I. The cat leaped up on the shelves Mrs. Priddy made along the back of her garage, to put her home-canned fruit and jam on. But those shelves weren't as high as the cat thought they were, or else Amos could jump higher than she thought he could. Amos missed the cat the first try. I got banged up when he dragged me over the hood of the car, but I got to my feet and yelled at him again.

It just took a second to see that he was going to make another try for that cat, and this time he probably wouldn't miss. The only thing I could think of to do at that moment was to get between Amos and the cat. So I did.

Well, the cat decided my head looked safer than those shelves, and she made a jump and held on tight! Wow! I did a kind of somersault just as Amos jumped for her again. Only this time my leg got in the way. Amos got his mouth on it instead of on the cat, and the shelf fell down and hit me in the head.

180

Mrs. Priddy was nice about the whole thing, since nothing happened to her cat, and since my mom helped me clean up everything in the garage. Amos made it home all right, but the lady didn't pay me for walking her dog.

"Do you still want to be a veterinarian?" Dr. James asked, laughing and putting the last piece of tape on my leg.

"Not any more, I don't," I answered.

Well, Barney, it was no joke to me. Right now I haven't got any more good ideas. When are you coming for a visit?

Your best friend,
Hank

Dear Barney,

Something nice happened to me for a change. I got elected president of the Math Club. It sort of made up for what happened the day before, which is what I want to tell you about.

You see, I'd been watching this TV show about a lawyer who was so good he got up in the courtroom and saved a guy's life and even discovered who the real criminal was right there in front of the judge and jury! So I started thinking about how it might be fun to be a lawyer some day.

I didn't know how good I'd be at it, and I didn't know any lawyers I could talk to about it; but then this golden opportunity came along. Remember how Miss Fring in English used to talk about golden opportunities and taking advantage of them? Well, this golden opportunity was the kid next door—Charlie.

He doesn't look much like a golden opportunity. In fact, he looks pretty awful most of the time. His face and hands are always dirty, and his nose is always running, and Mom says it's because he's only seven. Well—I came home from school and found Charlie sitting on our front porch, crying.

"I had an accident with the car," he said.

"You're kidding," I said. "You don't drive!"

"I wasn't driving. I was carrying rocks and boards in my wagon, and it turned over and the rocks and boards fell against the car. There's little marks on the car."

"Just a couple little marks?" I asked.

"I guess you could call them dents," he said, "but my dad is going to be mad at me. He said if I got in trouble once more this week he was going to throw the book at me."

"Charlie," I said, "how'd you like me for your lawyer?"

"Am I going to jail?" he asked, looking scared.

"No. But I can explain what happened to your dad. Maybe he won't get so mad. And it won't cost you anything."

"Can you do it right now?" Charlie asked. "Here he comes."

"Sure." I followed Charlie to his house, said "hello" to his father, and then went into the house with them.

"Charlie had an accident," I said, "and I'm his lawyer." I turned to Charlie. "You were carrying a load of things in your wagon when the accident happened, right, Charlie?"

"Yeah," said Charlie.

"Then the load fell off the wagon," I said. I turned back to Charlie's dad. "You can see how an accident like that can happen, can't you, sir?" I was trying to act like that TV lawyer.

"Well...I guess so," Charlie's dad said.

"Well," I said, "according to the accused, there are a couple of very small marks—uh, dents—on the side of your car."

"What?" Charlie's dad yelled, running outside.

I followed behind him, still representing Charlie, and there he stood by the car, holding his head and moaning.

I gulped. The little dents Charlie talked about weren't exactly little. In fact, it looked as though somebody had really bashed in the side door on the car.

"Where's Charlie?" his dad asked, staring at me.

That was a good question. Charlie was gone. If I knew him, he was probably under his bed.

182

"Sir," I said, "as Charlie's lawyer, I think I..."

"Well," Charlie's dad yelled at me, "as the judge and jury, I find Charlie guilty and he's going to get it!" He stomped past me, going back to the house, then turned around and yelled again: "And you're fired!"

Well, I was really upset. Mom gave me some more cookies.

"I think it's a fine idea," she said, "trying out different occupations to see which you might like to follow. But you've got to think about whether you have the right qualifications. Then ask yourself if you have special interests or talents for the job. Do you see what I mean?"

"Sort of," I said. "Like being too small for pro football?"

"That's right," she said. "You've got a talent you haven't even thought about. And it's not just a talent. It's something you like to do very much."

I thought for a moment. "You mean math?"

"Yes," she said. "Have you ever thought about working in mathematics when you grow up? Maybe you'd like to become an accountant and take care of the finances for a big corporation or individuals at income tax time."

"That's really something that would be fun!" I said.

So there it is, Barney. How does "Hank Dellfield, accountant" sound to you? Great, huh?

Mom said your mom wrote to her that maybe you could come back and visit for Christmas vacation, and I'm keeping my fingers crossed. We're going to have a lot to talk about!

Your best friend,
Hank

CHECKING PROGRESS

1. Name three careers that Hank was interested in and tried out. Which would you have said was his worst choice? What is your reason for making that choice?
2. What was Hank's favorite school subject? How did he use it at home? How was he recognized at school for his interest and ability in it?
3. From his experiences of "trying out" careers, what are some of the things Hank found out that you think will help him in selecting his career?
4. In what way do you think Barney helped Hank at this time in his life? Do you think that a friend like Barney is important when you are growing up? Why?

CHOOSING NEXT STEPS

1. Write a friendly letter to one of your friends or relatives who has moved to another city.
    A) Tell about something you have done at school recently.
    B) Tell about something you and your family did together this past summer.
    C) Tell about your favorite pet.
    D) Tell about a book you've recently read.
    E) Tell about a job you have. Or tell about a hobby in which you are interested.
2. Read the ads in your newspaper. Look for jobs you can do.
3. What is your best school subject? List all the careers you can think of that would involve the use of skills you are learning in this subject area.
4. Choose a partner. Write a letter to this person. Tell something in the letter about yourself that you think your partner does not know. Ask your partner to do the same thing when he writes back to you.

YOU ARE ALIKE, BUT DIFFERENT

THINKING THINGS THROUGH

The following story is a good one to read aloud. The language of the characters in the story will make it interesting to the listeners. You might even form a group with several of your classmates and record the story on tape. Here are some suggestions for reading aloud:

1. Read the selection silently first for practice before reading it out loud.
2. Find a comfortable standing or sitting position.
3. Face your audience and read loud enough for each person to hear clearly.
4. Pronounce all words correctly.
5. Read as if you were talking.
6. Show the feelings of the characters with your voice level and speed.

ABOUT WORDS

The author of this story has used descriptive words to give more feeling to the characters and to the story. These words are called adjectives and adverbs. Make a list of the adjectives with the nouns they modify, such as: "heavy nets," "keen eyesight." Make a list of adverbs with the verbs they modify, such as: "dipped dramatically."

Another form of descriptive language in this story is *personification*, or describing objects as if they were people. For example, "the sun smiled lazily." Find another example as you read the story.

185

INVESTIGATE

YOU ARE ALIKE, BUT DIFFERENT

It was a glorious summer day. The sun smiled lazily down on Harl Saunders, lounging at the edge of the pier. The smell of the salty sea air drifted by his nose, as Harl waited for his Uncle Bart to bring in the shrimp boat. A seagull broke the calm as it dipped dramatically from the sky to spear a small fish with its sharp beak. Harl studied the gull with interest, amazed at its keen eyesight, natural grace, and perfect aim. Up it soared as Harl's eyes followed, and disappeared into a drift of white clouds.

Into sight appeared the shrimp boat, Uncle Bart waving eagerly. He was sunburned and there were permanent wrinkles in his face, etched from years on the water. The rough hands of a fisherman, who had pulled a lifetime of heavy nets, grabbed Harl with warmth and friendliness.

"Your aunt said we could expect you today, Harl. Good to see you, young man!" Uncle Bart said and jumped onto the pier. "Come here and look at what we've brought in today."

Harl peered into the boat, dodging to avoid a collision with the other fishermen as they climbed onto the pier. The smell of the shrimp bothered Harl, and he wrinkled his nose and turned away.

"What's the matter, Harl?" Uncle Bart laughed heartily and put his arm around the boy's shoulder. Harl shrugged and turned to watch the fishermen as they gathered their gear and headed down to the end of the pier.

"We had good weather today, so our quota ought to be pretty good this week," continued Uncle Bart. "Say, Harl, it looks like you aren't listening."

"Well, it's just that shrimp are so boring!" blurted out the boy to the astonishment of his uncle.

"Boring!" Uncle Bart threw back his head and roared.

"They don't do anything," Harl stammered, fearful of his uncle's reaction. "Shrimp can't soar and dive like seagulls."

"There's nothing boring about the sea, young man," Uncle Bart replied sternly. "Tomorrow I'll take you out on my shrimp boat. It's time you learned the family business anyway. If you're to spend summers with your aunt and me, I'll expect you to do your share on the shrimper."

Harl listened hopefully for heavy rains all that night. But the sun mischieviously peeked through his window shade the next morning. He lay in bed waiting for the sound of his uncle's footsteps, signalling the time to head out to the shrimp boat.

"Come on, Harl," called Uncle Bart, "the men are waiting for us down at the pier." The door slammed. Harl rushed to dress and tore down to catch the boat moments before it pulled away.

Everything went wrong for Harl on the shrimper. The men laughed at his clumsiness, but Uncle Bart couldn't hide his disgust. Harl tripped over nets and equipment, dropped things, and generally got underfoot. Shortly before the boat headed back to shore, Harl noticed that the sea was getting

rougher. He stood and began studying the sky for signs of a storm. Carelessly, Harl lost his footing. "Yee-oww!" he screamed, tumbling into the choppy waters. All activity ceased as the men struggled to rescue the frightened Harl from the water.

Uncle Bart's temper flared. "We've always been a family of fishermen, Harl, and it looks like you can't even swim!" He turned away from Harl. "Let's bring in the boat, men."

Harl was very unhappy. He knew that his uncle was disappointed in him. He sat alone at one end of the boat as it moved toward shore. How could he explain to his uncle that he really did love the sea? How could he make him understand that they were alike, but different?

Harl was lost in thought as the boat, heavy with shrimp and tired men, swayed through the waters. If only he had remembered to bring along his sketch pad, he mused, this was a perfect setting for some drawings. And he could interview the fishermen, perhaps even write a feature story with illustrations for the fall edition of the school paper!

Clunk! The sound of the boat hitting against the pier jolted Harl back to reality.

"Let's get this boat empty and cleaned up before the storm hits, men," Uncle Bart called. "Harl, help them with the nets over there!"

Harl scurried to lend a hand, slipping on the wet patches of the boat. Scattered raindrops warned of the approaching storm, just as the work was finished and the fishermen gathered their gear to hurry home.

Uncle Bart had been unusually quiet during the cleanup. Harl was worried that there would be an argument between them. It came as a surprise, then when his uncle approached and put an arm around Harl's shoulder.

"Your aunt will have hot soup waiting for some wet fishermen...," Uncle Bart said.

"Uncle Bart," Harl interrupted, "please don't be disappointed with me. In my heart I am a fisherman."

188

Uncle Bart looked surprised and bewildered. "There are some things a man can't be taught, Harl. It just has to come by nature. What makes you think you'll ever be a fisherman?" He shook his head as they walked through the rain toward the house.

"I know that I was clumsy on the shrimp boat today. And you are right, I am not going to be your best helper on the shrimper this summer. But I'm going to learn everything I can about fishing and the sea, Uncle Bart. My teachers say that with practice someday I will be a good writer and an artist." Harl hesitated and then continued. "I like everything about your life, Uncle Bart. Being with you and the other fishermen this summer will help me to learn more about fishing and the sea. I want to share it with everyone I can. So if you can put up with me, I promise to do my best."

Uncle Bart said nothing for a few moments. As they approached the door of the house, the smell of soup greeted them. "It takes a real man to work on a shrimper, Harl. Welcome aboard!"

CHECKING PROGRESS

1. After reading this story, what does the title "You Are Alike, But Different" mean to you?
2. How does this idea of alike, but different relate to people? How does it relate to choosing a career?
3. Look up the meanings of these words: personification, adjective, and adverb. Read over the section on *About Words* at the beginning of the story. Then try to write your own examples of descriptive language.

CHOOSING NEXT STEPS

1. Try to describe the feeling you had when you read this story, or when you went to the ocean or beach. Use your senses to remember. Describe the sights, smells, tastes, and feelings of your experience.
2. Do you ever go off by yourself just to think? What kinds of things do you think about? Do you have a special place you like to go?
3. Read books and stories from the library about the sea and fishing.
4. If you live near the sea, go down and look for fishing boats as Harl did.
5. Take a look at your classmates. Make a list of all the ways your classmates are alike. Then list all the ways that they are different. You can either do this by yourself or in a discussion group.

MONTE: A LAW ENFORCEMENT PROFESSIONAL

THINKING THINGS THROUGH

Picture in your mind a police officer. Probably most of you pictured a man. Maybe in the future this will not be true. More and more women are becoming law enforcement officers. Maybe more and more of you will begin picturing women as police officers. This is the story of one girl who decides to train for the police force and what she thinks the duties of a woman on the police force should be.

ABOUT WORDS

Match each of the meanings from the list below to an italicized word in one of these sentences taken from the story. Use context clues, or other words around the italicized word, to help you select the correct meaning.

make businesslike	act as an assistant
familiar	genuine
likeness	beginners
conduct, behavior	

1. She is a *bona fide* professional with a college degree in law enforcement.
2. Today in the United States she has her *counterpart* in many cities.
3. She had gone with the family to police conventions where the *demeanor* of police officers also impressed her.
4. She was also always *accustomed* to discipline.
5. The purpose of the new university program was to try to advance education for law enforcement personnel and to try to *professionalize* the field.
6. Right out of college, she went into a twelve week training session at the Police Department Academy for *rookies* . . .
7. During her last year in college she did an *internship* in the Alpine Police Department.

191

MONTE: A LAW ENFORCEMENT PROFESSIONAL

Once upon a time there were jobs that were considered to be "man-sized" jobs. They definitely excluded women! Not any-more, though. The rules have been changing over the years. Women are welcome today in all former "man-sized" jobs, in-cluding jobs as police officers.

Monte Kay Johnson certainly doesn't look like one's image of a law officer. She is in her twenties, is very slender, and not too tall. She has medium brown hair which hangs to her shoulders, brown eyes, a pleasant personality, a soft voice, and a lovely smile. Her uniform is a softly pleated skirt of a dark gray material, a knit crewneck top in the same color, a dark blue jacket with the police emblem on a pocket, and dark gray shoes. She sometimes wears matching pants instead of the skirt. She is a bona fide professional with a college degree in law enforcement. Today in the United States, she has her counterpart in many cities.

Monte Kay Johnson doesn't think of herself as a pioneer in a man's world. It seems natural for her to have a career in law enforcement. Her father is a captain with the Department of Public Safety in Lubbock, Texas. Her brother is a highway patrolman. In college she dated a highway patrolman. She has always been surrounded by law enforcement people.

At first she didn't intend to go into law enforcement as a career, although the hidden motivation may have been there. She had always been impressed by her father's uniform. She had gone with the family to police conventions where the de-meanor of police officers also impressed her. From her earliest recollections she liked the way her father and brother worked together as a family unit and were always ready to help out whenever they were needed.

192

She was also always accustomed to discipline, which is necessary on the force. She had not been allowed to date or drive a car until she was sixteen. Even then people used to tease her by saying, "I'll bet your father gives your dates the third degree. He makes them sit in the corner and turns a spotlight on them until they confess all." Of course, this never happened, but her parents did want to know where she was going, who would be there, and when she would be home. She used to resent these restrictions. Now she can see why they were made. Her parents simply wanted to protect her.

Still, law enforcement as a career wasn't on Monte's mind. When it came time to choose a career, she went into the business world right out of high school. She worked as a secretary for an insurance company—typing, taking shorthand, and filing. But none of these things really interested her. She decided to go to college.

At Sul Ross State University in Alpine, Texas, she started taking the courses needed to become a teacher. The more courses she took, though, the less interested she became. Through her boyfriend, who was a highway patrolman, she met other highway patrolmen, security guards at the university, the border patrolmen (Alpine is located near the border between Mexico and the United States), and even United States Customs officers. One day while talking with her boyfriend and some other law enforcement officers, the conversation turned to a new program the university was going to offer in law enforcement. The purpose of the new university program was to try to advance education for law enforcement personnel and to try to professionalize the field.

Monte wondered aloud to these men if there were many opportunities for women in law enforcement. It sounded to her like an interesting career. The men told her there were some openings now for women, and more to come in the future.

Shortly after hearing about the new program, Monte changed her college major from education to law enforcement. She took such courses as Patrol Administration, Legal As-

193

pects of Law Enforcement, Police Role in Crime and Delinquency, Police-Community Relations and Procedure, Criminal Evidence and Procedure, and Probation and Parole. During her last year in college she did an internship in the Alpine Police Department. As part of her job, she worked with young people who were on probation.

While serving her internship, Monte set her own personal goal. She would try to bring a better image to the public of what law enforcement is. For she believes in professionalism. She thinks it is a way to help people see police officers as human beings, and more importantly, as individuals. She thinks a professional police officer can be of greater service to citizens. And service is very important to Monte. She is especially eager to work with young people.

Right out of college, she went into a twelve-week training session at the Police Department Academy for rookies of the Midland, Texas, Police Department. She is now studying all phases of police work. Some of it repeats her college training. But she is becoming better acquainted with a wide variety of police work that she didn't learn about in college. For instance, one phase of her training is defense tactics (mechanics of arrest), firearms training, and riot control. Anyone who might feel that a professional thinks he is "packing a pistol on his hip," can forget it. The weapon training and wearing of the weapon is part of the defensive training program. A professional law enforcement officer knows how to handle a weapon and knows its ultimate purpose.

What kind of assignments will Policewoman Johnson be given? She may do anything that has to do with regular police work. She personally feels women shouldn't be given patrol duty. She thinks that a woman patrolling an area and spotting a gang fight would have more difficulty handling the fight than a man would.

Monte thinks a woman police officer can respond better to another woman in cases involving attacks on women, examining a woman offender, and working with female juveniles. She thinks we'll be seeing more women officers in the future.

Already in the larger metropolitan areas of the United States, women in law enforcement are receiving equal opportunities to work on the police force. Fifty percent of New York's 1973 recruits to its police academy were women. They will be assigned jobs equal to men's jobs. Women are now in the Federal Bureau of Investigation, State Highway Patrols, and private detective agencies. Police work is no longer only a man-sized job. It is a woman-sized job, too.

Policewoman Monte Kay Johnson is participating in opening doors to the future for women interested in law enforcement as a professional career. And for each of us, the fuller use of the talents of all of us—female and male alike—will eventually bring about better protection of all citizens.

CHECKING PROGRESS

1. What are some of the law enforcement jobs for which a woman is especially needed?
2. What type of law enforcement job did Monte feel might be better for a man than for a woman?
3. Form a discussion group with several of your classmates and discuss the personality traits and qualifications you think a person who is interested in becoming a law enforcement officer should have.

CHOOSING NEXT STEPS

1. Try to think of a situation where you have recently observed a man or woman working on a job that in the past had always been filled by the opposite. Make your first sentence begin with "Once upon a time..." Then write a brief statement about the job. For example:

   Once upon a time the person who carried a flag in road work was always a man or a boy. This past summer on my vacation, I saw several girls carrying flags and stopping cars in places where the highways were being fixed.
2. Read a factual book about law enforcement or a fictional book about a law enforcement officer.
3. Visit your city police department and other law enforcement offices in your city.
4. Interview a policeman or a policewoman. Ask them such questions as these:
   (1) Why did you decide to become a law enforcement officer?
   (2) What kind and how much training did you have?
   (3) What do you like most about your work? What do you like least about your work?

I'LL ALWAYS REMEMBER
THINKING THINGS THROUGH

Many times the events of a person's childhood may affect his or her decision about a career. This story of Annaliese Parschat Hyde's childhood is a story of a child raised during the war in Germany. It is a story of an escape to a freer world. It is a story about being poor and hungry. This is not a story about her career as a nurse, but about the events which shaped her decisions to become one.

ABOUT WORDS

As you are reading this story, find words which answer the questions below. The first letters of these words, listed in the same order as the questions, will spell another word that relates to Annaliese and her life.

Who is Annaliese's brother?

What is the name of the disease that Annaliese and her brother Gunter got?

What word was used to describe the Russian soldiers?

Where was Annaliese's father going to be sent when he decided to escape?

Who was the main character in the story?

What did Annaliese choose for a career?

What is the last letter of the word that tells where Annaliese and her family lived when her father worked in Hanover?

BEFORE YOU READ

197

INVESTIGATE

I'll Always Remember

Annaliese Parschat Hyde is a lovely young woman, tall and blonde. She now lives in the United States, is married, and has two boys. This is her story of her early life.

I had always wanted to be a nurse. I had known it from the time I was eight years old and saw all the sick and wounded soldiers in a German Army hospital. But my daddy didn't want me to become a nurse. He finally said, "Before you do, you have to go to a household school where you will learn how to keep house, sew, and milk cows."

The school was a big country household. There were three students there. We learned to run a household, to raise chickens and calves, and to garden. How I hated it!

When my year at the household school was over, my daddy enrolled me in a secretarial school. But I had made my own decision. I had found out about a nursing school in Osnabruck. I wrote to them behind my daddy's back. Then I went to my daddy and told him that was all I wanted to do, nothing else. So he gave his consent, and I left home. I was just fifteen and was frightened about the trip.

But I got there, and I started my training. I received the equivalent of a high school education as well as nurses' training. We could leave the hospital only one evening a week, and then we had to tell the supervisor where we went and with whom. We weren't charged tuition but had to work two years after graduation to repay the hospital for training us.

During those six years I felt very secure; I couldn't have chosen a better place to be after my unsettled childhood during the war. It made me grow up and develop strength. When I finished there, I felt I could cope with anything.

198

I had grown up in Leipzig, Germany. My father had been a soldier from before the time of Hitler. After the conquest of Norway, he was transferred there, where he stayed until he was captured by the English and placed in an American prison. All during the war my mother, my little brother Gunter, and I lived in Leipzig. I still remember the capture of our city. I was just a child of ten or eleven, but I know that I will never forget it.

During the war, we had food in limited quantities. But we did eat and didn't suffer much except for the bombs. But after we lost the war, we really began to feel the impact of it. I can remember looking out the bedroom window and seeing Russian soldiers. The soldiers were the wildest looking people I have ever seen. They were ruthless. They had been told, "When you get to Germany, everything is yours."

Their food supply was low, and they took most of what little we had. For our school lunch, they gave us a little slice of black bread—it was so heavy it was like stone. It was really half sawdust, but we ate it anyway.

We lived on about five pounds of flour a month. I can remember my mother trading everything she had at the black market for food. Anything of value went for just a sack of potatoes. Even with all the money in the world, you couldn't buy food from the stores. They only opened a day or two a month when it was announced that we could get a certain amount of something that day. One month we lived only on split peas. Even now I can't look a split pea in the eye.

My father returned to the Russian Zone when the prisoners were freed. He was in a work camp taking apart machinery for shipment to Russia. When he discovered he was to be sent to a uranium mine, he escaped over the border into West Germany and managed to get word to my mother.

"We have to leave everything behind," my mother said to me. "We have to make a choice now. Either we're going to live in a freer world with our daddy or just stay here and continue to live this miserable life."

199

Right after midnight we took a train to the border. After we left the train, we had to cross the Harz Mountains on foot. We arrived at the border just before daylight. The man with whom we were going said, "We're real close to the border now. We have to be quiet and go over two at a time."

However, each person was thinking only of himself. You couldn't expect help. It was a kind of animal instinct. We had to cross a river, and there was no bridge. The river was a no-man's-land between the American Sector and the Russian Sector. Off to one side was a clump of bushes, and across the river we could see American soldiers. The people got excited and started running for the river. Then two warning shots were fired. Out of the bushes came Russian soldiers. They were drunk and teased and laughed at us. Finally they marched us back to a camp where we stayed in a sheep stall.

After quite a few days my mother came to me and said, "I don't want you to say a word or make a sound. We're going to leave right after lunch."

I replied, "Mother, have you lost your mind? How can we get out of here with this high steel fence all around?"

200

"Well, I've talked with the man who owns that guest house over there," she explained. "He told me there would be a period of several minutes when no one would patrol the gate."

We took very few things because it was just run, run, run the whole way. We came to the spot where we had been captured before. When my mother saw those bushes, she sank to the ground in despair and began to cry. She sobbed, "I just can't take it any more; I can't stand another defeat."

I told her to sit with Gunter. I crawled to the bushes on my stomach. No one was there. I said, "Let's run."

And we ran. I don't know how my little brother got over the river because he was such a little fellow. We were over the border when they shot at us. The American soldiers called to us, "Fall down! Fall down!" We threw ourselves on the ground. The Americans came running to help us.

We finally reached my father. He was working for a farmer in Hanover; that was all the work he could get. Besides, he thought if he worked for a farmer we could get good food. We lived in a pigsty; yes, literally, a pigsty. But Mother had cleaned it, and we had straw on the ground. We could sleep without being afraid. We had food, but after a few weeks Gunter and I developed hunger edema—we got big water stomachs. When a child has been hungry for a long time, he must be fed very carefully at first or the food will do as much damage as the hunger. We were sick for three months but finally became strong enough to go to school.

Now perhaps you can understand how much security there was for me in nursing school. There was a routine; we knew exactly when, what, and why we were doing the things we did. Each group of girls had an older nurse to look after them—kind of a den mother. It was a very secure, sure feeling, and I loved what I did. I'll always remember those years.

CHECKING PROGRESS

1. Name two types of schools which Annaliese Parschat Hyde attended when she was growing up. Describe each school. Tell something unusual about her training at each.
2. Why did she become interested in nursing? How old was she when she discovered this interest?
3. List several words that describe the feelings you think Annaliese had the night she and her family took a train and just left their apartment.
4. What kind of person was Annaliese's mother?
5. With evidence from the story, point out some of the personal strengths exhibited by Annaliese.

CHOOSING NEXT STEPS

1. Interview a nurse you know, either male or female. Find out why this person wanted to be a nurse. When did he or she become interested in nursing? How much training was needed? Where did this person get his training?
2. Read a biography or an informational article about a doctor or a nurse.
3. Find out about the types of medical careers that can be entered. Work with several of your classmates. Use library books and other informational material. Compile a chart of information about medical careers. Your chart may be arranged like this one.

Medical Careers

Occupation	Training	Personality Traits	Approximate Salary

HELLO, OPERATOR!

THINKING THINGS THROUGH

What's of more use around the house than the telephone! Sometimes the whole family seems to need it at the same time. Even though most telephoning is done through automatic equipment, there is still the need for people to work behind the scenes in the telephone operation. How very important they are when an emergency requires their assistance. The following selection tells about a young man who has found working as a telephone operator rewarding.

Study this selection using subtitles or section headings as a guide. Quickly preview the introduction and subtitles of the selection. Turn the first subtitle into a question. Your question will probably be something like this one, "Is there a chance for advancement in the telephone company?"

Now read to the end of the first section to find the answer to the question. Look away from the book and recite the answer to yourself. If you can answer the question, go on to the next section. If not, reread the section.

The questions below are examples you may use for studying the rest of the sections.

What skills, talents, and interests are needed to be successful in working for the telephone company?

Why are goals important?

What are the advantages versus disadvantages in working for the telephone company as an operator?

What does "incentive leads to success" mean?

ABOUT WORDS

Look up the root words, *tele* and *phone*. Try to think of as many words as you can which include them. Then see if you can find others in the dictionary.

203

INVESTIGATE

HELLO, OPERATOR!

Ever since the time when people had to crank a telephone while shouting into the transmitter, "Hello, operator!", a female voice has answered the call. However, during the last few years there have been some changes in telephone company operations. One of these changes involves a young man named Robert Carter, of Midland, Texas. He was one of the first male telephone operators hired in his area by Southwestern Bell Telephone Company.

When asked how it feels to hold a job in a world that has traditionally belonged to women, Robert answered, "It's not just a woman's world. Things are changing. One of the women who worked on the switchboard with me is now working at a job in which she climbs ladders all day long. This was once strictly a man's job, but she requested it."

According to Robert, the telephone company will let an employee transfer into almost any department, depending, of course, on his service record and experience with the company. There are no longer any sex barriers. Any employee who wants a certain job can work to get it.

Advancement Within the Company

Robert thinks the telephone company gives workers many opportunities to advance. Many members of minority groups have been hired under the company's policy of helping them learn and advance to higher jobs. There is also a plan to hire more male operators in Southwestern Bell operating areas.

In line with his hopes for advancement, Robert is going to college and taking courses in management. He hopes to soon

204

work into a management position. His goal is to go as high as he can. He would like to stay within the traffic department, the department where calls come through. There he could continue to work closely with people. He feels there is no limit on where he can go or how far.

Skills, Talents, and Interests

It takes skill to be a telephone operator. At times Robert laughs when he hears someone say how easy his job must be. It's not as easy as it sounds. It takes definite skills to be able to accurately complete the connections for a call within a few seconds. And it takes a sense of responsibility and an understanding of people to better serve the customers of the telephone company.

Robert has always liked being with people. He became interested in becoming a telephone operator because of the close contact with people that the job demands.

"It's important to have compassion for people," Robert stated, "because an operator can run into all sorts of problems. An operator has to be someone who understands people and knows how to talk to them. In trying to help them, if he doesn't understand their needs, he might say something that would cause an adverse effect and would alienate a customer."

Robert has an interest in speech and choir, too. He took first place in a high school drama tournament and also has worked with small theater groups. According to Robert, these interests helped him learn to express himself with other people. And he feels that it is important for an operator to be able to express himself clearly.

Goals Are Important

It was important to Robert all of his life to be able to set definite goals for himself—something he wanted to achieve within a certain amount of time—and to work toward these goals. He doesn't consider that he has failed at anything he has tried. Even when he lost in competition, for example, he still felt he had gained and learned through his practice and work for that competition.

Advantages Versus Disadvantages

"The job presented a challenge," Robert said. He explained that the telephone company only had one male operator when he was hired in 1972 at the age of eighteen. That man was transferred to another city soon after Robert came to work. Robert became the only male operator, and so he had to make a few adjustments.

"When our baby daughter was born," Robert said, "the other operators gave me a baby shower! I am probably the only man in history to have had a baby shower!"

Robert feels that the advantages of being a telephone operator are tied in with the benefits the company offers: medical policies, retirement policies, vacations, overtime pay, and good working conditions.

The disadvantages are few. Hours in which an operator works are called *tricks*. They are based on seniority. A new operator is at the bottom of the list and takes the trick the other operators don't want. Robert began working on the 1:00 p.m. to 10:00 p.m. trick—the last trick on the schedule.

Sometimes operators must work nights, Sundays, and holidays. In other departments, such as the business department, the workers have regular hours with Sundays and holidays off. The operators who handle calls do not.

Some people don't like these hours and consider them a disadvantage. But Robert thinks that they work out to his advantage. He can attend his college classes in the morning and still hold a job by working at night.

Incentive Leads To Success

In thinking about what his friends from high school have done since graduation, Robert can see some who'll never advance from the jobs they have now. He can see others who have gone on in their work and studies and have set goals. He feels that a personal incentive to succeed must be the key, and he feels that those who have it are lucky—as he is.

His interest in people, his enjoyment of the dramatic arts, and his belief in setting personal goals—all of these have combined to put him in the job he is so enthusiastic about today. He likes being a telephone operator. He likes working for the Southwestern Bell Telephone Company. And he sees a good future ahead for himself and his family.

CHECKING PROGRESS

1. Look back at the study questions. Check your memory by reviewing your questions and answers with a friend.
2. Do you think it's important for a telephone operator to be patient and understanding with other people? Why?
3. Have you set goals for yourself? If so, what are they? Has anyone encouraged you? Who? If you don't have goals for yourself, write several that you might like to have and talk them over with a teacher or a friend.
4. Read the sentences below which have been taken from the selection. Each has one or two words underlined which may have been unfamiliar to you. Read the sentences again and look in a dictionary for the meanings of words that you are not sure about. Write a sentence of your own using each of the underlined words.
   (1) . . . he might say something that would cause an <u>adverse</u> effect and would <u>alienate</u> a customer.
   (2) Hours in which an operator works are called tricks. They are based on <u>seniority</u>.
5. Two common words, *trick* and *traffic*, have special meanings in the telephone business. What are they? Why do you think these words were chosen for the meaning they have in the telephone business?

CHOOSING NEXT STEPS

1. Read books in the library about various communication systems, such as the telephone, telegraph, and radio.
2. Arrange to take a field trip to the telephone company with several of your classmates.
3. The telephone directory offers a great deal of information about your community. Study it with several of your friends. Make a list of the other types of information it gives you besides telephone numbers.
4. Make a picture story of the telephone. Start with its invention and continue to the present day. Collect pictures of as many phones as possible that are now being used.

MAN BEHIND CITY SCENES

THINKING THINGS THROUGH

How many people doing their jobs do you see during the day? As we go through the day, we usually see many different types of workers, such as bus drivers, salespeople, and waiters or waitresses. But what about the people behind the scenes? There are many people that we never see doing their jobs. This story is about Mike Anderson, who is one of these kinds of workers. He is the assistant director of the Public Works Department. He is the man who is rarely seen, yet he is responsible for street repair, water distribution, sanitation, and sewage collection in his city.

As you read this story use the same method of study which you used for "Hello, Operator." Remember to:

1. Preview or survey the entire selection. Read the introduction and skim the subtopics or section headings.
2. Read the first section, keeping your question in mind.
4. After you have finished the first section, recite the answer to yourself or write it down on paper.
5. Continue using the same procedure—question, read, recite—with each section.
6. After you have completed the entire selection, review your questions and answers for all sections.

ABOUT WORDS

Look up the word *civil* in the dictionary. Which of the meanings do you think applies to the term *civil engineer*? what kind of work do you think a civil engineer does?

INVESTIGATE

man behind
city scenes

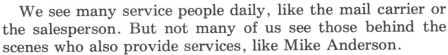

We see many service people daily, like the mail carrier or the salesperson. But not many of us see those behind the scenes who also provide services, like Mike Anderson.

Mike is the assistant director of the Public Works Department in a city of about 60,000 people. His responsibility is to see that crews are available for street repair, water distribution, sanitation, and sewage collection.

"People take these services for granted," Mike says. "For example, there's the woman who calls the department because her garbage hasn't been picked up yet. What she doesn't understand is that perhaps that day five truck drivers were home with the flu, and the others in the department were working extra hard to try to keep on schedule."

Mike has worked in towns and cities of various sizes in a number of states. Before working he completed three years of college in civil engineering and a "hitch" in the army where he did the same kind of work. What kind of work is it?

What Does Mike Do?

Civil engineering includes care of streets and roads, water distribution, sewage, and pick up and disposal of garbage.

Mike's job is different every day. He travels the city in a car with a telephone, so that he can be reached at all times. He must go out to check on a large hole that has developed in one of the streets after a heavy snow. He must make sure the drainage system is working properly during a sudden rainstorm, so no flooding develops. He must check on a complaint that the garbage pickup truck missed one of the alleys.

210

He is also a go-between with the people of the city and the employees of the Public Works Department. He must do his best to make sure the workers are satisfied with their working conditions. He wants them to feel an interest in their jobs and recognize the importance of the work they are doing.

Benefits of Working for a City Government

There are many benefits in working for a city government, according to Mike. For one thing, there is no problem with a layoff from work because of bad weather or because supplies haven't come in on schedule. The workers for a city are paid a guaranteed salary for a 40-hour week. If bad weather keeps them from going outside to work, there are other jobs that can be done inside. Even if the men are sent home for the day, they are still paid. Even though starting salaries are not high, they do increase with experience.

The government also offers a generous vacation schedule. Aside from the legal holidays, many employees get vacations of three weeks or more. In addition to social security benefits and medical benefits, a retirement program is offered.

Many other things help a man working for a big organization like city government. One is new equipment. Most of the large sanitation trucks in Mike's city have automatic transmissions which make them easier to drive.

Also, the workers are assigned uniforms. These are good identification and save workers' clothes. It's much less expensive for a worker to wear city-issued uniforms.

Qualifications for City Workers

People who apply for these jobs must go through a screening and a police check. The city feels responsibility for the actions of its employees.

Reading and writing are necessary in some jobs. Drivers are given written instructions and must write notes about problems they have during the day. Those who drive large trucks must have a commercial driver's license.

The Way to Advance

Those who want to learn and can take job responsibility are

quickly promoted to a higher classification. A high school graduate has no limit in his future in public works administration providing he is willing to take the time to learn. He must acquire the skills needed to operate equipment, know why he must use certain materials to do certain jobs, and know the reasons behind the way things are done. To be successful, Mike thinks a man must be observing all the time. He must see what is needed, what conditions the streets are in, and why barricades are placed a certain way.

212

Often short educational courses can be taken, but learning by experience is important, too. Sometimes an experiment in operations is tried, and it doesn't work. The right approach is, "We have learned something from this. Now, how will we approach the problem the next time? Let's try another way."

"A man must be willing to accept a challenge," Mike says, "if someone asks him if he can do a certain job, his answer should be, 'I'll give it a try.' "

No Longer Jobs Just for Men

There no longer exists a rule that certain jobs can only be held by men. During the summer many college students apply for work, boys as well as girls."

"Last summer," Mike says, "a college girl applied for a summer job working a mowing tractor. She had experience on her father's farming equipment. She was hired and turned out to be the leader of the crew she was assigned to because she could easily read the maps."

Preparation for the Future

"A summer job is good experience to help prepare young men or women for the job they choose in life," says Mike.

He would like to see something like a junior achievement program for all students in high school. "Too often the students have no idea of the business world," he says. "Some kind of program is needed to help students realize what is going on in the world, what they really need to know, and what they are going to do with their education or degree."

He thinks that with more knowledge of the functions of a city's Public Works Department, many more young people would be attracted to jobs within its structure. "It's good to be working at something you really like to do," Mike says.

213

CHECKING PROGRESS

Review the questions and answers for all sections of the selection you have just read.

CHOOSING NEXT STEPS

1. The last four selections you read are about a law enforcement officer, a nurse, a telephone operator, and an assistant director of the Public Works Department. From the information you have gained from reading the selections, compare these four careers according to the following:

Qualifications and training	Chance for Advancement	Advantages of Job	Disadvantages of Job

2. Interview someone in your city who works in one of the areas mentioned in this selection. Ask such questions as:
   (1) How can you advance?
   (2) What are some advantages of your job? What are some disadvantages of your job?
   (3) What type of training did you have for your job?
3. Prepare a slide presentation including pictures of persons in public works in action on the job. Ask a classmate to work with you. You might start your work on the project by visiting the director of public works. Ask him to direct you to locations for taking photographs. Record on tape an explanation of each slide and present this project to your entire class.
4. On a map of your city, locate all of the public works projects and work centers. Write a brief description of each and attach it to the map.

CAREER CLUSTERS

THINKING THINGS THROUGH

Did you ever hear of career clusters? These are groupings or *clusters* of occupations according to different career fields. In the United States we can divide careers into fifteen different clusters. These are: Agriculture; Clerical; Communications and Media; Construction; Fine Arts and Humanities; Finance, Insurance, and Real Estate; Health; Managerial Occupations; Manufacturing; Marine Science; Marketing and Distribution; Mining; Personal Services; Public Services; and Transportation.

Do you know what career cluster you are most interested in? As you read the following article, you will learn more about each cluster. You may also learn about careers which seem new to you. To help you in finding information, each career cluster has been divided into four paragraphs. Each paragraph answers a particular question: (1) What is this cluster? (2) What are the future opportunities? (3) What kind of training is needed? (4) What specific jobs are in this cluster?

ABOUT WORDS

Before you read the article, let's see how much you already know about careers. Try to match up the jobs in the left column with the correct career cluster in the right column. Then read the article to see if you did well.

carpenter	agriculture
artist	health
diver	public service
cashier	communications and media
petroleum engineer	clerical
reporter	fine arts and humanities
pharmacist	marine science
farm manager	construction
fireman	health

215

Career Clusters

Agriculture

This area is associated with farming or the production of foods and grains. Agriculture is a multi-billion dollar industry.

Outlooks for the future in agriculture are very good especially for large and middle-sized farms. Since the world's supply of food is growing smaller, more nations are spending money on American farm products.

The best background for entering this career field is to grow up on a farm. Many high schools offer courses and clubs for experience in agriculture.

Jobs in this field include: farm managers, soil scientists, agricultural engineers and plant scientists.

Clerical

Clerical refers to operating office machines of all types, keeping records, and communicating in business.

As American business continues to grow, more clerical workers will be needed.

For most positions, a high school diploma is required. Some companies give students an opportunity to learn on the job while still attending high school. For many clerical positions it is necessary to know typing, arithmetic, spelling and grammar, reading skills, and how to meet people.

Clerical jobs include: bookkeepers, cashiers, file clerks, secretaries, timekeepers, mail clerks, and bill collectors.

Communications and Media

This area deals with the sending of messages either by letters, by spoken word, or by picture. Included in this area are newspapers, telephone and telegraph, recording, radio, and television broadcasting.

The future outlook is best for technical and news writers. In other fields such as radio, television, and movies, there will be much competition for jobs.

Most of the positions in this area require some form of training or *apprenticeship*. A college degree is not always necessary for obtaining a job.

Jobs related to this area include: reporters, copywriters, editors, directors, costume managers, designers, disc jockeys, stuntmen and cameramen.

Construction

Any activity in building is part of this area. About half of these jobs are in electricity, air conditioning, and plumbing. The other half is in constructing buildings, roads, dams, and bridges.

The outlook for future jobs will depend upon the nation's economy. Economy and construction grow together.

Training as an apprentice is probably the best way to enter this field. A high school diploma is desirable but not always necessary.

217

After experience, one may be promoted to foreman. Some craftsmen are often required to have a license.

Some occupations related to construction are: bricklayers, carpenters, asbestos workers, painters, roofers, pipe fitters, electricians, and machine operators.

Fine Arts and Humanities

The values and ideals of our society are included in this area. It deals with the arts, architecture, religion, languages, social science, and teaching.

Future opportunities may be favorable for architects, clergymen, commercial artists, and for people who speak foreign languages. The performing arts will continue to be competitive.

In this area much training and practice is needed, especially in the performing arts. College degrees are needed for architecture.

Jobs in this area include: commercial artists, painters and sculptors, interior decorators, photographers, musicians, composers, choreographers, singers, dancers, actors, novelists, playwrights, interpreters, archeologists, historians, and museum directors.

Finance, Insurance, and Real Estate

This area relates to a person's money matters. Nearly everyone uses some of these services.

Jobs in this area are expected to increase somewhat due to population growth, business activity, and rising incomes.

Most persons in this area have completed high school. Bank guards may need less education. On-the-job training is given in banks and insurance companies. People in real estate must pass a test in order to get a license.

Occupations related to this area are: bank clerks, tellers, bank officers, managers or workers in finance, sales managers, sales persons, underwriters, brokers, and adjustors.

Health

The health area deals with the physical and emotional care of people.

218

Because the population is growing and more people are concerned with their health, there is a tremendous need for health workers.

The amount of training needed is different for each position. Professional health workers such as doctors, dentists, and pharmacists must complete many years of professional school and pass a state exam. Other workers such as a dental assistant may require only two years of college.

There are many jobs in this field including: medical technologists, psychiatrists, dentists, dental assistants, laboratory assistants, x-ray technicians, school nurses, doctors, nurses, ambulance attendants, veterinarians, pharmacists, dietitians, and therapists.

Managerial Occupations

This area concerns anyone who manages a business or is in charge of other workers. A manager's decisions can affect the success of the business.

Large firms are depending more on managers who have had special training. In the future, the employment of salaried managers is likely to increase.

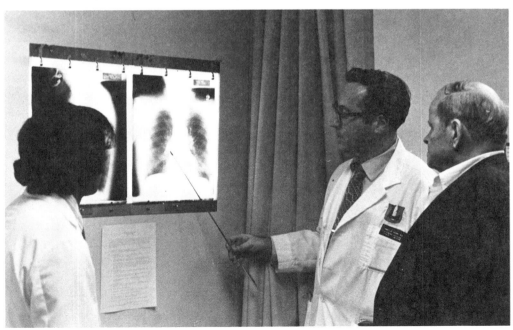

Many employers look for people who have college degrees in business administration. Other employees look for people who have technical training. A person who does not have a degree may work his way up as he gains experience.

Jobs include: store managers, office managers, service managers, presidents and vice-presidents of firms, chairmen of the board, city managers, executive secretaries, and traffic managers.

Manufacturing

Manufacturing is the process of making products by

hand or by machinery. It has over 8,000 kinds of jobs.

Due to automation, employment in this area may increase at a slower rate. Still this industry will continue to employ the greatest number of people.

The amount of training depends upon the type of job. A college degree or experience is desirable for a management position. Scientists and engineers have at least a bachelor's degree. Technicians need two years technical or junior college education. Craftsmen usually have a four-year apprenticeship.

Skilled workers usually need several years of experience. Semiskilled workers are given on-the-job training. Unskilled workers do not need a high school education. They are trained on the job also.

The occupations relating to this field are varied: presidents or vice-presidents of industries, chemists, physicists, engineers, draftsmen, metalurgists, engravers, pattern makers, electricians, tool and die makers, mechanics, printers, and plant maintenance jobs.

Marine Science

Marine Science is the discovery and growing of food and minerals from fresh and ocean waters. Many jobs are involved with research.

Since man needs to find new food and mineral sources in the future, fish farming and ocean mining will grow as industries.

There is a need for unskilled and technical people as well as people with college degrees. Many workers are needed for *aquaculture*, or raising aquatic plants and animals. Occupations dealing with research require specialized training.

Some jobs related to this area are: oceanographers, marine biologists, drillers, surveyors, fishermen, divers, marine biologists, and hydrologists.

Marketing and Distribution

This area refers to the buying and selling of products and services. One out of every fifteen persons employed in the United States works with some form of selling.

Employment in the marketing and distribution area is expected to increase moderately in the 1970's.

People with less than a high school education and no previous experience can qualify for several jobs in this career cluster. However, many jobs do require advanced training, especially at the manager level.

Occupations in this area include: managers, clerks, researchers, salespersons, importers and exporters, analysts, buyers, warehouse attendants, and advertisers.

221

Mining

Mining refers to the taking and developing of petroleum, natural gas, and ores from the earth. This is the smallest major industry in the United States.

Employment in mining is expected to decline slowly in the 1970's even though more materials will be taken from the earth.

Most workers begin as helpers and get on-the-job training. It may last several months or several years. For professional occupations, college training with at least a bachelor's degree is required.

Occupations related to mining are: paleontologists, geologists, petroleum engineers, geophysicists, mining engineers, drillers, pumpers, draftsmen, surveyors, metallurgists, landmen, and welding engineers.

Personal Services

This area is concerned with the care of a person, his clothing, appearance, comfort, and recreation. Nearly ten million persons work in the service occupations.

Employment in the personal services area is expected to increase rapidly through the 1970's. In the future, man will have more time for relaxation and pleasure.

The service industries are an important source of employment to new or experienced workers. Often people can go to commercial schools for special training.

Some occupations related to personal services include: housekeepers, cooks, motel or hotel managers, butlers, gardeners, maids, camp managers, hair stylists, cleaners and pressers, tailors, porters, entertainers, animal trainers, chefs, athletic trainers, athletes, lifeguards, and bakers.

Public Services

This area deals with positions of service to the public. These can be either at the local, state, or national levels.

Rapid growth is expected in state and local public service. Federal employment is expected to grow more slowly but the trend here will also go upwards.

The majority of government jobs are filled through a civil service test. Some jobs have special requirements. The Armed Forces is a voluntary career.

Opportunities in this area include: policemen, firemen, Social Security workers, postal clerks, mailmen, forest rangers, servicemen, conservationists, environmental control workers, gas meter technicians, and sewage treatment workers.

Transportation

Transportation is the transfer of people and objects from place to place.

Transportation systems will grow in the future. This field will continue to offer many career choices.

Usually training is more important than education. Pilots and stewardesses must be trained. Some jobs such as airplane mechanics and truck drivers must have special licenses.

Occupations related to transportation are: parking lot attendants, taxi drivers, train crew members, pilots, dispatchers, baggage handlers, train yard workers, stewards or stewardesses, pumpers, canal lock attendants, and seamen.

CHECKING PROGRESS

1. What is the best background for entering the agriculture cluster? How else can you learn about agriculture?
2. Which area of the fine arts cluster is overcrowded?
3. What kinds of jobs are there in the manufacturing cluster? Would you like to do any of these?
4. What is aquaculture? In which career cluster would it be found?
5. Which clusters have good outlooks for the future? Which do not have good outlooks?
6. Which career clusters do not require much education? Why do you think this is so?

CHOOSING NEXT STEPS

1. Which career cluster seems the most exciting to you? Which seems the least exciting?
2. Would you rather have a job out-of-doors or a job inside in an office? Tell why.
3. What kind of job would you most like to have? Did this article change your feelings at all?
4. Choose a job from the health cluster such as a doctor or x-ray technician. Try to imagine yourself doing that job several years from now. Describe how you might spend your day.
5. Try to speak with some people who have jobs in different career clusters. What do they have to say about their jobs?
6. You can find out more about any job in the *Occupational Outlook Handbook* in your public library.

PARTS OF A BOOK

A book has several important parts which you should know how to find and use. Before and after the body or main part of the book are certain aids, such as the table of contents and the index, which help you to locate specific information contained in the book. Other parts, such as the title page with the copyright date help you decide whether or not the material in the book is appropriate and current enough for your purpose. Glossaries and other supplements at the end of the book add to the information in the body of the book.

TITLE PAGE

The title page is found at the beginning of the book. Both the front and back of the title page carry important information about the book. Study the title page in at least three books. Then write the correct answer for each question below on a separate sheet of paper. There may be more than one correct answer or each book may have a different answer.

1. Where is the title of the book located? (a) on the front of the title page (b) on the back of the title page (c) on both sides of the title page
2. Where is the publisher's name listed? (a) on the front of the title page (b) on the back of the title page   (c) on both sides of the title page
3. What other information does the title page give about the publisher? (a) other books the company has published (b) place of publication (c) name of president of the company
4. Where would you find the copyright date? (a) on the front of the title page (b) on the back of the title page (c) on both sides of the title page
5. Where is the subtitle found? (If there is one.) (a) on the front of the title page (b) on the back of the title page (c) on both sides of the title page
6. Where would you find the name of the author? (a) on the front of the title page (b) on the back of the title page (c) on both sides of the title page

Were there differences in the title pages of each of the books you referred to? Draw some general conclusions about the location of the title, publisher's name, author's name, and copyright date. Why do you think you would need to know this information? What other information did you find on the title page?

The table of contents is located in the front of the book between the title page and the main body of the book. Find and skim through the table of contents of at least three books in addition to the example given below. Then answer the following questions.

1. Are the listings in the table of contents given in alphabetical order?
2. Are the listings in the table of contents grouped by chapters? by sections? by units? by topics?
3. What determines the order of the listings which appear in the table of contents?
4. Would a selection found on page 12 in a book be listed in the table of contents before or after a selection found on page 39? Explain your answer.
5. Would a selection, "Wonder Star," beginning on page 20 be listed in the table of contents before or after a selection, "Blue Seas," beginning on page 78? Why?

Contents

The index is usually found at the back of a book following the main body of reading material. Study this example of an index. Then answer the following questions.

1. Are the topics listed in the index in alphabetical order?
2. Are the listings in the index grouped by chapters? by units? by sections?
3. What determines the order of the topics listed in the index?
4. Are page numbers given in the index? If so, in what order do they appear?
5. Between which two entries in the index below would you list the topic *cocoa*, p. 305?
6. Between which two entries in the index below would you list the topic *LaMont*, p. 37?

Index

GLOSSARY

The glossary is found in the back of the book. It includes words used in the book that are difficult to understand and/or pronounce. It also may contain a special vocabulary that is related to the content of the book. Study the glossary in at least three different books. Then answer the following questions.

1. In what order do the words in a glossary appear?
2. How can a glossary help you with the pronunciation of a word?
3. How can a glossary help you understand the meaning of a word?
4. In a glossary, which of the entries below would come before the entry *ceremony*?

   Columbus   California
5. Which of the entries below would come after the entry *kayak*?

   indignant   lizard

WHAT DID YOU LEARN ABOUT PARTS OF A BOOK?

Read each of the statements below and then decide whether it is usually true or false.

1. The copyright date is found on the back of the title page.
2. The name of the illustrator of the book never appears on the title page.
3. The author's name usually appears on the back of the title page.
4. The publisher's name is listed on the title page.
5. The topics in the table of contents are in alphabetical order.
6. The topics in the index are listed in alphabetical order.
7. The words in a glossary are listed in numerical order by the page on which they appear.
8. The index is usually found in the back of a book.
9. A glossary lists only the proper names used in the book.
10. A glossary gives the definition but not the pronunciation of the words listed.
11. The entry words in a glossary appear in alphabetical order.

Put the following topics in the order that they would appear in an index. Then put them in the order that they would appear in a Table of Contents. Write them on a separate sheet of paper.

George Washington, p. 6   Abraham Lincoln, p. 15
Benjamin Franklin, p. 45   Theodore Roosevelt, p. 75
Thomas Jefferson, p. 30   Amelia Earhart, p. 60

paths of my choice

Paths come in all shapes and sizes. Here is an interesting, scenic path; here is a rocky, stumbling one. Here is a wide path; there is a path that is uphill all the way.

Which path will you choose to take? Will the smooth path meet your needs? Will the rocky path lead to a goal that is worth the trip? How will you reach your goals? The choice is yours.

UNIT 4   PATHS OF MY CHOICE

THE GOOD LIFE
THINKING THINGS THROUGH

As you read this story entitled "The Good Life," think of some answers you might give if someone were to ask you what a "Good Life" is.

As you read, pay particular attention to the characters in the story. Do you have a favorite character? Why? Do you think there is good teamwork in the group? Do you think the students are really accomplishing what they set out to do? Why or why not?

Would you like the opportunity to work on such a project? How do you suppose it might help you now with choosing your career? Would there be any additional questions you might like to take an opinion poll on?

ABOUT WORDS

In this story you will find words which have a special meaning. They are related to what is happening in the story. The list below gives some of the special words. Using the dictionary, make a glossary of your own, giving the definition of each word as it is used in the story. Underline this definition. Then write any other definitions the words might have.

script	camera
film	scene
screen	projection
lights	narrator

BEFORE YOU READ

INVESTIGATE

THE GOOD LIFE

"Jan, it can't be done!" exclaimed Tom Dale as he looked at the group's English assignment.

"There must be a way," said Jan Schilling, "or Mr. Richardson wouldn't have given us this assignment."

"Oh, yeah! Then let Mr. Richardson do it!" Oscar Hamrick said. " 'Come up with a visual communications project on the quality of life,' he says. I don't even know what that means."

"Well, I think we can do it," replied Maria Robles, the fourth and last of the group members to speak.

Tom spoke up again. "O.K., Miss Smarty. You and Jan tell me and Oscar what *quality of life* means."

"I'm not too sure," Jan said. "It's more of a feeling I have about it. But *quality* means worth of something and *life* in this example means how you live. So I guess it means how worthwhile your way of living is."

"I'll look it up," said Maria as she picked up the dictionary. "It says *quality* means degree of excellence. That means to me, How good is your life?"

"Neat!" burst out Oscar. "We have quality of life meaning excellence, goodness, or worthwhile. But tell me—how will that help us to come up with a visual way to communicate it?"

"You don't have any faith in us, do you, Oscar?" said Jan.

"We'll have to put our heads together and think for a while. All right, everybody. THINK!" Jan urged.

The four students in Mr. Richardson's eighth grade English class at Coronado Junior High School, in Riverside, California, bowed their heads in serious thought. Once every few minutes one of them raised up, and then shook his head. There seemed to be no easy way to solve their problem. Suddenly Jan Schilling threw back her head and cried out:

"We can make a Super 8 movie on the quality of life! We can use my parents' camera and each of us can chip in from our allowances to buy film and pay for the processing."

"Great! I'll be the director," Oscar said.

"And I'll be the star," said Maria.

"Get serious, guys," said Jan. "First we've got to have a story line, or some angle. How are we going to do that?"

"Easy," Tom said. "We'll ask Maria. She always makes A's." He turned to Maria: "What do you want out of life?"

"It's simple. I want to go to college, then get a good job, have a nice salary, get married, and have two kids."

"Ugh!" said Oscar. "That's not a good life. That's a disaster. I want a motorcycle, fun, and pretty girls."

"Your answer, Maria, isn't what most girls want today," Jan put in.

"I don't think any of us knows what most boys and girls want today," Tom said. "Let's find out by asking the class."

"How are we going to do that?" asked Maria.

"We can take an opinion poll," Tom answered. "I'm sure Mr. Richardson will let us. We can ask him right now."

233

Tom went up to Mr. Richardson's desk. In a few minutes he was back.

"He says it's fine with him," Tom said. "But he wants to see our questions before we ask them."

"What are we going to ask?" Jan was puzzled.

"One thing we could ask is the same question we just used—'What do you want out of life?'" said Tom.

"That sounds so general," Jan said. "Some people won't know what we mean."

"Let's say, 'What are your ambitions?'" Maria suggested.

"Same difference," said Oscar. "But let's use Maria's words. O.K., Tom? Jan?" They nodded their agreement.

"We could ask something about pollution. Everybody is interested in that subject," said Jan. "We could say, 'How do you feel when you see pollution?'"

"Good suggestion," said Tom. Jan smiled at Tom as he supported another one of her ideas. He smiled back.

"How about a question on money?" inquired Oscar.

"Sure thing," replied Jan. "How will we word it, Maria?"

"Let's say, 'What would you do if you had $500?' Their answers should tell us what they think is important in life."

"I want to add one more question, 'What does the world mean to you?'" said Jan. No one objected to this idea.

"All right," said Maria. "Let's see what our opinion poll questions look like when written down." She wrote on her paper these questions:

1. What are your ambitions?
2. How do you feel when you see pollution?
3. What would you do if you had $500?
4. What does the world mean to you?

Tom took the questions up to Mr. Richardson for his approval. He returned in a short while.

"Mr. Richardson said to go ahead with the opinion poll. These are good questions."

The bell rang. The group decided to get to class early the following day and write their questions on the chalkboard.

234

The next day Jan arrived first. She wrote the group's questions on the board. When the class began, she explained what her group's project was and asked the students to fill out on a piece of paper their responses to the questions. After a few minutes, Jan and her group collected the papers.

"How are we going to tally these?" asked Oscar.

"Let's make a column for each question and jot underneath it what the student said," suggested Maria.

The group agreed. They made four columns—one for each question—and tallied the responses as follows:

Question #1	Question #2	Question #3	Question #4
Happiness	Clean up	Buy clothes	Beautiful
Stewardess	Move away	Spend it	Interesting people
Have fun	Get a horse	Motorcycle	Wonderful
College	Scream	Save it	Work together
Scientist	We'll die	Help poor	Holds secrets
Housewife	Angry	Pay bills	Nice people
Fish	Burn trash	Fishing rod	Natural wonders
Pro sports	Say stop	Travel	Fun to live
Doctor	Fight pollution	College	Lots of sickness
Lawyer	Pass laws	Stereo	Justice

"This talley sheet looks like a jigsaw puzzle," Tom said.

"Let's ask Mr. Richardson to figure it out," Oscar said.

The group went up to Mr. Richardson and showed him the tally sheet. "Do students believe the quality of life is determined by the amount of money a person has?" the teacher asked. "Compare the responses they gave you to questions one and three."

"Oh, I see what you mean," said Maria. "In answer to question number one, someone has said his ambition is to fish, and for question three, he wants a fishing rod. If he doesn't have money to buy it, he can't enjoy the sport. So the quality of his life is related to money."

Jan said, "But look at the answer to question one which says 'Scientist' and question three which says 'Help poor.'

235

That person obviously doesn't think he needs money to enjoy an excellent life."

"Without money how could he help the poor?" asked Oscar.

"I think you have the idea now," said Mr. Richardson. "Money is needed for some things. But you can help the poor without giving them money." The teacher looked at the tally sheet again. "Let's compare a few answers to questions two and four— pollution, and what the world means:

Question #2	Question #4
Clean up	Beautiful
Scream	Work together
Fight pollution	Lots of sickness

These people could improve the quality of life for themselves and others without the help of money."

"I think we can go ahead with our project now," said Tom.

Maria looked at the tally sheet. "I see that there is no one career for everyone."

"Mostly everyone wants to stop pollution," Oscar said.

Jan spoke up. "Everyone wants to spend money on things. But students appear to be nice people and in column four have a wonderful outlook on life."

"Let's use a theme of value—what's important for our visual communications project," Tom said.

"We could call our film, 'Paths of Choice,' " Maria said.

"That's great," Jan said. "Let's get started tomorrow!"

The group met at Jan's house. The camera was all ready with film. Jan led the way for writing a script by saying: "We could show Tom and Maria tutoring handicapped children after school. This would show how we care about others. And Oscar could be sitting on a pile of goods he bought with his money—clothes, motorcycle, stereo, fishing rod."

"We could all go outside to clean up a city block," Maria said. "That would show our concern about pollution."

"What about the world full of nice people?" Jan asked.

"That's easy," Tom said. "We'll take pictures of people working and helping others. Smiling people."

236

"Super idea," said Oscar. "I'm ready to shoot now."

A week later the group presented their film to Mr. Richardson's English class. Tom was the narrator, Jan worked the lights, and Oscar and Maria took care of the projection.

On the screen the words "Paths of Choice" appeared, and in the background were different paths leading off in several directions. Tom began to speak:

"The good life is having enough money to buy necessary things and other things we want, too. (The picture of Oscar sitting on a pile of goods was shown on the screen now.)

"In order to have money, we must choose a career which will give us a salary to do the things we need and want to do. (Pictures of different careers were flashed on the screen.)

"The good life also must include helping others. (Maria and Tom were shown helping handicapped children. Then the picture changes, and they are cleaning up a city lot.)

"The good life means having a positive outlook and enjoying people around you. (Scenes were shown of people in Riverside doing their daily activities.)

"And who is responsible for the 'quality of life'?" (A surprise picture was shown of the students in the English class.)

Tom finished the project with these words: "The choices you make—how you look at things and people around you—will determine the quality of your present and future life. Where is the good life? All around you!"

CHECKING PROGRESS

1. What did the student committee decide the term "quality of life" really meant?
2. Why did the committee chose the title "Paths of Choice" for their visual communication film?
3. What scenes from your own life could the committee have used to illustrate:
   A. The title of the film
   B. Use of money for necessary items and things we want
   C. A career choice
   D. Helping others
   E. Positive outlook on life
   F. Who is responsible for the quality of life
4. Write a short paragraph about the person or thing that has had the most influence on the quality of your life.

CHOOSING NEXT STEPS

1. Work with a committee of three other people and take an opinion poll in your class. Decide on several questions that relate to something in which your committee is interested.
   A. Make a bar or circle graph showing results of the poll.
   B. Make a picture story interpreting the results through the use of slides, movies, or pictures.
2. Make a visual representation showing your interpretation of the meaning of "the quality of life."
3. Make a poster showing pictures of people enjoying a good life. Cut these pictures out of magazines or newspapers.
4. Make your own personal poster. Use the title *My Idea Of A Good Life* for the center. Then find words in magazines or newspapers that describe what you think a good life is. (For example: clothes, camera, books.)

GOALS FOR ALL PLAYERS

THINKING THINGS THROUGH

Everyone enjoys cartoons. No doubt you have been reading cartoons and comic strips ever since you learned to read. Your first reaction to a cartoon is usually a chuckle, but often your second reaction is more serious. The picture along with the *caption*, or explanatory comment, makes you think. By expressing an opinion in an amusing way, the cartoonist catches your attention and helps you get a point of view.

To get the full message of a cartoon you should study the picture and read the caption carefully. The picture and the caption work together to put the message across.

As you read the following selection, give special attention to the cartoons which are included. Decide what message each cartoon conveys in relation to the whole selection.

ABOUT WORDS

Before you read the following selection, you should be able to understand several words which relate to *economic* goals. Economic means having to do with wealth and its use. These words are: *growth*, *stability*, *security*, *justice*, and *freedom*. See if you can match these words to the definitions listed below. Use a dictionary if you need help.

(1) Certainty; a feeling of being safe
(2) Rightfulness; fair dealing
(3) Development; process of growing
(4) Independence; power to do as one likes
(5) Unchangeableness; constancy

After you read the selection, see if you have increased your understanding of these words.

INVESTIGATE

GOALS FOR ALL PLAYERS

Do we often forget what work is all about? Some people believe that we work to obtain money for material things we need and want. That is, we work in exchange for money with which we buy food, clothing, shelter, and a few luxuries.

But do we work merely to satisfy our material needs and wants? Many people become very involved in their careers. Most of us would choose to work at something whether we needed to or not. Working is one way of making ourselves feel useful to other people. We work to contribute something to this world.

As Americans, we strive to better ourselves and our families. That is, we attempt to make our material lives better, and we try to gain recognition for what we do. There are five economic goals we try to achieve. These goals are: growth, sta-

240

bility, security, justice, and freedom. Each of these can be examined through our everyday comic strips.

Economic Growth

As we work, we expect to increase our standard of living. In other words, we want more material things. We want to be able to afford more next year than we can buy this year. We normally think of a raise in income as an improvement to our standard of living. A cartoon illustrates this idea.

Economic Stability

We work so that the economic system stays in balance. We want our wages to be sufficient to pay for goods and services that we need. When the system is out of balance, we don't have much purchasing power. In the cartoon above, the prices are going up. Yet, our ability to pay for goods we need is going down.

Economic Security

By working we attempt to put ourselves in situations where changes in the eco-

nomic system won't affect us so severely. We want to be adequately prepared with savings and company benefits in case unfortunate situations should arise. The king on the next page illustrates this idea. He may have a lot of worries, but from the looks of the gold in his wheelbarrow he is prepared for anything. Like the king, many people select jobs they don't particularly like because they feel they must have more security.

241

Economic Justice

This economic goal is based upon equal opportunities for every person no matter what sex, race, or religion he is. It has been one of the major concerns of our nation during the last ten years. Blacks, other minorities, and women are striving to get job equality. This includes equal opportunities, salary, advancement, and benefits. The cartoon below illustrates this idea of justice. It points out that there are really very few "entrance ramps" or opportunities for minorities to become equals in all situations.

242

Economic Freedom

A well-known element of our society is economic freedom. No one tells us what we must do to make a living. No one tells us what to buy or how to spend the money we earn. These decisions are left to the individual in a free society.

will completely achieve all five. We may wish to surrender some economic security for economic growth. For example, we may take a job that we know will continue into the future, and reject one that is higher paying but more risky. Or we may be more satisfied to give up

In the American system, manufacturers are free to make any product they wish. In fact, many businesses are constantly in search of the product that everyone would want. The cartoon above shows a salesman who thinks his new product will soon be in great demand.

Each of us attempts to obtain these five goals as we participate in our economic system. Yet very few of us

some economic freedom in exchange for economic justice. For example, we may choose to work in a certain area of the country where there is less discrimination against racial minorities. This is not uncommon.

As wise citizens we must choose the goals that are most important to us. Then we must find job opportunities which will allow us to express these goals.

243

CHECKING PROGRESS

1. What are the five economic goals we try to achieve? Explain what each means.
2. In which economic goal might a woman be most interested? a newcomer from a foreign land? a black? a poor married couple? a man who is often laid off at work? a woman whose husband is seriously ill?
3. Try to analyze the messages presented in the cartoons. In several instances, the author has helped you. Write down in your own words what each cartoon says.

CHOOSING NEXT STEPS

1. Think of the five economic goals that are discussed in this selection.
   (a) List them in order of their importance to you.
   (b) If possible, compare your list with a classmate's list. Discuss the likenesses and differences in the lists.
2. Think of a career in which you are presently interested. How does this career relate to each of the five goals? Does this career emphasize the goal you think is most important? Tell why you think so.
3. Think of an opinion that you have about a current issue in your school, city, or nation. Then draw a cartoon and write a caption for it that will convey your message. Remember to make it humorous, but keep the message clear.
4. Make a collection of cartoons and comic strips from newspapers and magazines. Organize them according to subjects such as economics, pollution, family affairs, or politics. Place them in a notebook for others to read.

SCOUTING THE GROUNDS
THINKING THINGS THROUGH

Have you ever used the expression, "scouting the grounds"? When and how did you use it? Have you ever heard this expression used? What does it mean to you? As you read the following selection, you will find out what it means as used by the author. Also in this selection, a high school counselor gives clues on how to make a game plan. The game plan he suggests is likened to game plans used in football. Read the selection and find out how scouting the grounds and making game plans can point the way to a future career.

ABOUT WORDS

Divide the words in each group below into syllables. Can you find a similarity between the words in each group? What is the similarity?

(1) person   select   complete
     campsites   surface   problem
     ahead   compare   college

(2) listed   wisely   showing
     scouting   forded   forging
     mixing   rushing   routings

(3) unknown   prefer   invest
     explore   review   become
     resource

245

INVESTIGATE

Scouting The Grounds

One person rode ahead to scout the area. Where could the streams be *forded*, or crossed, best? How could the hills and rough surfaces be crossed with least risk? Where were the best camping sites?

The frontiersmen would not have thought of forging into unknown lands without exploring for best choices. They sent a scout ahead to inspect the grounds before deciding routes.

So it is, too, if you are looking for things you need. You look at more than one pair of shoes before deciding which to buy. You want to see, touch, try on, ask about, get advice, or compare in any way you can to get the item that you will like best. You want the item that suits you and the item that will serve your needs best.

Scouting the grounds for a career is no different than exploring to get what you want

246

and need, except it is about the most important thing you must choose. You will want to scout the area ahead, plan carefully and wisely.

You don't have to choose right now. However, you need to start exploring now—scouting the grounds, inspecting different trails, deciding preferences today, and reviewing for further decisions at a later time. Your final choice may take years.

A necessary part of the area to explore is school itself. Where can you get help—the map to study, the means to scout ahead, and the resource person who can lead you to the right course?

Your teachers are glad to help. The librarian can lead you to information in print. The principal can guide you to the helps you need. The counselor is an expert in helping students.

What should you look for? Look for people in careers

you think you might like. Read about their work, activities, interests, talents, problems, and rewards. Compare yourself with those you read about; talk with others in similar careers.

Investigate what to study in school. Ask the counselor to help you explore ahead to see what courses you might prefer to study in high school. If you do not have a school counselor, ask your teacher and your principal.

You may be interested in how Mr. Murphy, the school counselor, helped a student map plans for study. He says, "Decide on your game plan." His ideas are patterned like a game plan because he used to be a coach.

"Any game plan," says Mr. Murphy, "must include the basics. In football, the basics are facts of the game and required formations that you start with before deciding on game *strategies*, or plans of attack. You plan passing and rushing plays, and ways of mixing them. Your strategy depends upon the skills and the talents of your teammates and the odds you must overcome.

"In planning your high school studies," he advises, "you list the required courses first. Then, you plan *electives*, or courses chosen based on preference. These are chosen to fit your talents and interests.

"Let's look at a study plan which I have worked out for a student.

"The sample game plan on page 248 was worked out for Ralph last spring for the four-year period. Ralph is a first-year student. Twice a year Ralph's plan will be reviewed to see if any changes need to be made. Sometimes students change their minds about what they like and need. Sometimes their schedules won't work out to include all they first plan. Reviewing game plans keeps them on course.

"Ralph does not plan to go on to college. His father, who is in poor health, owns a sheet metal business. Ralph expects to take over the business after graduation."

Study Ralph's *choice card*, a card for showing courses a student plans to take.

247

Year	Required	Elective
1	English (reading - writing) Related Math 1, 2* Physical Science 1, 2 Physical Education 1/2	Shop (Metal 1, 2)
2	English 1, 2 Related Math 3, 4 World History 1, 2 Physical Education 1/2	Shop (Metal 3, 4)
3	English 3, 4 Biology 1, 2 Physical Education 1/2	Shop (Drafting 1, 2) Business Arithmetic 1, 2
4	American History 7, 8 American Government 1/2 Physical Education 1/2	Shop (Technical Drafting 1, 2) Business Law 1/2 Plane Geometry 1, 2

Total Units   11 1/2 +   6 1/2 = 18 Units

*Most whole year courses are numbered by half units, as: 1 and 2 for first year, and so on through the number of years the course moves forward (2-3, 4; 3-5, 6; 4-7, 8).

"Sometimes a course that is listed as required on one plan may be an elective on another. Electives vary with individual students, depending upon their main career interest. Most required courses are about the same for all students, however, there are some variations between high schools. For instance, at our high school we offer a variety of courses with many various subjects in each field including art, music, business, English, foreign languages, social studies, industrial arts, physical education, homemaking, mathematics, and science. Not all high schools have as many subjects to choose from, but most high schools do.

Mr. Murphy pauses and then advises, "Get acquainted with what is offered. You are chief scouts for your grounds. Keep scouting the grounds. Or, if you prefer, begin making your game plan."

CHECKING PROGRESS

1. What does the expression, "scouting the grounds," mean as it is used by the author of this selection? Think of an illustration of "scouting the grounds" from your own past experience or an experience you are planning.

2. Mr. Murphy compared the mapping of plans for a student's high school courses with a game plan for football. What parts of the game plan for football did he compare to required courses? What did he compare to elective courses?

3. Can a required course on one student's plan be an elective on another student's plan? Explain your answer.

CHOOSING NEXT STEPS

1. Idioms are expressions that have special meanings other than the ordinary meanings of the individual words in the group. For example, decide on your "game plan." The meaning here is that students should prepare their courses of study carefully.

   (1) Illustrate an idiomatic expression with drawings and let your classmates guess the idiom.

   (2) Write several sentences which can be completed with idiomatic expressions.

   (3) Write definitions for several idioms and ask your classmates to think of the idioms.

2. Ask your high school counselor to come to your class and give suggestions about planning for high school courses.

3. Make a tentative high school plan for yourself. List required and elective courses which you plan to take.

THE
MYSTERIOUS MESSAGE MYSTERY

THINKING THINGS THROUGH

Everyone likes to read a mystery story. Follow along with Jimmy Monroe as he accidentally comes upon some very unusual circumstances.

As you read the story try to determine what kind of appearances the characters have. How does Jimmy look? Captain Schulevitz? Parky? Mr. Monroe? Note how the author's descriptive words and the character's dialogue add to these appearances in your mind.

Also, stop to study a moment any sentence or paragraph that suddenly captures your interest and creates suspense. Try to determine why the author uses the words in the way she does. For your own experiment, you might take the same words and rewrite them into sentences of your own, and then judge to see if your sentences hold the same interest.

ABOUT WORDS

The jumbled words below were all used in the story. The definition following each word should give you the needed clue for recognizing the word.

suemum	a place where a mummy is kept
ogarc	load carried by a ship
rbluy	strong, rough
ymulas	refuge, shelter
fedcte	leave one's own country for another
gtnea	someone who works for a country

BEFORE YOU READ

251

INVESTIGATE

THE MYSTERIOUS MESSAGE MYSTERY

The captain strolled through the waiting room of the suite of offices of the United States consul, his rolling walk showing that he was a man whose life was spent at sea. He pushed back his cap and nodded to the secretary, saying in a deep voice, "Captain Schulevitz to see the consul."

The secretary spoke to the consul on the phone. Then the captain pushed through the big doors of the consul's office.

Jimmy Monroe, seated in the waiting room, watched the captain enter the consulate offices. He was waiting to walk home with his father for lunch. It was summer and school was out, and Jimmy had nothing to do. But it was interesting to live in the small European country of Paratania, with a father who was a consul with the United States Foreign Service.

Jimmy wondered what the captain wanted his father to do. He was a big burly man, and Jimmy had been on his ship a number of times to visit a friend—a seaman named Parky. Parky must have had a first and last name, but he claimed to have forgotten them over the years at sea. The sun and salt spray had tanned and weathered his face so that he looked like one of those mummy heads in the museum. Parky enjoyed the sea, and Jimmy enjoyed knowing Parky. But for some reason Jimmy was afraid of Captain Schulevitz.

The office doors flew open, and the captain came out, saying loudly, "Thanks to you, Mr. Monroe. Now that the papers are approved, we'll be leaving port within two days."

Jimmy waited until the captain was gone, then went inside his father's office. Mr. Monroe was putting away some papers. "So you're going to walk me home, are you?" he smiled.

Jimmy leaned on his father's large polished desk. "What did Captain Schulevitz want?" he asked.

252

"You know that a United States ship captain must bring his sailing papers and the custom clearance of his cargo to the consulate when his ship comes into port. It's a law. However . . . there's a minor problem. Do you know Parky?"

"Of course I do!" Jimmy said. "Parky's a friend of mine!"

"He isn't feeling well," his father said. "He's in the hospital and won't be sailing with the ship."

Jimmy was alarmed, "Is it serious? Will he be all right?"

"Something's wrong with his back. But Captain Schulevitz didn't seem too worried. He was more concerned about getting my permission to sign on a new hand in Parky's place."

"What will happen to Parky if he stays behind?" Jimmy asked.

"Captain Schulevitz will take care of his hospital bill and find a way to get him back to the United States."

"Could I visit Parky?"

"I don't see why not," Mr. Monroe said, "as long as it's all right with the hospital rules." He smiled sympathetically. "I'd go along with you, but I've got to prepare a speech for a reception the Mayor is holding tomorrow."

Jimmy was eager to finish lunch and visit Parky. He kept thinking about Captain Schulevitz—wondering if he had something to do with Parky's sudden illness.

253

Jimmy had no trouble getting permission from the nurse on duty to visit Parky in his hospital room. As he entered the room he saw two tall men at the end of the hallway coming his way. When they saw Jimmy, they stopped and quickly turned their backs to him, but not before he had gotten a good look at their faces. He was puzzled. He had never seen the men before, so why were they hiding from him?

Parky was sitting up in bed reading a newspaper. "Hello there, Jimmy!" he called out happily.

"I thought you were sick!" Jimmy blurted out.

"Why I am, boy!" Parky tried to look miserable now but didn't succeed. "It's the terrible pain in my back."

"Where in your back?" Jimmy asked.

"Uh—all over my back," Parky answered.

"My dad said the ship will sail without you. Captain Schulevitz has already signed a seaman to take your place."

"Has he now? That's good." Parky smiled.

"Don't you want to leave with your ship?" Jimmy asked.

"Of course I do." Again Parky tried to look miserable.

Jimmy knew there was something strange going on. Parky wasn't really suffering from pain in his back. Then why was he pretending? It was a mystery Jimmy couldn't figure out.

"Don't just sit there, Jimmy," Parky said. "Bring over the checkerboard. We'll have ourselves a game before you go."

Jimmy quickly forgot the unanswered questions in his mind as he enjoyed playing checkers with his friend. Then suddenly it grew late. "I've stayed too long," he said.

"Come back tomorrow," Parky said. "I'll have lots of time to spend here until—well, until they cure me."

"When will that be?" Jimmy asked.

"Why, in a couple of weeks," Parky said. "Of course the ship will be safely back in the United States by then, so they'll probably have to fly me home."

Jimmy smiled at his friend. "I'll be back tomorrow."

As Jimmy left the room he saw a quick movement at the end of the hall. Turning about for a better look, he realized

254

that the hall was empty. But someone had been there a moment ago, watching him leave Parky's room.

A few minutes later Jimmy left the hospital. He walked over to the seawall and gazed down at the harbor, the salt air of the sea stinging his cheeks. In the distance lay the big freighter which belonged to the American company that Captain Schulevitz worked for. Wednesday it would be leaving for the United States without Parky.

Suddenly Jimmy remembered he was supposed to ask Parky something—would it be all right if his mother sent him some cookies? He hurried back into the hospital.

This time he nearly bumped into the two tall men as they rushed out of Parky's room. Were they friends of Parky's? If they were, why did they act so strangely?

Jimmy poked his head around the edge of the door, expecting to see the cheerful Parky he had left. But Parky was lying in the bed, the sheet pulled to his chin. His hands were shaking and his face was wet with perspiration.

Jimmy hurried to his bedside. "What happened, Parky?"

"Nothing," Parky said. "Better get away from here. Jimmy took a step backward, then Parky suddenly raised himself on one arm as though he had just thought of something. "Wait! I need you to take a message for me."

"Sure," Jimmy said. "Did those men hurt you?"

"Never mind about those men," Parky said. "Listen carefully! Find Captain Schulevitz and tell him not to wait till Wednesday to sail. Tell him to get out of port as fast as he can! He's got his clearance papers, hasn't he?"

"Yes," Jimmy said, "but . . ."

"That's well and good," Parky said, lying back on the bed. "Find him quickly, Jimmy. It's important!"

"I will!" Jimmy said.

Jimmy hurried from the hospital. It took nearly fifteen minutes for a cab to get to the dock area, and he was lucky to have enough money for the ride. If Parky wanted him to deliver the message in a hurry, he had better get there fast!

255

Jimmy found a cab on the street. When he got to the dock area, he paid the driver and ran to the guard station.

"It's important!" he told the guard. "Can you call the ship and see if Captain Schulevitz is aboard?"

"He's over there on pier two," the guard said.

Jimmy ran outside and called to the captain.

"I was with Parky," he said breathlessly. "Two men came out of his room, and he looked terrible! He said you shouldn't wait till Wednesday but to sail as fast as you can!"

"But the cargo's not loaded yet," the captain said, staring hard at Jimmy. "You're sure you got the message right?"

"I'm sure," Jimmy said. "Will those men hurt Parky?"

"Parky knows what he's doing." The captain scowled now, grabbing Jimmy's arm. "Don't speak of this to anyone!"

Jimmy watched him rush off. The sky was darkening, and he remembered he had better hurry home, too. But now he had no money for a cab. He got on the nearest bus.

When he got home, his mother scolded him for being late.

"I've got to talk to you and Dad," Jimmy said. "I think Parky's in serious trouble."

Jimmy then told his parents everything that happened.

"I had better talk to Parky," Mr. Monroe said quickly. "Come along, Jimmy."

It didn't take long to drive to the hospital. When they got there the first thing Parky asked about was the message. Mr.

Monroe told him that Jimmy had delivered it. "That's what we're going to talk about, Parky."

"There's nothing much to talk about, sir," Parky said.

"Nothing to say about smuggling into the United States a young man famous for his writings behind the Iron Curtain?"

Parky sighed heavily. "This man writes nothing but the truth, sir. He escaped from his country because they were going to put him in prison. We've got to get him to the United States. He's Captain Schulevitz's cousin!"

"I've heard through channels about his disappearance," Mr. Monroe said. "His country wants no one to know he's escaped. Do they know yet that he's here?"

"They suspect it," Parky said. "Two of their agents threatened me today, but I told them nothing."

Mr. Monroe asked, "Does this man want to defect—leave his country and ask for help in the United States?"

"Yes, sir. That's why I'm here. My back's just fine, but I want this young man to take my place on the ship."

"But he'll be entering the States illegally," Mr. Monroe said, "with forged papers. I could see that our embassy here in Paratania granted him asylum. Then we could fly him safely to the United States."

"Would you help him, sir?" Parky asked excitedly.

"Of course," Mr. Monroe said. "I'll get in touch with Captain Schulevitz immediately."

Just then the door burst open, and the two men whom Jimmy had seen before came up to Parky's bed. "We're taking this man to a sanitarium," said one of the men.

"Just a moment," Mr. Monroe said firmly. "He's a United States citizen." He turned to Jimmy. "Get the police!"

The men looked at each other and began to back slowly out of the room. "Maybe we made a mistake," the other one said.

Mr. Monroe watched them leave. Then he said, "Get up, Parky. Come with us. We have work to do."

Jimmy felt happy. Being a consul for the United States Foreign Service was the most exciting job in the world!

CHECKING PROGRESS

1. Tell what you thought about the following:
   A. Characters
   B. Setting
   C. Plot or plan of the story
   D. Climax or turning point of events
2. Using the following sentences from the story to help you, describe Parky and Captain Schulevitz in your own words or with a drawing.

   Parky: The sun and salt spray had tanned and weathered his face so that he looked like one of those mummy heads in the museum.

   Captain Schulevitz: The captain strolled through the waiting room . . ., his rolling walk showing that he was a man whose life was spent at sea.
3. What was the first "mystery" that Jimmy became aware of when he went to the hospital to visit Parky? List other mysterious happenings or circumstances that followed.

CHOOSING NEXT STEPS

1. Write a mystery story of your own. Remember how the author used her words in this story to create suspense and try to do the same thing.
2. Select a mystery story in the library and make a report. Tell what you thought about the characters, setting, plot, and climax of the story. Mention the high points of suspense that made you want to keep on reading.

TEAMWORK—
IN AND OUT OF ORBIT

THINKING THINGS THROUGH

How many careers can you think of where a person would work completely alone? Most of us will probably choose careers where we will come in contact with other people, so it is important to learn how to work well together. Astronaut Bill Anders knows the importance of group effort, not only on the job but at home as well.

ABOUT WORDS

Review the principles that apply when dividing words into syllables. Also remember:

(1) When an accented syllable ends with one or more consonant letters, it is closed. The vowel sound in that syllable is usually short.

(2) When an accented syllable ends with a vowel, it is an open syllable. The vowel sound in that syllable is usually long.

(3) The vowel sound in many unstressed syllables is the schwa sound /ə/.

Divide the following words from this story into syllables and pronounce them. Use a dictionary to check your work.

commander   astronaut
revolutions   adjustments
communicator   holiday
propulsion   insertion
environmental   celebration

259

TEAMWORK-IN AND OUT OF ORBIT

The communicator in Houston radioed the message: "This is Houston at 68:04 (sixty-eight hours and four minutes after launch). You are go for LOI (lunar orbit insertion)."

"O.K. Apollo 8 is go," came the quick reply.

"We'll see you on the other side," the Houston communicator called. "One minute to LOS (loss of signal). All systems are go. Safe journey, guys."

"Thanks a lot, troops," replied rookie Anders. "We'll see you on the other side."

At 4:59 a.m. on December 24, 1968, three astronauts, Frank Borman, James A. Lovell, Jr., and William A. Anders, began what would be ten complete revolutions of the moon. Space travel was new to only one man on the crew—William Anders, a thirty-five-year-old major in the U.S. Air Force.

Anders had been originally trained to be the pilot of the lunar module (LM) crew. "I spent eighteen months training to fly the lunar module," Anders explained. "When the decision was made to switch us to a circumlunar flight, I felt like I had lost an old friend. What does a lunar module pilot do without a lunar module?"

Anders had to be retrained. His new job was to learn the command modules and service modules inside out. He became responsible for the electrical power, environmental control, and communication and propulsion system during the flight.

Imagine what a letdown Anders must have had! He was switched from a major role in the mission to a backup position. But this is what teamwork is all about. Sometimes we must take a lesser role than someone else in the group. We must, like Anders, perform as team members and not always be concerned about being the leader of the group.

260

Anders was used to the military life and the teamwork it involves because his dad was a Naval Commander. This probably had some influence on his choice of careers. He was able to learn from his father about service life and what problems and rewards it has to offer.

Anders' wife and five children have also had to learn to work together as a team and to make adjustments because of Anders' career. Sometimes a career may interfere with family life. Through group effort, problems can usually be worked out. For example, Anders left on his space flight on December 24, the day before Christmas. Since Christmas is an important holiday for the family, they decided to hold their own pre-Christmas celebration the last weekend Anders was home. They exchanged some of their presents then, but they still kept others to open when Anders returned safely home.

Whether we are planning a military career or not, teamwork will be important to us in whatever career we choose. Most of us will be working with or for other people. We should try, like the Anders family, to think *we* instead of *me*.

CHECKING PROGRESS

1. What are some of the ways teamwork is important in Bill Anders' life as an astronaut?
2. Write a paper discussing the importance of team effort. Take the point of view of one of these people:
   (1) an astronaut.
   (2) a member of a school sports team.
   (3) a member of a school activity planning committee.
   (4) a member of a family group.
3. What are some of the ways that parents and relatives can help young people make their career choices? Think about how someone has advised you and helped you to make a choice in your life; that person might have been a parent, teacher, or friend.

CHOOSING NEXT STEPS

1. Read biographies of other astronauts and informational books about space flights and space exploration.
2. Study some words and terms used in space exploration. Start with those that are included in this story. For example, find the meanings of lunar orbit insertion (LOI) and lunar module (LM).
3. Write to one of the astronauts. Ask such questions as:
   (1) When did you become interested in space exploration?
   (2) What is most interesting about your work?
   (3) Did anyone influence you to enter this field? If so, who was it?

PLAYING WITH FIRE:
THE VOLCANOLOGIST

THINKING THINGS THROUGH

In this selection the author tells how volcanologists use seismographs and tiltmeters to help them predict and record volcanic eruptions. These instruments measure the disturbances in volcanoes with a great deal of accuracy. Although the exact time of the eruption is not predictable, it does allow time for warnings to be given to people in the area.

ABOUT WORDS

Look up the words in the left-hand column and match them with the correct meanings in the right-hand column.

cone volcano	1. An instrument made up of two pots of water connected with hoses, designed to measure the swelling of the earth.
crater	2. A dome-shaped volcano, from which nonexplosive volcanic materials flow.
crust	3. The melted rock below the surface of the earth.
lava	4. The outside shell of the earth.
magma	5. An opening in the earth from which hot gases and melted rock escape. Either they flow, as in a shield volcano, or they are thrown out with force, as in a cone volcano.
seismograph	6. A high mountain-like buildup of lava around the opening in a volcano.
shield volcano	7. A bowl-like depression in the sides or top of a volcano. The lava and gases come from these depressions.
tiltmeter	8. An instrument that records the movements of the earth, called earthquakes.
volcano	9. A scientist who studies a live volcano.
volcanologist	10 The name given to molten rock, or magma, after it leaves the earth.

263

BEFORE YOU READ

INVESTIGATE

Playing With Fire:
THE VOLCANOLOGIST

The volcano is erupting. Most people who hear these words would leave the area to get out of harm's way. But the *volcanologist*—the scientist who studies volcano activity—goes to the scene of the eruption.

Volcanoes are not all alike. There are the explosive volcanoes like *Krakatoa*, which suddenly blew up in 1883, with a sound so loud it was heard 3,000 miles away. There are the *shield volcanoes* like *Kilauea* on the island of Hawaii, in which eruptions flow from the floor or the sides of the crater. Kilauea is not an explosive type of volcano. Tourists come to see the huge *crater*, which is constantly steaming, and are excited when they see the volcano erupt the burning lava.

The *Paricutin* volcano in Mexico formed suddenly, pushing up from the earth with violent force in 1943, frightening the farmers in the area who hurried to get away. Paricutin rose from the flat farmland to become a mountain over 1,400 feet high. Not too many years ago a volcanic island was formed near the coast of Iceland and named *Surtsey* after the Norse god who was supposed, in legend, to have brought fire to Iceland. Recently a volcanic island has appeared near Japan.

What Is A Volcano?

What exactly is a volcano? It's an opening in the earth from which hot gases and melted rock escape. The melted material that flows in a liquid state—like molasses flows—is called *magma*. When magma reaches the cooler air of the earth, it hardens and is called *lava*. The lava begins to pile up around the opening in the *crust* of the earth, causing the building of a *volcanic cone*, which appears mountain-like.

Have you ever seen snow-capped Mt. Ranier in Washington State? Have you ever vacationed at Mt. Shasta in California? You probably didn't realize that these mountains are really volcanoes. Although they have not erupted for many years, they still test hot and someday could begin their volcanic activity again.

Each year many thousands of people visit Yellowstone Park. When they are sitting on the benches, admiring the power of the geyser called *Old Faithful*, they are really watching the activity of a live volcanic field. The volcano has many openings and is not a cone.

What Does A Volcanologist Do?

Why should anyone study a volcano? What can man learn from them that would be helpful?

First of all, scientists recognize that volcanoes are dangerous to man. When most volcanoes erupt they throw out the rocks of burning magma, ashes, and a poisonous gas. There are many cases in history in which a volcano has destroyed cities, towns, and villages. When Mt. Vesuvius, in Italy, erupted in the year 79, it destroyed many nearby towns. Among the most famous was the resort city of Pompeii. Many thousands of people were killed. They never suspected that the beautiful mountain was really a volcano.

Since then Vesuvius has erupted many times, sometimes remaining quiet for a period of 600 years or more. In 1944, during World War

II, our Allied troops helped to evacuate the people of San Sebastiano, which was in the path of a stream of hot lava thirty feet deep.

If people are taken by surprise when a volcano erupts, they have less chance to escape. It is important for man to learn how to predict when an eruption will occur so that a warning system can be set up.

There are volcano observatories all over the world, in areas in which active volcanoes exist. One of the oldest observatories, which was begun in 1847, is at Mt. Vesuvius. In the United States one of the most active observatories is at the edge of the crater Kilauea in the Hawaiian Islands. Kilauea has been erupting for many years, and its eruptions flow, rather than explode; so it is a good volcano to study.

In ancient years the Hawaiian people brought offerings of a special berry and other fruit to the volcano, because they thought the goddess of volcanoes, Pele, lived there and was

266

angry with them for something they had done.

Today, we know about the pressures that cause a volcano to erupt.

The Laboratory

The Hawaiian observatory is a small building with a view of the crater Kilauea. Inside are rows of *seismographs*, which are drumshaped cylinders covered with paper, on which needles record the movements of the earth. These seismographs record earthquakes from movements too small to be felt by man, to the larger quakes that accompany the eruption of the volcano.

Beneath the earth the molten magma is moving. As the gases build up, an outlet is needed for them. The earth moves. It moves again. The movement becomes stronger. Soon the earth is in almost constant motion, with up to 300 quakes recorded in one day. This is one way the volcanologists can tell when an eruption is coming. They record the number and the strength of the earthquakes.

As the earth becomes more and more disturbed, they can get ready to accept the next eruption. Seismographs are stationed in various places around the crater. In this way volcanologists can better tell where the strongest activity is and where the eruption most likely will take place next.

However, the seismographs alone can't tell the volcanologists that an eruption will take place. It is also necessary to know if the earth is swelling and how much swelling is going on. Scientists have worked out a device called a *tiltmeter*.

What Does A Tiltmeter Do?

As the pressure builds up inside the volcano, as the magma rises to the top, ready to break through the crust of the earth, a certain amount of swelling occurs. This swelling takes place slowly, so that it can't be noticed by the eye. Instruments which can record it are needed.

After many experiments in different volcano observatories around the world, a tiltmeter was developed. Basically, tiltmeters are instruments made up of two sealed water pots connected by two tubes. One tube connects the water-filled sections, and one connects the air spaces over the water. A pointer on each pot marks the top level of the water.

These pots are mounted on concrete and set apart from each other. Pairs of these pots are placed in various areas of the volcanic crater. When the ground swells, one of the pots becomes higher than the other in its pair. As it becomes higher, some of the water runs into the lower pot. The higher pot has a lower level of water than the one below it. The volcanologists measure these pots regularly to check on the water level, and in this way they can measure the swelling of the volcano. Because the heat of the sun can affect the water level, the tests are done at night.

With the combination of the information received from the seismographs and from the tiltmeters, the volcanologists have been able

to predict possible eruptions, so that people in the area can be warned. National park rangers, given the warning, are ready to fight any fires that result from a hot flow of lava, which sets fire to the trees as it moves through them. Tourists can be kept back from any dangerous flows, and villages in the area can be evacuated.

What Do Volcanologists Hope To Learn?

It is still not possible to predict the exact time an eruption will take place. After the prediction, the volcanologists might wait several days, weeks, or months for the eruption to happen. However, it is still better to be warned than to be taken by surprise.

During an eruption the volcanologists continue to take measurements of the activity with the seismographs and tiltmeters. They measure the heat of the magma as it comes to the surface. They take samples of the molten magma and volcanic gases, and they analyze them.

These facts give them answers to questions that still puzzle them: Why does the rock beneath the surface of the earth melt? What causes this great heat? Is there a way of knowing for certain when a volcano will erupt and where in its crater or sides it will choose to erupt? Is there a way of pinpointing it exactly so that people can be safely moved from the area? And is there a way of knowing when the activity will be over, so that people can return to their homes without endangering their lives?

Through their constant study of Kilauea, volcanologists are learning more about the differences in the magma that comes to the surface, about the structure of the volcano itself, and about the crust of the earth and the materials below it. As they study these things, they hope someday to know enough about the inner structure of volcanoes so that eruptions of any of the world's volcanoes will not be the danger to man that they have been in the past.

270

How To Read A Graph

A graph is a form of art which shows us quickly the answer to our questions. It is easy to see by looking at the graph below that the gases contain much more water vapor than they do anything else.

The numbers at the top of the graph mark the percentages. When we see that the line opposite "water vapor" is a little past the seventy percent mark, then we know the approximate amount.

This graph is marked off in units of five percent. If it were marked in units of one percent or in fractions of a percentage, our answers could be more accurate.

Look at the graph and find the amounts of the chemicals in the volcano gases.

Water Vapor
Carbon Dioxide
Sulfur Dioxide
Nitrogen
Other

How close were you to the exact percentage figures? Water Vapor, 70.75; Carbon Dioxide, 14.07; Sulfur Dioxide, 6.40; Nitrogen, 5.45; and Other, 3.33.

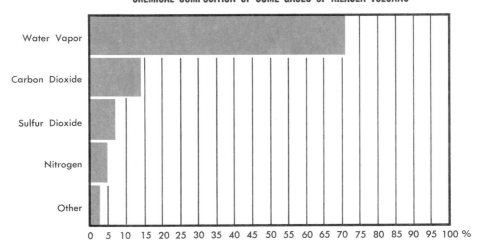

CHEMICAL COMPOSITION OF SOME GASES OF KILAUEA VOLCANO

CHECKING PROGRESS

1. Write a brief report about three or four of the most interesting facts that you learned about volcanoes.
2. For what purposes do volcanologists study volcanoes?
3. Where in the United States is a volcano observatory located? Why is it located in this particular place?
4. What are three locations where volcanoes have formed during recent years?

CHOOSING NEXT STEPS

1. Make a diagram of a volcano as described under the heading, "What is a Volcano?" Use labels to identify the characteristics of the volcano.
2. Do some follow-up research in the library on one or more of the following volcanoes or subjects which were mentioned in the selection you read. You may find information about the volcanoes listed by name and/or location.
   (1) geyser
   (2) Pele - goddess of volcanoes
   (3) Mt. Vesuvius - Italy
   (4) Paricutin - Mexico
   (5) Surtsey - Iceland
   (6) Old Faithful - Yellowstone National Park, Wyoming
   (7) Kilauea - Hawaii
   (8) Mt. Ranier - Washington
   (9) Mt. Shasta - California
3. Locate facts about the history of words about volcanoes.
   Example: Volcano (vol - ka - no), Italian, from Latin volcanus, VULCAN
   Vulcan (vul-kən) is the god of fire and craftsmanship.
   Other words might be: lava, magma, crater

UNDERWATER ARCHEOLOGY

THINKING THINGS THROUGH

Searching for hidden treasure seems to most of us like it would be exciting work. That is the kind of work underwater archeologists do. But they search for treasures that tell of people and customs of a certain period of time, rather than treasures of gold and silver. This letter to students from the director of an underwater archeological project explains what this career is about and what background you would need to do this kind of work. Following the letter is a picture story to take you along on a treasure hunt off the Gulf Coast of Texas.

ABOUT WORDS

1. The word *archeology* is made up of two word roots—*archaeo-*, meaning ancient times or early conditions, and *-logy*, meaning study of. Thus, the word *archeology* means the study of people, customs, and life in ancient times. Using what you know about the word *archeology*, define the following words and use each in a sentence:

    archeologist
    archeological

2. Included in the letter are these words which may be unfamiliar to you. Use your dictionary to help you with their pronunciation and meaning.

    artifacts   anthropology
    maritime   site
    alien   scuba

INVESTIGATE

underwater archeology

Texas Antiquities Committee

Box 12276, Capitol Station, Austin, Texas 78711

Dear Students,

Work in the field of underwater archeology is interesting and very exciting. Work beneath the sea is a challenge since man is in an alien environment. Recovering artifacts from the wrecks of ships hundreds or even thousands of years old is exciting and rewarding as well. As a member of an archeological expedition you are participating in a scientific project which will add not only to man's knowledge of maritime history and ship design, but also to man's knowledge of himself.

An archeological site on land can contain artifacts from a time span of hundreds of thousands of years which are often difficult or impossible to date precisely. Each shipwreck, however, can be regarded as a time in which the ship sailed. The analysis of the closely dated artifacts from such a site often tells us many things about the culture and society which built the ship. Often these details are not recorded in written history. There is, you see, more important treasure buried within a shipwreck than gold and silver. There are a variety of levels at which you could become involved in underwater archeology. As a diving technician the only training necessary is learning to use scuba equipment and becoming a qualified diver. You can take lessons from a dive shop or perhaps your local YMCA. Some training in anthropology and archeology on the college level would improve your chances of getting such a job.

To become an underwater archeologist, you must have a college education. You can receive training in archeology either in the Classics

274

Department or the Anthropology Department of many colleges and universities. If you want to be in charge of your own underwater archeological expedition, you will need to do graduate work and obtain at least a master's degree.

Underwater archeology is an expanding field, and at this moment there are jobs available. An exciting career may await you.

Sincerely,

Carl J. Clausen
Marine Archeologist
State of Texas

Texas Gulf Coast, Site of Underwater Archeology Project

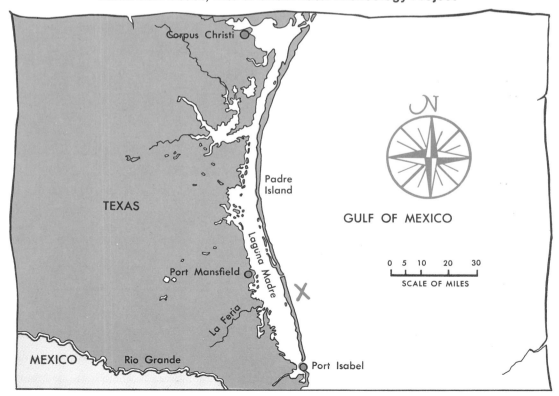

There are three vessels used by the underwater archeology project off of Padre Island on the Texas Gulf Coast. They are the crew boat, "Anomaly," (left); an inflatable rubber boat, "Anomaly II," (center); and a steel box barge which serves as a work platform (right). All are located above the site of a 1554 Spanish shipwreck.

Inside the cabin of the "Anomaly," Project Director Carl J. Clausen pilots the boat, while another crew member studies a seamanship reference book. They are off to search the wreck for treasures in the form of objects that will tell them more about the life style of sixteenth century Spanish people.

Assistant Archeologist Barto Arnold clamps backpacks onto the scuba tanks that will be used by the divers.

The divers prepare to go to work searching the wreck. They are assisted in putting on their gear by other crew members.

The divers finally go underwater. They are searching for treasures hidden below.

Project Director Clausen returns to the surface with an artifact, or manmade object. In this case the artifact is a small silver disc.

A crew member on the deck of the ship studies another artifact that has been brought aboard.

A close up of an encrustation shows that it is composed of shells and corrosion products. In the center of the encrustation is an artifact, a piece of broken pottery.

CHECKING PROGRESS

1. In the first paragraph of the letter, Mr. Clausen mentions that an underwater archeological expedition can add to man's knowledge in three areas. What are these areas?
2. What is the main difference between artifacts from an archeological site on land and artifacts from a shipwreck?
3. What are the training requirements for each of the following careers related to underwater archeology?
   (1) a diving technician
   (2) an underwater archeologist
   (3) a director or head of an archeological expedition
4. What do you think is the purpose of the underwater archeological project on the Gulf Coast of Texas?

CHOOSING NEXT STEPS

1. Find and view a 16mm film or a filmstrip on underwater archeology or scuba diving.
2. Invite a diver or an archeologist to come to your class and discuss his work.
3. Make plans to observe an underwater diving demonstration. Write a report on what you saw.
4. Read books related to archeological expeditions, diving, and underwater exploration.
5. Visit a museum to observe artifacts and to read information about various types of archeological exploration. Especially look for artifacts from underwater exploration.
6. Try to find information about the ways archeologists determine from what period artifacts come. Use an encyclopedia or books from the library.

KNIGHT OF THE ROAD

THINKING THINGS THROUGH

1. Before you read this story, make a plan for study. Remember to do the following:
   (1) Preview the entire story
   (2) Form a question about each subtopic
   (3) Answer each question after reading the section
   (4) Review all questions and answers after you have read the entire story.
2. This story includes a map of Bob Landry's trip. When reading a map be sure to:
   (1) Read the title of the map
   (2) Study the legends and symbols which will help you interpret the map.
      (a) Direction symbols—example:

      (b) Legends—example:

      ⋀⋀⋀ mountains   ≈≈ rivers   ○ city

      (c) Scale of miles—example: 0   100   200   300
   (3) Notice the kind of map you are studying.
      (a) A *political* map shows man-made features of the earth such as states and countries.
      (b) A *physical* map shows physical features of the earth, such as mountains and rivers.
      (c) *Others* might be transportation and highway maps, economic maps, or population maps.

ABOUT WORDS

Look up the meanings of the following words which were used in this story and add them to your vocabulary list.

interstate	friction	dispatcher
regulations	momentum	gauge

279

INVESTIGATE

Knight of the Road

His horse today is a truck. It is big enough to scare any dragon—with fifteen forward gears and one backward. And it is far more expensive than a horse—sometimes costing between $35,000 and $40,000.

His armor is usually blue denim or other work clothes. The accent on the road is the casual look.

The inn where he stops is a popular roadway truck stop. The restaurant menu is the equal to any eating place catering to family food tastes. The fast telegraph machine gives him an opportunity to receive messages and money orders, or to send these items. It is his bank away from home. The gas pumps are available to refill his tanks. And there is a motel where he can get a room for a few hours, stretch out, clean up, or spend the night. For entertainment the roadway lounge offers pinball machines, billiards, or television. The medieval inn was never like this!

Modern Knight of the Road

A knight today is a cross-country truck driver. As in olden days, this adventure holds the same thrill—to travel. Truck drivers have been known to be off the road for a few days and then yearn to be going somewhere.

Do you like to travel? If you do, then let's go along with one of these modern-day knights on a cross-country run, which is a driving schedule from the start of a trip to the end.

Bob Landry lives in Corona, California, which is located about 45 miles east of Los Angeles toward the desert country. He is married and has a boy twelve years old and a girl who is

280

nine. He owns his own truck and has been a driver for almost thirty years.

His destination this time is Homestead, Florida. It'll take about five days. Once there, he'll turn around and head back to Los Angeles, picking up other loads to move along the way. The whole run will take him about twenty days.

First, however, Bob will pick up a load of furniture in Riverside, California. After the truck is loaded, he'll be off on the first leg of the journey which will take him to Yuma, Arizona. This stop will be a major resting place from one to two hours in duration. Federal *regulations*, or rules, of interstate commerce require that truck drivers drive no more than ten hours at any one time.

Bob heads the big truck out onto the *interstate* highway, a superhighway connecting states. He's on his way to Florida!

Driving on Interstates

Do you wonder what driving is like on an interstate highway? Bob has a reply.

"It gets a bit monotonous out there. The long stretches of highway go on and on. There aren't any towns to go through like the old two-lane roads we used to travel a few years ago.

Bob paused, then went on, "The only thing that breaks the monotony is listening to the disc jockey in New Orleans. Louisiana, six nights a week from 9:30 until 5:00 the next morning.

There is a special program sent out over the airwaves to truck drivers. We can listen to music, receive important bulletins about weather or driving conditions along our route, or get a personal message over the air. For instance, we may hear a message something like this, 'Will Driver 203 please call your office? You have the wrong load. You need to go to Baltimore instead of New York.' The radio station is a big help to us truck drivers."

One hazard of travel on the interstate highway is the lack of stops. "Anyone can become hypnotized on an interstate because it's just a steady grind," says Bob. "You also have more tire failures on such long stretches. A driver used to go through a small town every thirty or forty miles, slowing down for stop signs and red lights. Your tires cooled off some before you hit the highway again. Today, you can go three or four hundred miles without stopping. The heat buildup on the tires is terrific! You have all kinds of tire trouble."

Truck drivers today usually stop every one hundred or one hundred fifty miles to check their tires and the general condition of the truck. It's possible to get a flat tire back on the rear of the truck and not realize it as you sit in the cab up front. When *duals*, or double tires, are used on a truck, the friction is greater with a flat, and the result is very often a serious fire.

Bob is quite busy as he approaches Yuma, Arizona. There are fourteen different *gauges*, or instruments, on the dashboard to watch at all times. Suddenly, a red light looms up. It's on the car ahead. Bob applies his air brakes and explains: "A lot of people tend to believe that because you have a sign on your truck that reads, 'Caution Air Brakes,' you can stop a truck on a dime. It just can't be done quickly. A loaded vehicle carrying sixty to seventy thousand pounds will roll forward on the momentum caused by its own weight. Though the wheels will stop, the truck won't for several yards. A truck driver must be sure to allow plenty of room between his truck and the car ahead in order to stop safely."

282

Yuma, Arizona to El Paso, Texas

After a coffee break in Yuma, Bob heads toward Tucson, Arizona. He'll spend eight to ten hours there, stopping at the roadway truck stop.

A truck passes Bob sixty miles out of Tucson in moderately heavy traffic. Bob blinks his lights several times to signal the driver that he may safely cut back into the lane again. Sometimes, when the road is clear to pass, Bob will wave a car ahead that has been following him for a long time. Bob has a better view for a longer distance of the road ahead because he sits up so high in the cab of his truck.

Early in the morning outside El Paso, Texas, Bob blinks his lights at an oncoming car. The distance is approximately five hundred feet between the two vehicles. There is no return blink. Bob blinks again. Still, no return blink from the oncoming car. When the car gets within one hundred feet of his truck, it drifts slowly over in front of him. CRASH! They hit head on. Fortunately, no one is seriously injured. All three persons in the car had been asleep.

283

Bob does not believe there is such a thing as an accident. Something is wrong when a collision happens. It is a failure— whether it's equipment failure, mental fatigue, driver failure, or some other failure. It's not an accident.

After minor repairs to his truck in El Paso, Texas, Bob is ready to drive again. This time he heads through Texas on his way south.

Traveling in Texas

The highway from El Paso to Sierra Blanca goes along a fertile valley watered from the Rio Grande River. There is almost no traffic. As the truck rolls along, Bob remembers many things as he reflects on how he got into this business.

First of all, he remembers how he started tinkering with motor equipment of all kinds when he was fourteen years old. Before driving this truck, he drove cement mixers, dump trucks, and tractors. He worked as a mechanic's helper in a

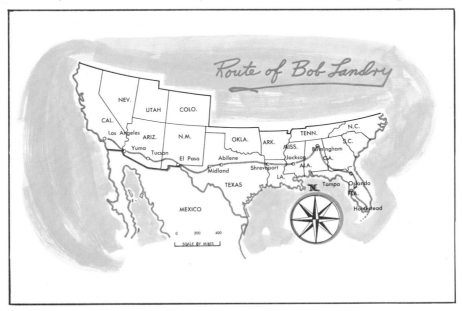

garage. Finally, after returning East from a trip to California with a friend, Bob drove a truck for the first time. His truck route took him through the East and Midwest. He recalled one winter in particular. He had to stop at a small motel in upper New York because of a heavy snowstorm. There was snow everywhere. When morning came, he was freezing in his room. He woke up and looked down at a foot of snow on the floor! That's when he decided he wanted to move to California. Bob Landry has never regretted this decision.

Outside of Midland, Bob becomes aware that he has been dreaming about his early life for the last several miles. It's now time for a stop. Midland is the headquarters for the company Bob works for.

It was time to turn in his paper work to the company. Federal regulations require a driver to complete a daily log, or report on his trip. The sample log on the next page shows where Bob went on this run, how long he drove, what hours he was off duty, and how far he went.

Bob finishes his business in Midland. Once again, he rolls along on Interstate 20. After brief rest stops in Abilene and Tyler, he arrives in Shreveport, Louisiana.

The Road From Louisiana to Florida

In Shreveport a company dispatcher is moving to Mississippi and wants Bob to move his Siamese cat. They place him in an orange crate on the seat next to Bob. During the day whenever he shifts gears, the cat tries to claw him. The cat refuses to eat, drink, or make friends with Bob. He feeds the cat tuna, steak, and other foods. But the cat still refuses to eat. He's one mad cat!

This incident reminded Bob of the time in California when he was asked to move a fish tank filled with rattlesnakes. He declined the job. He recalled also that other movers wouldn't take the man's business either. He wonders now whether he

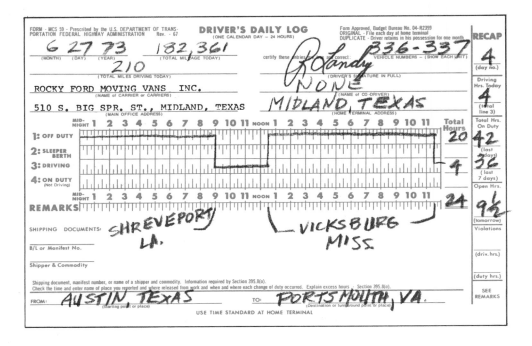

should have agreed to take the Siamese. Bob will be glad to get to Mississippi.

After delivering the Siamese in Jackson, Bob heads toward Montgomery, Alabama. A light drizzle is falling. As the water builds up on the highway, he knows he must be careful. Bob would prefer surfing at the ocean in California to riding on slick roads. The drizzle stops. Bob is glad to be driving out of the rain.

From Montgomery, Bob drives to Atlanta, Georgia. It is late at night, and he tunes in the New Orleans radio station.

Atlanta is a short stop and soon Bob is on the road again. Jacksonville, Florida will be his next intermediate stop.

The sun is shining. It is a beautiful day like so many he remembers back home in California. But it will be another week before he gets home. Bob thinks to himself that he'll stay off the road two weeks this time when he reaches Corona again. Most drivers cannot afford the loss in income by staying home that long. Bob, however, believes some time spent

286

with his family is more important than the extra money which a few days more on the road would bring.

"Homestead, Florida, here I come," he says aloud in the cab. The thought of heading home soon afterwards makes him a happy man.

Bob Landry's Advice to Young People Interested in the Trucking Industry

"When I started, very little education was needed. All you did was drive the truck, load it, and unload it. You had no paper work. Your log books were really simple to make out. You didn't have these big company records, IBM machines, and everything else.

"Today, I would say at least a high school education, especially mathematics, is needed. You've got to be able to figure out all your freight bills. Sometimes additional training is required and provided by the trucking company. Of course, education never hurt anyone. And if you're going into this occupation, you should take a mechanical course in school. It is important to know how to repair the truck, or at least have some knowledge about what's wrong with it.

"Anyone who would like to learn how to back up a truck could learn from a model truck because it will move in the same direction as the big ones. I had a friend who learned this way, and with some practice he got his driver's job.

"Another thing to do would be to build a model of a truck. There is everything in a model kit that's in the original, only scaled down to 1/50th of the original size.

"Truck driving pays well today. Some drivers make over $20,000 a year. A driver with his own truck can make more money than that. And the bigger truck stops today have facilities to make your life away from home more pleasant. If someone has an urge to travel, it's one way to see the country. And they'll also be well paid while doing it!"

CHECKING PROGRESS

1. Review the study questions and answers for the entire story.
2. Give several reasons why you think a person might choose to be a truck driver. List some reasons why a person might not choose this occupation.
3. What preparations does Bob Landry suggest a person make for the job of a truck driver?

CHOOSING NEXT STEPS

1. Interview a truck driver and ask such questions as:
   (1) What do you like most about your work? What do you dislike most?
   (2) What kind of preparation did you have for your job as a truck driver?
   (3) What kind of records do you keep? Ask to see the driver's daily log.
2. Read books on trucking and trucks, transportation, and other jobs relating to transportation.
3. Draw or prepare models of different types of road signs that you find in your city.
   (1) How is color used?
   (2) What shapes are used?
   (3) How are symbols used?
   (4) How are pictures used?
4. Prepare a map showing the route you or a friend of yours followed on a recent trip.
   (1) Give the title of the map.
   (2) Include a direction symbol.
   (3) Prepare a legend.
   (4) Include a scale of miles.

LET'S HAVE A DISCUSSION

THINKING THINGS THROUGH

Have you ever been asked to lead a discussion? When Luis was asked to lead a discussion, he did not think he knew how. As you read the story, use the suggestions below to help you decide how well Luis did.

(1) Keep the discussion only about the question or problem that needs to be talked about.
(2) Guide the people in the discussion to take turns.
(3) See that no one talks too long or too much.
(4) Take part in the discussion by asking questions and adding your own ideas.

ABOUT WORDS

Find synonyms in the dictionary for each of the underlined words in these sentences taken from the following selection. Then replace the underlined word with the synonym. Read the sentence with the new word to see if there has been any noticeable change in meaning.

(1) Luis Sanchez sat up abruptly in his seat and stared at Mr. Langdon.
(2) "Mom's worried about if I'd miss my friends too much,..."
(3) "Maybe some of the experiences you've had will help Luis reach a decision."
(4) Luis sat up eagerly.
(5) "Then suppose you lead the discussion, Luis."
(6) Laura raised her hand timidly.

289

LET'S HAVE A DISCUSSION

"You're not paying attention, Luis."

Luis Sanchez sat up abruptly in his seat and stared at Mr. Langdon. "I'm sorry," he sputtered. "I was thinking about something else—about a job my dad might take. He was offered a big promotion and a lot more money to work for his company in Singapore."

"Singapore!" David shouted. "But that's far away!"

"But he doesn't know if he'll take it or not," Luis said. "Mom's worried about if I'd miss my friends too much, and if the schools there would be good. He left it up to me, but I think he wants to go."

"I have an idea," Mr. Langdon said. "Some of you have lived in other countries with your parents. Why don't we have a discussion about this problem? Maybe some of the experiences you've had will help Luis reach a decision."

Luis sat up eagerly. "That's a good idea," he said.

"Then suppose you lead the discussion, Luis."

"But I don't know how," Luis said.

"Then this is a good time to learn," Mr. Langdon said. "To have an orderly discussion, everyone who wants to speak will have to take a turn. Come on, Luis."

Frank began the discussion. "We lived in Turkey for three years," he said. "What I can tell you would take hours."

Before Frank could continue, Luis said, "Maybe you could tell me some of it after school, Frank. We have to keep things short to give everybody a chance to talk."

Luis saw Mr. Langdon smile and nod in approval.

"Okay," Frank agreed good naturedly. "I liked meeting the people in Turkey. They ate different food and followed different customs than we have here."

290

"How did you meet them?" Luis asked. "In the schools?"

Frank shook his head. "No," he said. "My dad's company sent over teachers from the United States, and we had our own school. If we had gone to Turkish schools, it would have been too hard to learn the language well enough to understand the teacher. We met the interesting people through my mother. She taught English to the army officers. Some of them invited us to their homes. It was a lot of fun."

Laura raised her hand timidly. When Luis called on her she said, "My best friend moved with her family to Canada. She likes it there, and she goes to Canadian schools. The only thing she says makes her feel funny is that they learn Canadian history instead of United States history..."

"She wouldn't have a language problem," Alice said.

Luis frowned. "Don't interrupt," he said.

Frank jumped in his seat. "But it's fun to learn another language—even if you can't speak it very well."

"What about the food in other countries?" Luis asked.

"We ate American food most of the time," Frank said, "—from a store the company set up. But I liked Turkish food, too."

"He likes any food," Nancy said. "He eats all the time. He'll eat anything that isn't running down the street!"

The class burst into laughter, but Luis was finally able to get order again. "We're not having a discussion about Frank," he said, frowning again.

Luis called on Debbie. "My father is an engineer," she said, "and we lived in Colombia for a while. But he got out of his contract, and we came home because we were in danger."

"What kind of danger?" Luis asked.

"There were people who were trying to take over the country. They bombed office buildings or shot at people in the streets," Debbie said. "They shot in the air around our village sometimes and tried to scare us. My father didn't know if they'd decide to really do something bad, so we came home."

"You lived in a village?" Luis asked.

"Yes," she said. "Our oil company built it because there were no houses to rent or buy in the nearest town ."

"I have a question," Mr. Langdon said. "Did any of you who lived in other countries have any problems finding doctors?"

"There was a company doctor from the United States with us," Frank said, "but he was for small things. When a man needed an operation, he had to be flown to Paris for it."

Mr. Langdon moved to the chalkboard and wrote: people, food, medical, safety, schools. "Now, Luis," he said. "you should have learned some things about these items which might help you make up your mind."

Debbie spoke up. "But Mr. Langdon, we haven't talked about if our families ever want to go back."

"That's a good point. Would your family?" Luis asked.

"No." she answered. "My father changed jobs so he wouldn't have to work outside the United States again."

"My dad would like to," Frank said. "He is on a waiting list with his company for the next overseas opening. He likes getting a larger salary for overseas work, too."

Luis sighed. "I've learned a lot, but I still don't know just what it will be like in Singapore. Things are different in each country. How will I know if I'll like the way things are in Singapore?"

"You can find books in the library that will tell you how people live there," Nancy answered.

Luis thought a moment. "I won't have to worry about schools, I guess. And I won't have to worry about food because my mom is a good cook. And I'll let my dad worry about what kind of house we'll live in. I guess it will be as safe living in Singapore as it is in the United States because the people there aren't anti-American."

He sighed again. "So it just comes down to whether or not I want to live in a country different from my own. I think I know now what I'm going to tell my dad."

"What?" Nancy asked. "What did you decide?"

Luis smiled. "I'd better tell my dad first," he said. "I'll tell *you* how it came out tomorrow."

CHECKING PROGRESS

1. What would you have done if you were in Luis' place?
   (1) Did the facts you learned from Luis' classmates influence you in any way? How?
   (2) Did anything else influence your thinking? What?
2. Write an ending to the story. Have Luis tell his parents about what he decided to do. Write the ending in conversational form. Be sure to give the response of Luis' parents when he tells them his decision.
3. Do you think Luis was a good discussion leader? Did he follow the suggestions given before the story? Support your answer with examples from the story.

CHOOSING NEXT STEPS

1. Form a discussion group with six or eight of your friends. Select a problem or question and discuss it.
   (1) Choose a leader.
   (2) Choose two judges. Ask the judges to observe the discussion and to decide whether or not the group followed the suggestions given before the story.
2. Think of an experience you have had that took you to another state, country, city, or even to the home of a friend.
   (1) What differences did you find in the food, the houses, and the people who lived there as compared to that of your own family?
   (2) What likenesses did you find in the food, the houses, and the ways of the people as compared to that of your own family?

THE CHOICE

THINKING THINGS THROUGH

Even though we may have a strong interest in one area, there may be other things we like to do, too. Mamie Williams is a very talented musician. She also likes to work with young people. It was because of her interest in young people that she finally decided to become a teacher. Yet music is still a part of her life. Do you have more than one interest which may lead to a career later in life? Even if your career does not turn out to be in one of those areas, do you think you will still have these interests as an adult?

Be sure to notice as you are reading Mamie's story, what her attitude is towards achieving what she wanted out of life. Also note whether or not she feels that being black has hurt her in any way.

ABOUT WORDS

Do you remember what antonyms are? If not, look up the definition in the glossary at the back of the book. Then choose a word from each list to form pairs of antonyms.

segregated	easy
difficult	boundless
worthwhile	useless
confident	encourage
seriously	national
limited	integrated
deter	jokingly
local	unsure

295

INVESTIGATE

THE CHOICE

Even though Arturo Toscanini, the great symphony orchestra conductor, told her that she had a great deal of talent and should continue with her music, Mamie Williams decided to rebel when she went to college. "Well, I am *not* going to work that hard, and I am *not* going to study music," she remembers thinking at the time. So she took her bachelor's degree in English with only a minor in music and her master's degree also in English. She is now coordinator of English in the secondary schools of a city with over 16,000 students.

Her parents were plain, hardworking people; neither of them was educated. But Mamie repeatedly refers to the debt she owes her parents for the start they gave her. She said with a chuckle, "I had dancing lessons, piano lessons, violin lessons, horn lessons, drum lessons, voice lessons—you name it, and I had it."

She also feels her parents helped her by giving her a spirit of independence. They sent her to an out-of-state college when she was sixteen. She was glad she went to a small, predominantly black college. "The competition was not as great, and I got more attention on a small campus," she said.

Mrs. Williams doesn't feel that being black has limited her in any way. "Of course I have encountered discrimination—some heartaches—but nothing that would deter me from doing what I feel I am here to do...I've had all sorts of opportunities handed to me, and I've tried to grasp at almost all of them," she stated.

"I suppose I have been sort of a pioneer," she continued. "I have tried to be an example and, hopefully, have done a little to pave the way for others. I was one of the first black teachers to go to a newly integrated high school. I was also one of

296

the first blacks to go to an administrative position on the central staff in my school system. I was one of the first blacks to become a member of one of the local chapters of a teachers' honorary society. But on the other side of the coin, I am also a member of several professional and civic organizations of my own race..."

Although Mrs. Williams sometimes regrets not choosing music as a career, she said she wouldn't be as interested in a concert career as in teaching. She likes young people.

At one time Mrs. Williams seriously considered going back to music school to prepare for a teaching career in music. Even now she finds time to give piano lessons on Saturdays. However, she has decided that she would like to get a certificate in counseling. She explained, "I have this confident feeling that I can help young people. My teaching experiences in an all-Negro school, along with those in an integrated situation, make me feel I could do well as a counselor. I feel that I can work with students and help them grasp things that are worthwhile. In fact, I'm going to take some courses in counseling very soon. I'm going to pursue it—I really am."

297

CHECKING PROGRESS

1. Mrs. Williams gives her parents credit for helping her to become a well-adjusted person in her adult life and work.
    (1) What were some of the things her parents did that helped her?
    (2) What have your parents done, or are now doing, to help prepare you for the future?
2. Even though Mrs. Williams did not go into a career in the field of music, in what ways does music make a contribution to her life today? What are some ways she might use her musical background in the future?
3. What are some of the reasons why Mrs. Williams is interested in becoming a counselor?
    (1) How do you think her past experiences will help her be of assistance to students as a counselor?
    (2) How can she be of assistance to parents, teachers, and other adults?

CHOOSING NEXT STEPS

1. Interview a teacher or counselor and ask them such questions as:
    (1) Why did you choose a career in this field?
    (2) Have you ever changed the course of your career? If so, when and why?
    (3) If you should change the course of your career, what would the change be?
    (4) Do you have any hobbies or special interests? How do they contribute to your life and work?
2. Write a short autobiography describing your life and work as it might be ten or fifteen years from now.
3. Read biographies of both black and white teachers, musicians, and counselors.

EXPLORING YOUR LIBRARY:
THE DEWEY SYSTEM OF CLASSIFICATION

Have you ever wondered how libraries are organized? Have you ever been amazed at how neatly and accurately the books are arranged? Libraries use a special system to classify books and materials. This system serves as a guide to the arrangement of the library. It also helps students to locate books and materials they wish to read.

The most widely-used system in school and public libraries is the Dewey Decimal System of classification. It is named after Melvil Dewey. He worked out the idea of using whole numbers and decimals to classify materials and organize the library in a new manner.

In the Dewey Decimal System, books are classified according to their subject. In this way, all books about a particular subject, such as science or art, are classified together. Then they can easily be located. Also, other books on the subject are within close reach.

All books in the library are either fiction (not true) or non-fiction (true, factual). In most libraries, fiction books, biographies, and story collections are not given Dewey decimal numbers. Instead, fiction books are designated with "F" or "FIC." Individual biographies are usually marked "B" (but collective biographies, or biographies grouped together in one book, are classified under 920 in the Dewey system). The letters "SC" are used for story collections.

All non-fiction books are assigned Dewey decimal numbers. These numbers range from 000 to 999, using both whole numbers and decimals. They are used to designate the subject of the book. Below are the numbers used for the subject classifications:

000-099   General Works (information, newspapers, magazines)
100-199   Philosophy (man learns to ask questions and to think about himself in relation to the universe)
200-299   Religion (man thinks about God)
300-399   Social Sciences (man thinks about other people)
400-499   Language (man learns to use words, communicate)
500-599   Pure Science (man learns about forces of nature)
600-699   Technology (man makes things for his comfort)
700-799   Fine Arts and Recreation (man learns to express himself and make use of his spare time)
800-899   Literature, Including Poetry and Drama (man becomes a storyteller)
900-999   History, Travel, Geography (man writes of people, places, events)

CLASSIFICATION OF NON-FICTION BOOKS

Using the list of Dewey decimal numbers of 000 to 999, write down the correct classification numbers for each title. Be sure to use a separate sheet of paper.

World Religions
Folk Songs of America
Young People and Parents
Man's Conquest of Space
Round the World Plays for Young People
Familiar Insects of America
The Language Book
Battle of Little Big Horn
The World Book Encyclopedia
Looking at Sculpture
The Realm of Algebra
100 Story Poems
Picture History of Astronomy

CLASSIFICATION OF BOOKS IN SUBDIVISIONS

Each main division of non-fiction books may be divided into ten subdivisions. The subdivisions of classification 500, Pure Science, are:

510 - Mathematics
520 - Astronomy
530 - Physics
540 - Chemistry
550 - Geology
560 - Paleontology (prehistoric life)
570 - Anthropology (humans)
580 - Botany (plants)
590 - Zoology (animals)

Choose the right classification number for each book listed below. Be sure to use a separate piece of paper.

The Great Apes
Quick and Easy Math
Patterns in the Sky
The Romance of Physics
Great Ideas of Science

Books are arranged in the library according to call number. This consists of letters or numbers and letters which are found in two lines on the spine of the book. (The spine is the center backing which connects the front and back covers.) The top line classifies the book either by fiction, biography, or Dewey number. The second line consists of a single letter which is usually the first letter of the author's last name. But in the case of biographies, this letter stands for the subject's last name.

Fiction is shelved alphabetically by the author's last name:

Biography is shelved alphabetically by the subject's last name:

Non- fiction books are shelved numerically beginning with small numbers and going to larger numbers:

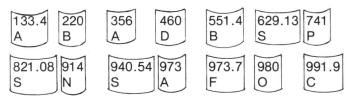

Non-fiction books with the same classification number are then shelved alphabetically by the author's last name:

For each section listed below, put these books in order as they would be on the shelves of a library. Use a separate sheet of paper. Make sure that you have first read and understood Activity Three.

A. Fiction

F O   F D   F L   F A   F F   F W   F R   F G   F J   F C   F P

B. Biography

B S   B P   B B   B F   B D   B L   B E   B T   B Z   B H   B A

C. Non-fiction:

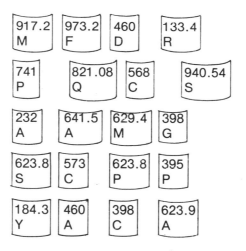

917.2 M	973.2 F	460 D	133.4 R
741 P	821.08 Q	568 C	940.54 S
232 A	641.5 A	629.4 M	398 G
623.8 S	573 C	623.8 P	395 P
184.3 Y	460 A	398 C	623.9 A

footprints of life styles

Footprints, ladies and gentlemen! Step right up and try them.

You say you like the prints made by cowboy boots, young man? And you, Miss, you're trying on the dancing shoes? There are footprints over there, left by a pair of heavy construction shoes; and a light pair—used by a young woman working in an office. There's a life style in footprints for all.

UNIT 5   FOOTPRINTS OF LIFE STYLES

VOLUNTEERS IN ACTION

THINKING THINGS THROUGH

Volunteer workers devote some of their time to helping others. They may help by painting walls, caring for the young—or the old, working on political campaigns, or even feeding animals at the zoo. Age is not important. All of the volunteers you will read about in this selection are teen-agers. Some of them began doing volunteer work when they were only thirteen.

These young volunteers have not only been helping others, but they have been helping themselves, too. As you read this selection, see what influence their volunteer work has had on their plans for the future. How can being a volunteer worker help you decide whether or not you want to follow a particular career choice?

ABOUT WORDS

Below are some words that can be used as either nouns or as verbs. On a separate piece of paper, write sentences using each word in both forms.

Example: They *tutor* a class of young children. (verb)

The *tutor* was able to help the child with her math homework. (noun)

volunteer	sign
work	design
call	range

After you have written the sentences, see if you can find other words in this selection which can be used both ways.

305

INVESTIGATE

Volunteers in Action

A job without pay? Who'd look for a job like that? There are a great number of young people who see a need for volunteer workers and do their best to fill this need. In most any activity you will find teen-agers giving their time. Need a responsible person to teach a Sunday school class? Need someone to tutor young children in English? Just send out the word, and soon a teen-ager will be answering the call.

Seventeen-year-old Butch Traeder began working at the YMCA as a volunteer teacher when he was only thirteen. The YMCA in Butch's town uses about twenty volunteer teachers during the year. Butch usually works ten hours a week, except during basketball and football seasons when he spends extra time coaching the teams. He estimates that in the last three years he has served close to 3,000 hours.

"You don't have to be an expert in order to teach at the 'Y'," Butch explained. "They have clinics that teach the instructors how to conduct the classes." When Butch began teaching gymnastics, for example, he had never tried the exercises himself. After working with the children, he became interested in gymnastics himself and learned some of them.

"It sounds funny, but I'd rather not be paid for the work I do at the 'Y'," Butch said. "Later when I have to support myself, it will be a different matter; but right now I want to give my time."

Working at the "Y" has influenced his future plans. After college he would like to become a park and recreation director.

But for now Butch is happy doing volunteer work. "A volunteer can work out his own hours and teach what he wants when he wants," he explained. "There is freedom in it."

306

Eileen Nixon's first volunteer job was during the summer when she was thirteen. She worked with small children at her city's Community Day Nursery.

"I wanted to be busy," she said. "I didn't want to spend the whole summer just being lazy when there were things that needed to be done."

At the nursery, she worked with small groups of children. She taught them their alphabet and numbers, gave them a mid-afternoon snack, and played games with them.

The following spring Eileen took an entirely different kind of job—as a volunteer at the zoo. On Saturdays and Sundays she worked the full day helping to feed the animals, cleaning the cages, answering the phone, answering questions the visitors had about the animals—and even cautioning them to keep their fingers out of the cages!

The volunteer work she did gave her a direction toward her future plans. "I decided I would really like to work with children. Maybe I will become a counselor."

Eileen likes to do volunteer work. "You don't go away each day thinking how noble you are," she said. "You just leave with a feeling of 'that was fun. I'd like to do it again.'"

Eileen's older brother, seventeen-year-old Joe, also does volunteer work. He has been doing volunteer work in politics since he was twelve.

At first he was assigned the job of going door to door with campaign literature for national and local candidates. As he became older and developed more depth in his study of political issues, his workload increased.

"A political volunteer must be willing to do the work, or he shouldn't get involved," Joe said. "A volunteer can be called at any hour to handle any kind of job. If you offer to do something, you must do it responsibly, and you must plan to work hard and long hours just before the election. It takes a lot of work to make sure people know about your candidate and what he stands for."

He added, "A person who gets involved in volunteer work has to remember he has other responsibilities, too—like homework and household chores. Taking part in this work has helped me develop a greater sense of responsibility."

Joe admits he began doing the work for fun and excitement; but as he grew older he felt a sense of service to the country and to the party he chose to work for. "If the party is made better, it would be a great service to the country; and if the country is made better, it would be a great service to the world," Joe stated.

Joe has become very interested in the political world through his volunteer work. He hopes to someday become a congressman or senator himself.

Work with the elderly is sometimes difficult, but thirteen-year-old Sarah Woods enjoyed her volunteer job at a retirement home for the aged. During the summer Sarah worked at this home every Monday. Usually she would perform any task that needed to be done. At times she read to the elderly women. Sometimes she helped them to sign their names to things. She brought them fresh water and ran errands.

There were about twenty or thirty patients Sarah visited, and the biggest need they all had was to talk to someone. "It really was interesting," Sarah said. "I met so many fascinating people and they had so many things to talk about!" Sarah smiled. "The only problem was finishing the chores quickly enough to have time left to talk," she added.

Sarah got the job by calling a volunteer headquarters in her city. Like other teen-age volunteers, she wanted to do something worthwhile during the summer. She had to drop the job when school began, but she plans to volunteer for work again next summer. She would like to work at the same job again—one day a week as before—but she would like to try something new during the rest of the week.

"To do volunteer work you have to be willing to give up some of the things you like to do," Sarah said. "If you really don't enjoy it, you don't make a good volunteer."

Sarah feels that her volunteer experiences eventually will help her decide what she'll want to do when she's grown. At the moment, however, she said, "I want to be busy, because if you're busy you're happy; and if you're doing something helpful, you're even happier."

After three years of work with Teens to Aid the Retarded (TARS), high school senior Jo Ann Ellis knows that this is the work she would like to do as an adult. Jo Ann is president of TARS. She devotes her entire weekend along with many additional hours during the week to help the retarded children, mostly teen-agers, who come to the TARS center for classes and social activities.

"What we try to do is give them friendship," Jo Ann said. "Everyone needs friends, and this is something retarded children often lack because many people forget them. Some of

these kids have made real progress just by having friends their own age."

The teen volunteers have set up a club at the center called "The Pop Bottle." In it they have two pool tables, a coke machine, and puzzles and games. The club is designed as a place to relax and have fun. And there are always TARS members on hand to help.

In the summer the volunteer workers' hours increase. Arts and crafts programs are held every day. Each Friday outings are planned, such as visits to a bakery, a bottling company, or an ice skating rink. One week in August the youngsters have the opportunity to attend a camp at a dude ranch in the Davis Mountains of Texas.

Volunteers in TARS range in age from eighth graders to high school students. "I hear kids say there is nothing to do in our town," Jo Ann said, "but with all the volunteers we need, I don't think anyone has to make that statement."

Being a boy scout sometimes requires doing volunteer work in the community, and eighth-grader Craig Seal had to work out his own community service project in order to qualify for Eagle Scout.

Craig heard that Casa de Amigos, a community center which aids citizens of Mexican-American heritage, needed the rooms of their house painted. So Craig and two of his friends volunteered. After the walls were freshly painted, Craig added a few touches of his own. He decorated the walls with cartoons that he designed himself.

This was not Craig's first volunteer job, and it won't be his last. He plans to do more volunteer work next summer. "I don't know what it will be yet," Craig said, "but I feel that now is a good time to try different things and explore career ideas. I don't know yet what I want to be, but I can get some idea through the volunteer work I do."

Age doesn't matter in volunteer work. Too young to get a job? That didn't stop these people. They learned of some group or individual who needed help, and they were there to give it. That's what volunteer work is all about.

CHECKING PROGRESS

After reading the experiences of six teen-agers who have served as volunteers in their communities, you should be able to draw some conclusions about teen-agers and volunteer work. The following plan of study should help you.

1. Make a chart with the following headings and fill in specific information about each teen-age volunteer.

Name	Type of Work	Personal Satisfaction	Influence on Future

2. Answer the following questions with one summary statement based on the information given in the chart. Remember that a summary statement gives one or more main idea drawn from specific information.
    (1) What kind of volunteer work can teen-agers do?
    (2) What personal satisfaction do teen-agers get from doing volunteer work?
    (3) How can volunteer work influence teen-agers' plans for the future?

CHOOSING NEXT STEPS

1. Prepare a list of volunteer jobs that are available to teen-agers in your community.
2. Prepare a report for your class on volunteer work that you have done.
3. Take a survey in your class to find out the kinds of volunteer work being done by your classmates.
4. Invite a person from a community organization to come to your class to discuss opportunities for volunteer work.

BETTER BE SAFE THAN PATRICK

THINKING THINGS THROUGH

Have you ever tried so hard to do something just right and found that the harder you tried the more mistakes you made? If so, you can probably identify very well with Patrick in the following story, "Better Be Safe Than Patrick."

ABOUT WORDS

There are some words in the story that are pronounced the same as other words you may know. The words may be spelled differently or may have different meanings, but when you say them they sound alike. These kinds of words are called *homophones*. Select the proper word for each of the sentences below. Then try to find other homophones in the story and write your own sentences for them.

1. The boys waved their arms (*higher, hire*) in the air. The teacher didn't know which one to (*higher, hire*) for the job as head of the safety committee.
2. "I didn't realize I'd find (*to, two, too*) such eager volunteers (*to, two, too*) head the safety committee."
3. The class had to (*weight, wait*) while Patrick set the crate in front of the room. The crate couldn't hold his (*weight, wait*), so he came crashing down.
4. When Patrick tried to do any (*feat, feet*), he managed to trip over his own (*feat, feet*).

313

INVESTIGATE

BETTER BE SAFE THAN PATRICK

Patrick Felton stretched his arm higher and higher in the air. Howard Thomas was also eagerly waving his hand.

"Relax, boys," Miss Williams said. "I didn't realize I'd find two such eager volunteers to head the safety committee for our school. I really don't know who to choose."

Patrick leaned forward, holding his breath. The job could not mean as much to Howard. Howard didn't have a big brother who practically collected titles in school. During seven years of school, Patrick hadn't even been appointed to clean erasers.

"I have an idea," Miss Williams said. "Let's have a contest to see who has the qualifications to be chairman."

Patrick let out a sigh. There went his chance. He sized up Howard. . .tall and strong for his age, popular with everyone, and an "A" student. He knew himself only too well. . .too short, too clumsy, too everything. He slumped in his seat.

Miss Williams smiled. "Patrick, you have a chance to get started on safety practices right now. We're going to practice for a fire drill so when the fire captain visits our school, things will run smoothly. Since you sit near the windows, see that they're closed before taking your place in line."

The drill began. Patrick moved to the first window and quickly closed it. But the next window was stuck.

"I think something is caught up here," Patrick said and leaned out to reach up and give the metal frame a pull.

Before he knew it he had sailed out the window and was sitting in the zinnia bed. The window flipped down with a bang. He slowly picked himself up and looked through the window into the classroom. The boys and girls were doubled up with laughter. Howard was laughing hardest of all.

314

Patrick clenched his teeth and removed a zinnia from behind his left ear. Laugh, would they? Well, he'd show them.

When everyone left the room for lunch, he approached Miss Williams. "May I make a safety poster to show the class?" he asked. "I could work on it tonight."

She nodded. "Very good, Patrick. I like that idea."

Patrick worked hard on his poster. He knew he was only passing in art ability, but at least his work was neat and it put across a basic safety rule. He drew lunch bags, books, and papers left in an aisle between two rows of desks. He wrote the words, "WATCH YOUR STEP!"

Right before class, Patrick began to worry about how to present his poster. If only he weren't so short! Then he remembered the wooden supply crates in the custodian's closet. If he stood on one of them, he would be tall enough and important enough to get his point across to the rest of the class.

When everyone was seated, Miss Williams invited Patrick up to the front of the room. He placed the crate on end and climbed on it, holding his poster high over his head.

Then he realized the crate was splintering under his weight. He came crashing down, knocking books and papers helter-skelter out of the first row.

Miss Williams helped him to his feet.

"I'm all right," he muttered, brushing off his shirt.

Miss Williams handed him his poster. "It's a fine poster, Patrick," she said. "Tack it up on the bulletin board in the hall so the whole school can see it."

Patrick brightened a bit. At least his poster would get some recognition. He cautiously opened the glass door that protected the bulletin board. This time he would make no mistakes. He carefully pinned up the poster, then stood back to survey his work. He sighed with relief.

This time he hadn't messed things up. Happily he grabbed the door with both hands and swung it shut.

"Yeeeeooo!" he screamed.

His yell echoed down the hall. He grabbed his squashed thumb and held it tightly, hopping up and down in circles.

The fire bell rang. Miss Williams stuck her head out the door. "Get in line, Patrick," she sighed.

They marched to the front of the school. Everyone was extra quiet because the fire captain was watching. He looked at his watch, nodded his head, and said, "Very good timing."

Miss Williams suddenly remembered she left her record folder on the desk. She asked Patrick to hurry and get it.

Patrick dashed up the short flight of steps to the door. He barely missed the captain, who was climbing the steps to speak to the group. He saw the fire extinguisher the captain was holding. Swish...swoosh, he thought, any fire would be out in a minute. He ran down the hall, into the room, and grabbed the folder from Miss Williams' desk.

Back down the hall he ran. He threw the door open and sailed through. He tripped and landed right on top of the fire extinguisher. He must have kicked the release button because when he looked up, he saw that the fire captain's trousers were dripping wet.

316

In the shocked silence, he held up the folder of papers. "I brought your records," he told Miss Williams.

"So I see," she replied, looking behind him.

He turned and looked, too. The contents of the folder were floating in the puddle of foam.

Patrick felt like he was in the middle of a nightmare. The students began marching back to their classrooms. The captain left. Patrick knew he had lost the chance to be safety chairman. After cleaning things up, he dragged his unwilling feet back to the classroom.

"Come in and sit down, Patrick," Miss Williams said as he entered the room. "You are our new safety chairman."

Safety chairman! Patrick's mouth fell open.

Miss Williams smiled and said, "The class felt that you were the one person in the entire school who would benefit the most from a safety campaign, so we elected you."

Patrick grinned as his friends clapped and shook his hands. Howard even offered his help.

"Good," said Patrick, feeling taller already. "From now on, Howard, YOU can close the windows!"

CHECKING PROGRESS

1. Describe characteristics of Patrick's personality that were shown during these parts of the story.
   (1) Miss Williams said, "Let's have a contest to see who has the qualifications to be chairman."
   (2) Patrick clenched his teeth and removed a zinnia from behind his left ear.
   (3) "May I make a safety poster to show the class?" he asked.
   (4) He sighed with relief.
   (5) After cleaning things up, he dragged his unwilling feet back to the classroom.
   (6) "Good," said Patrick, feeling taller already. "From now on, Howard, YOU can close the windows!"
2. Did you like the way Miss Williams handled the selection of safety chairman? Why?
3. Do you think Patrick should have been selected chairman of the safety committee? Why or why not?
4. Why did the writer of this story give it the title, "Better Be Safe Than Patrick?" From what familiar expression was the title taken?

CHOOSING NEXT STEPS

1. Make a poster or cartoon story about safety. Use a familiar expression such as "a stitch in time saves nine." Change it so that it becomes a safety slogan such as "Careful drivers save lives."
2. Select and read books which contain information about careers in the field of safety.
3. Invite a safety engineer or highway patrolmen to come to your class and discuss career opportunities in the field of safety.

MY ABILITIES?
I THOUGHT YOU'D NEVER ASK

THINKING THINGS THROUGH

The selection, "My Abilities? I Thought You'd Never Ask," is about Gene Martin, a student the author wrote about in a previous selection entitled, "An Interest Profile." In this selection, comparisons are made from information gathered in an interview with Gene Martin and information obtained from a DAT, or Directional Aptitude Test. Some evaluations are also made after rereading the article, "An Interest Profile," with those results obtained on the DAT. Read this selection and find out how information about ourselves is obtained and evaluated.

ABOUT WORDS

The following article discusses results of a DAT. In order to have a clearer understanding of what the measured categories mean, learn the meanings of each as explained below.

Verbal Reasoning - Measures your comprehension and understanding of what is read.

Numerical Ability - Indicates possible success in mathematics, physics, chemistry, and in engineering if scores are high.

Verbal Reasoning and Numerical Ability Combined - Indicates that a student should definitely expect to do well in college if scores are high.

Abstract Reasoning - Measures your ability to think without numbers or words to guide you.

Clerical and Speed Accuracy - Assesses your ability to accurately compare and mark lists of names and numbers.

Mechanical Reasoning - Measures your grasp of common laws of physics.

Space Relations - Measures your ability to visualize the shape of surfaces from drawings to the real object.

Language Usage - Tells how well you do in spelling, punctuation, and grammar.

319

INVESTIGATE

My Abilities? I Thought You'd Never Ask

Talking about ourselves in junior high school is rather easy. But finding out information about ourselves is a lot harder to do.

Let's go back and interview Gene Martin, the seventh grader who let us use his interest survey. In this interview, we'll try to find out how much Gene knows about his abilities. Later, we'll compare what Gene knows about himself to what we learn from his aptitude test.

The Interview

We find Gene in the school library and ask him if we might discuss the results of his recent testing surveys, and what he has learned about his abilities.

"Well, some of the tests I have taken show that I'm good in reading," Gene tells us proudly. "In fact they show my reading level above most pupils my age."

"How do you know this?" we ask.

"Well, some of my teachers thought I'd like to know that, so they told me," Gene replies.

"Does this give you any clues about a possible career you should consider?" we ask Gene.

"I guess I should plan a career in which I would do a lot of reading. At least I'd be able to get information fast from reading material," says Gene.

"Let's look at some other school subjects, Gene."

"Science is a subject I do well in, and I also like health courses. I really dislike social studies. This subject really bores me."

"Do you read many science books?" we ask.

"As a matter of fact, I'm reading some interesting things about lasers. I'm also reading about UFO's, and I like chemistry."

320

Gene smiled and said, "My best subjects in school are math and science."

We decided to ask Gene how he spends his free time.

"I like to build things like model gliders, airplanes, and rockets. I really had a *blast* (a great time) last Sunday. Last spring I built a two-stage rocket called 'Black Widow.' I'd put off launching it because I thought I'd put it together wrong. Last week my brother had a birthday and got a new rocket launching panel that connects to a car battery. The flashlight battery type doesn't work very well. He got a new rocket, too, so we decided to launch. We tested everything we had.

"Boy, it went a mile high!" Gene continued excitedly. "We thought we'd lost the second stage for a while. It floated off downwind, dangling from its recovery chute. Dad and I looked for an hour before we found it. The model ended up about a mile down range in somebody's yard. The engine mount blew out when the second stage fired."

"Sounds exciting, Gene. What else do you do?"

"Well, I like music. I take piano lessons and play cello in the orchestra."

We thanked Gene for the interview and left.

Gene knows some things about his abilities. Ability tests give information about a person, but are only one source for information. These must be analyzed along with other kinds of information we have about ourselves.

Let's review what Gene has told us. He knows that he has done rather well on at least one reading achievement test. He also reads a lot, especially subjects in the science area. Gene said that he does well in science and math. As a matter of fact, his school performance is above average.

Now, let's turn to Gene's special aptitude test and compare the interview data with the test results.

It is also *apparent*, or easily seen, that Gene is interested in building things. Another subject in which Gene shows ability is music.

	VERBAL REASONING	NUMERICAL ABILITY	VR + NA	ABSTRACT REASONING	CLERICAL SP. & ACC.	MECHANICAL REASONING	SPACE RELATIONS	LANGUAGE USAGE SPELLING	GRAMMAR
Name MARTIN, GENE H.					**Year** 1974F	**Form** L	**Grade** 8	**Sex** M	
Raw Score									
Percentile	97	99	99	99	20	99	97	99	97

A Test Analysis

The DAT, or Differential Aptitude Test, is a popular test often used in junior and senior high schools. It contains both the general and special aptitude parts of a measurement test.

As you can see, Gene does well in all subjects except one. His high scores in verbal reasoning and numerical ability show that he can do well in college. His high score in the numerical ability area indicates possible success in the fields of mathematics, physics, chemistry, and engineering. This ability is also useful in many technical careers not requiring college training.

Looking at the abstract reasoning, mechanical reasoning, and space relations together backs up Gene's strengths in the mechanical and technical areas.

Abstract reasoning is the ability to think when there are no numbers or words to guide you. The mechanical reasoning tells how well a person grasps common laws of physics. Space relations is the ability to visualize the shape of surfaces from drawings to the real object.

The language usage section tells how good a person is in spelling, grammar, and punctuation. This strengthens the results Gene obtained in the verbal area. The clerical speed and accuracy section measures a person's accurate ability to compare and mark lists of names and numbers. This ability is important in many office jobs and warehouses; insurance companies, banks, and business firms require this skill. Gene did not do very well on this portion of the test so he really should

322

not think of a career in which this skill is necessary. He does have other areas of ability from which to choose.

When we compare Gene's interview with the test information, we can verify his reading ability. His performance in science and math appears on the DAT, too. It is not unusual, however, to find a difference between test performance and school performance. If this exists, it does indicate that there may be a problem. This would require further investigation to determine why the student is not working up to his or her potential.

We have another source of information on Gene, in the article, "An Interest Profile," which you read about earlier in this book. Since Gene's aptitude shows a high potential in both the verbal and numerical portions of the DAT, his interests in the musical and literary areas can be pursued. His abstract reasoning score supports this position. His tested interests in the career areas of mechanics and science could be followed also.

There are many ways we can gain information about our abilities. We have used two here, the interview and the special aptitude test. Each method has its advantages. No one source of data can be used by itself. In this article it is obvious that one source adds information unavailable from a separate source. For example, we cannot measure Gene's ability in either the language or the scientific area through the type of interview we used. The results of the DAT test extend our information.

Wouldn't this kind of information be valuable to you in planning a career?

CHECKING PROGRESS

1. What are the two sources of information about Gene Martin's abilities which are used in this article? What are some other sources that could be used?
2. According to his interview, in what school subjects does Gene have the greatest ability? What does he like to do at home?
3. According to Gene's results on the DAT, in what areas does Gene have the most aptitude or ability? The least?
4. One area in which Gene scored high was numerical ability. What careers might Gene consider on the basis of his high scoring ability?
5. Gene made a low score on the clerical area on the DAT. What career fields should he avoid?

CHOOSING NEXT STEPS

1. Pretend you are being interviewed instead of Gene. Answer each question that was asked. Compare your answers to Gene's. How are you alike? How are you different?
2. Invite your school counselor to come to your class and discuss the kinds of tests which are given to students in junior and senior high schools in your school system.
3. Plan for a conference with your favorite teacher, your principal, or your counselor. Ask this person to give you advice on how you can improve in your school work. Also ask for some suggestions for choosing electives in the future.

STUDENT INVOLVEMENT THROUGH COMMUNITY ACTION

THINKING THINGS THROUGH

Sometimes high school students complain that their school clubs and extracurricular activities are too heavily centered around school and are not involved with the outside community. Students feel that a club should relate to the city and to people in the area. They want an activity to have some overall purpose of improving the community.

In many schools, new organizations have been formed for students who wish to improve their community. One such organization is SITCA, or Student Involvement Through Community Action. The next article tells about the SITCA organization in Midland, Texas.

ABOUT WORDS

The word SITCA is an *acronym*, or a word formed from the initial letter or letters of several other words. By taking the first letter of each word in the phrase Student Involvement Through Community Action, we come up with the word SITCA. This abbreviated word is more convenient to use. Here are some other acronyms:

UNICEF	United Nations International Emergency Children's Fund
NASA	National Aeronautics and Space Administration
NOW	National Organization of Women
CORE	Congress On Racial Equality
NATO	North Atlantic Treaty Organization

It is not necessary for every letter of an acronym to stand for a separate word. Sometimes two letters refer to a single word in the phrase. For example, RADAR stands for RAdio Detecting And Ranging.

BEFORE YOU READ

INVESTIGATE

Student Involvement Through Community Action

Did you ever hear of high school students being full-fledged members of their city's Chamber of Commerce? This may seem unusual, but it's a fact. In Midland, Texas, students are able to join the Chamber of Commerce through their participation in SITCA. This organization, Student Involvement Through Community Action, is made up of students who work for the betterment of the community in which they live.

In Midland the SITCA organization has been in operation for three years. It is the prestige organization of the two high schools in the city. Membership is limited to fifty students—twenty-five from each of the two schools. These twenty-five consist of ten seniors, ten juniors, and five sophomores.

Students may apply for membership in the fall. Af-

ter the beginning of school, application blanks are distributed to anyone wishing to apply. There are three requirements for membership. A student must: 1) be a full-time student in high school, 2) have passing grades the previous semester in all subjects, and 3) have good character. Applicants are also asked for a brief statement explaining why they wish to join.

After the applications are received, they are screened for passing grades. Then a selection committee makes final decisions. It is difficult for the committee to choose fifty students from as many as 150 applications.

After the members are chosen, the first meeting is held in the conference room of the Midland Chamber of Commerce. Everyone is excited and eager to learn about the year's plans. Members are assigned to committees, and a vice-president of the Chamber addresses them with a challenge for the coming year. Then the SITCA members decide upon projects.

The SITCA group in Midland has decided upon the following projects: building a miniature playground on the east side of the city, helping with the annual used-book sale, decorating a car for the Christmas parade, planning a party in December, organizing a clean-up week, helping with "Christmas in April," and having monthly breakfast meetings. Besides these, SITCA helps with any special projects the Chamber of Commerce organizes.

The playground project is a special one for this year. SITCA members plan to make a play area using large, gaily-painted trash cans and other kinds of playground equipment.

The book sale begins with a book drive for the new junior college library. Students collect over 60,000 vol-

umes, and the college chooses the books it can use. The remainder of the books are sold at the annual used-book sale in October. The books are dusted, sorted, and attractively displayed by SITCA members. Approximately eight hundred dollars is made. This money goes into the scholarship fund. At graduation, a scholarship is given in each of the two high schools.

At Christmas, a car is decorated for the local parade. Several SITCA members dress up in costumes and march along in the procession. Then a party is held which may include a hayride, Christmas caroling, and hot chocolate.

In spring, the major effort of SITCA is the annual clean-up project. Dressed in jeans, members arm themselves with hoes, rakes, and shovels. They work with vigor. For the past two years, SITCA has been awarded a certificate of recognition from the governor's achievement program.

"Christmas in April" sounds amusing. Actually, it is a Y.M.C.A. sponsored project which is directed towards helping elderly property owners who are not able to have repairs made on their homes. These repairs consist mainly of carpentry, plumbing, roofing, and painting. SITCA members work where their abilities best fit in.

Every month SITCA members have a breakfast meeting. They discuss how their projects are going.

At the end of the school year, two new directors are chosen for the coming year. Although SITCA does not function during the summer, its directors are busy making plans for new projects to be done the following school year. SITCA has been a very successful organization in Midland. Not only are students working together to help their community, they also are learning responsibility and ways of helping others. What better outcome could an organization have?

329

CHECKING PROGRESS

1. What is an acronym? What phrase does the acronym SITCA stand for?
2. How many students can become members of SITCA in Midland, Texas?
3. What are the requirements for membership in SITCA?
4. What are SITCA's projects and activities? Choose two of these and explain in more detail.
5. When are new directors chosen?

CHOOSING NEXT STEPS

1. Try to make up some words which would fit these acronyms: WAY (Where Are You?) ROCK, STONE, BAG.
2. Make up some of your own acronyms. Be sure to include the phrase that the acronym stands for.
3. What do you think is the main advantage of using acronyms? Explain your thoughts.
4. Find out if your city has a SITCA organization. If so, ask one of the sponsors or directors to come to your class and explain what is being done.
5. What do you think would be the most rewarding feeling that would come from working in an organization such as SITCA?
6. What other kinds of volunteer work are available for you to do in your community?

CLUES FOR CAREER CHOICES

THINKING THINGS THROUGH

A seventh-grade student wrote the following poem:

The things we could do;
The heights we could reach;
If only we knew the outcomes of each!

The student has expressed a desire to know what will happen in the future. We all wonder what the future will bring. What will we be doing ten or twenty years from now? It's fun to wonder and to think imaginatively about the future. But we can do more than just imagine. We can scout around now and make plans for what we will be doing in the future. Now is the time to look for clues which will help us in making career choices. The following article will tell you about such clues. Where will your clues lead you?

ABOUT WORDS

Besides using clues as guidelines for career choices, we can also use clues to play word games. Here is a game to broaden your word skills. You can play it with a partner.

1. Choose a word which you want your partner to guess.
2. Think of a one-word clue which suggests the word.
3. Tell this clue to your partner.
4. Let your partner guess what the word is.

If he guesses, you get ten points. If he is wrong, give him another clue. After the second clue, you get only nine points when he correctly guesses the word. For each clue that is given, you will get one less point when he identifies the word. Keep track of your score. Then let him think of a word and clues. Fifty points wins the game. For example, the word "brave" might have clues such as: bold, valiant, courageous, daring. But a word like "fox" might need several clues (such as animal, red, sly) to be guessed.

331

BEFORE YOU READ

INVESTIGATE

Clues For Career Choices

"What am I able to do? How do I find out what I can do well?"

These two questions come to mind when we consider what careers we should choose. Luckily, we have clues which can provide us with guidelines for career choices. There are five sources which serve as clues: tests, school performance, home performance, hobbies, and health.

Tests

Educational tests can give us information about ourselves. The achievement tests tell us how well we are performing compared to others like us. Interest tests show what activities we like or dislike. Aptitude tests predict our future success in a certain area. If we like and do well in a particular field, maybe we should consider some aspect of that field as a possible career.

Performance at School

School performance includes grades, classroom participation, and activities. School cannot be used alone to predict success, but it does indicate much about your behavior. These patterns tell future employers something about what they can expect from you. They also tell you what you can expect from yourself. In what areas have you performed best? Have you explored a wide range of courses? Junior high and high school should be the times when we explore. We should be trying new things to find our special abilities.

Performance at Home

Our behavior in one place is often different than in another. This is very true in the home. Here we can find clues about responsibility and about how we will react under certain situations.

For example, do you finish your chores? Or, if your five-year-old brother skins his knee, are you able to take care of him?

Hobbies

Hobbies are a means of exploring your interests and developing your skills. Depending upon the hobby, you may choose to develop it into a career. For example, a person who enjoys pets may choose to to become a veterinarian.

Health

This area includes physical health and personality.

Some jobs may require us to have physical strength and endurance. Other jobs call for certain types of personalities. We need to look at our abilities to get along with other people. How tolerant are we of others? How flexible are we? Can we adjust to situations easily?

Some of us can get along with a greater variety of people than others can.

By using these five clues, you can more easily be guided into a career that is right for you. Now is the time to play detective and see where your clues will lead you.

CHECKING PROGRESS

1. What are five sources of information which can offer clues to our career choices?
2. Why should junior high and high school be the time for exploring new courses and trying new things?
3. What two clues can be found in home performance?
4. What may a hobby develop into?

CHOOSING NEXT STEPS

1. Make two lists of behavior patterns at school which:
   (a) predict probable success in a future career.
   (b) predict possible problems in a future career.
   Make similar lists of behavior patterns at home.
2. Take a look at yourself. How do you get along with yourself? How do you get along with others? Which personality traits help you most in:
   (a) getting your work done at school and at home?
   (b) getting along with other people?
   (c) getting along with yourself?
3. What are some of your personality traits that you wish were different? How could you change these traits?
4. Invite a person who has an interesting hobby to come and share it with your class.
5. Make a family tree of careers. First find out about the careers of family members as far back as possible—such as grandparents, aunts, and uncles. Then list people's names and their careers on a poster, beginning with the person who goes farthest back in time and ending with the person who is most recent. You may wish to illustrate the poster.

BEYOND BARRIERS

THINKING THINGS THROUGH

No doubt you have known persons with handicaps who were able to do things which seemed impossible for them to do. These people have gone "beyond barriers." Many people go beyond barriers, and some even make them into bridges that lead to success and happiness. As you read this selection, watch for instances where barriers have become bridges. Keep a list of the people who have gone beyond them to find happiness.

ABOUT WORDS

For each sentence, choose a word from the list below that means the same as the definition found in parenthesis.

aristocracy	ludicrous
credence	mediocre
dynamic	misshapen
insurmountable	rigorous

1. He never complains, although his entire back is (out-of-shape, deformed).
2. Helen Keller's life typifies a struggle against what seemed to be (impossible to overcome) barriers.
3. Every day he did (difficult or strict) exercises and gradually strengthened himself.
4. Even in a wheelchair he was still a (powerful) individual.
5. Abraham Lincoln was so tall compared to other men that people considered him (ridiculous) in appearance.
6. Since the United States does not have a born (nobility), wealth has been the measurement for social success.
7. Mental barriers can occur . . . when others don't give full (acceptance or belief) to your ideas.
8. Louis Pasteur was rated as (neither good nor bad, average) in chemistry when he attended college.

335

INVESTIGATE

BEYOND BARRIERS

Swoosh!! The cement came out in one big rush. The man never had a chance to jump aside. He was badly battered and covered with cement. Soon he realized that he was paralyzed. His nerves were permanently damaged and he could not control his hands. But Glen Holmquist never gave up. He had real grit. Even though he could not use his hands, he found ways to do his carpentry work. For example, he can drive nails by using a special nail holder which straps around his hand and holds the nail.

People *like* Glenn Holmquist. They admire his spirit and his cheerfulness. He never complains, although his entire back is misshapen. His attitude is an inspiration to all who know him. Glenn is a fine example of the many persons in the United States who have overcome barriers.

There are several types of barriers: physical, social, mental, and cultural. This article will tell about many people who have encountered and gone beyond such barriers during their lifetimes.

Physical Barriers

Helen Keller's life typifies a struggle against what seemed to be insurmountable barriers. She was left blind and deaf from a childhood illness when she was nineteen months old. Eventually she could "see" by feeling a person's face. She was able to "hear" by putting her fingertips on a person's throat. Also she learned to speak. Years later she graduated with honors from Radcliffe College. Helen Keller's story has given encouragement to many people who cannot see or hear. Never again would anyone be able to say that being blind and deaf is an impossible barrier to overcome.

Theodore Roosevelt is another example of a person who went beyond physical barriers. As a boy he suffered from asthma. He was very sickly and weak. But he was determined to do something to improve his condition. Every day he did rigorous exercises and gradually strengthened himself. For a while he even worked as a cattleman in the West. During his lifetime he worked hard to maintain his physical strength. History remembers him as the man

with a strong will who accomplished many things and was a great President.

Still another example is Franklin Delano Roosevelt. At the age of thirty-nine he was handsome, personable, rich, and seemed to have a promising future. But he began to feel tired and his legs ached. Gradually his condition got worse. He realized that he had polio. His legs withered and he was paralyzed from the waist down. Yet he refused to accept the life of an invalid. With the help of his wife and close associates, he gradually regained strength. Soon he

could walk with a cane. He could drive his own car with its hand-operated controls. Even in a wheelchair he was still a dynamic individual. During this period he was elected governor of New York and later served as President.

Often a young person without a handicap feels that he does have one. Many people think they are too tall, short, ugly, or fat. Others think their noses are too big or their feet too flat.

No one looks like he would like to look—even the most beautiful girl or the most handsome boy. Jewelers remark that even the most beautiful diamond has a flaw that may not be seen with the naked eye. So it is with human beings. Everyone usually thinks he has a flaw somewhere. But a flaw can be turned into an asset.

Abraham Lincoln was so tall compared to other men that people considered him ludicrous in appearance. But when they learned to respect him, his height only added to his stature as a person. Napoleon was only

five feet tall but men learned to respect him for his great military genius. Wilt Chamberlain has used his tallness to make thousands of dollars as a top basketball player. Willie Shoemaker has used his shortness to become a successful horse jockey. Being tall or short should not be a barrier to success. A physical condition only becomes a barrier when it is thought to be one.

Kate Smith was considered fat. When she went to New York to enter show business, she became the object of comedians' jokes. But she accepted these jokes good-naturedly and went on to become the number one radio star in the late 1930's and early 1940's. The model Twiggy turned her thinness into a trademark of modeling. Being fat or thin should not become a barrier to success or happiness.

Phyllis Diller became successful largely because of her ability to make jokes at what she considered her ugliness. Eleanor Roosevelt was told by her mother that she was not an attractive

girl and that she would have to develop her personality to get along with people. She later became one of the most admired women in the world. Bert Lahr thought he had one of the ugliest faces in show business. Yet few people considered him ugly since he was an outstanding actor, a great humanitarian, and a funny person. Paul Newman, on the other hand, believes that his handsome face has kept him from receiving certain serious acting jobs. The view of ugly, handsome, or beautiful is in the eyes of the beholder.

Social Barriers

A person does not have to be from a wealthy background in order to achieve success and happiness. A wealthy person may have an easier time in life, but this is not necessarily true. Many rich people work long hours a day. Physical handicaps occur in wealthy families, as in the case of Franklin D. Roosevelt. Tragedy visits the rich and poor alike.

Since the United States does not have a born aristocracy, wealth has been the measurement for social success. Today more and more

people are being judged on their uniqueness as individuals. To fully assess your social development, you need to consider factors other than personal wealth.

Abraham Lincoln was a poor farm boy who became a successful lawyer and then President of the United States. George Washington Carver was a black who came from a slave background. He became famous for his experiments with the peanut. Amelia Earhart earned money on her own for flying lessons. She became the first woman to fly over the Atlantic Ocean. Benjamin Franklin was from a very poor family and became a great statesman.

It is important to find outlets in school activities to develop social poise and confidence in your abilities. Lack of the social graces can be a barrier to future employment in certain jobs. It is important to know how to meet and converse with people, and how to conduct yourself in a social setting. Your social development depends a great deal on you.

340

Mental Barriers

Mental barriers can occur when you doubt your ability or when others don't give full credence to your ideas. You may believe that you're not as smart as you would like to be. However, history is full of examples you should consider before you decide you're not smart. Einstein was four years old before he could speak and seven before he could read. Beethoven's music teacher once said of him, "As a composer he is hopeless." F.W. Woolworth got a job in a dry goods store, but his employers would not let him wait on customers because he didn't have "enough sense." A newspaper editor fired Walt Disney because he had "no good ideas." Louis Pasteur was rated as "mediocre" in chemistry when he attended college. Abraham Lincoln went into the Black Hawk War as a captain but came out as a private. Louisa May Alcott was told that her stories would never be popular.

What may appear to you now as a mental barrier may

not be a barrier later on in life. Many people have been misjudged about their intellectual capacities. You may just be a "late bloomer," a person whose abilities improve at a later time in life.

Everyone can learn something. There is probably at least one thing or maybe more at which you are especially good. Hardly anyone is equally good at every task. Your job is to find out what you can do best.

Cultural Barriers
There was a time in the United States when having white, black, yellow, or red skin meant having a different life style. Even today all cultural barriers have not been lifted. But the door to opportunity is open much wider than it used to be.

It is important to remember all barriers—physical, social, mental, and cultural —can influence your development. Depending upon your attitude, these forces can help you or they can hinder you. With determination, you can overcome most of them. What lies beyond barriers? Happiness. Success. Self-fulfillment. The decision of overcoming your barriers is up to you.

CHECKING PROGRESS

1. Make a list of the people in this article who have gone beyond barriers and have found happiness.
2. What are the four types of barriers? For each type, name a person who overcame that barrier.
3. Compare two persons from this article who had physical handicaps.
   (a) At about what age did each person become handicapped?
   (b) What things did each person do in order to overcome the handicap and find success in life?
   (c) What type of career did each person have?
4. When can a mental barrier occur?
5. Give some examples of people who seemed to have poor mental ability but who really had extraordinary talents.
6. What is a "late bloomer"?

CHOOSING NEXT STEPS

1. Which barrier do you think is the most difficult to overcome? Tell why.
2. Do you have any mental barriers, or do you ever doubt your ability? How can you overcome these barriers?
3. Read biographies of some of the persons mentioned in this article. Share what you read with your class.
4. Interview someone who has overcome a barrier. First ask this person's permission for an interview. Then ask such questions as:
   (a) How did you overcome your barrier?
   (b) Who is the person who helped you the most?
   (c) Have you been able to help others with the same barrier?

THINKING AND PROBLEM-SOLVING

THINKING THINGS THROUGH

The world in which we live is largely a technical and auto-mated world. We use machines every day. For many years people worried that machines would take away all the jobs. But actually they have created new jobs. These new jobs call for workers who have more skills than just reading, writing, and arithmetic. Workers today must have a more important skill: the ability to think.

Thinking involves solving problems. When we solve a problem we often get a new outlook. Then we have learned something. No one can afford to stop learning today. Most situations and problems have solutions which we can discover if we know how to think.

The next article tells about skills in thinking which are to be used for solving problems. Read the article. What do you think?

ABOUT WORDS

The following article contains words you may not under-stand. Some of these words are listed below. Copy the words in the left-hand column. Then find the correct definition for each word in the right-hand column and write it after the word. Use your dictionary if you need to.

automated   related to
ongoing   piece of metal that acts as a safety
relevant   device for an electric current
fuse   mechanically operated
electrical circuit   complete path of an electric current
     continuous

343

INVESTIGATE

Thinking And Problem-Solving

Learning to think requires the development of certain skills for solving problems. Life itself is an ongoing experience of solving problems. Successful individuals in all occupations know how to work effectively with any problem which may arise. To solve problems, a person must be able to:

1. identify the problem.
2. find information relevant to the problem.
3. draw conclusions.
4. act appropriately on the conclusions drawn.
5. cooperate with others.

These skills are useful in all career areas. Let's see how well they work with a simple problem.

A Problem to Solve

Suppose that you and your friends are talking in the living room. You turn on the lamp but it doesn't light. Now try to use the five basic skills of problem solving.

344

First, identify the problem. You need light but the lamp does not go on.

Second, find information relevant to the problem. Maybe you remember some things about electrical circuits. Or you can look in a book for information.

Third, draw conclusions. You learn from the information that there may be several sources for the problem: the light bulb, the plug, the wire line, and the source of electrical power.

Fourth, you act on these conclusions. Try a new light bulb. It still doesn't work. Is the lamp plugged in? Yes. Is the line frayed or cut? No, it looks fine. Finally, you check the source of power, the fuse system. You find that one fuse has blown out. When you put in a new fuse, the lamp goes on.

Fifth, and perhaps the most important thing to remember is to cooperate with others. Whenever possible, protect the feelings of other people. It is wise to ask questions such as: "Is the lamp plugged in? Can I check it for you?" Offer your help but never try to hurt people. If you say: "You knucklehead, did you ever think to change the bulb?", you are sure to make people angry. Always approach a problem carefully. We need to have consideration for other people in order to work well with them. Cooperation is a necessary skill.

These five basic skills can help you to solve problems effectively. The ability to solve problems is important to your future. Employers want people who are ready to think and act under any circumstances. Thinking people can adjust to new situations. They are easily retrained for any new jobs that may arise. If you become effective in finding solutions to problems, you will be more valuable to yourself and more useful to your employer.

CHECKING PROGRESS

1. What are the five things a person must be able to do in order to solve problems?
2. Which skill in question 1 does the author think is most important? Tell why. Which skill do you think is most important? Explain why.
3. Why do employers want people who are ready to think and act under any circumstances?

CHOOSING NEXT STEPS

1. Which of these statements show a sense of cooperation? Explain why you think so.
   (a) "May I offer a suggestion?"
   (b) "How could you forget to do that?"
   (c) "Are you crazy? That could never work."
   (d) "How about if we try this."
   (e) "I think I have an idea."
2. Choose one of the following situations. Imagine yourself using the five skills of problem-solving. Tell how you would reach a conclusion.
   (a) Your basketball is not in the place where you remember leaving it.
   (b) The radio does not go on.
   (c) The library sends you a note that a book is overdue, but you think you already returned it.
   (d) Your sweater has a hole in it.
3. Make a comic strip or cartoon showing cooperation or lack of cooperation with others.

MISS CINDER RELLA

THINKING THINGS THROUGH

"Miss Cinder Rella" is a fairy tale with a not-so-happy ending. It tells the story of what might have happened to Cinderella if her fairy godmother had lost her magic wand.

This type of story can be described as a *parody*, a story which imitates another story in order to ridicule it or to make it seem funny. In this particular case the author changes the famous fairy tale about Cinderella to help him make his point in an amusing way.

ABOUT WORDS

There is a section, called the *prologue*, which is read by an announcer at the beginning of the play. There is another section, called the *epilogue*, which is read by the announcer at the end of the play. After reading the play, see if you can tell what the purpose of the prologue and epilogue is. Then look up both terms in the dictionary. How does the dictionary definition of the words differ from yours?

Here are some other words that appear in the story. If you don't know their meanings, look them up in the dictionary before you begin reading the play.

plight	composure
salable	domestic
sage	moral

347

miss cinder rella

Announcer: (Reading the prologue) Attention, audience! Pay heed to the plight of Miss Cinder Rella so you won't find yourself in a similar position one day. Her story shows the need for a salable skill in the job marketplace. It also shows the need for getting a high school education. A sage once said, "A word to the wise is sufficient." Let the play begin!

Scene: The scene opens in the office of Mr. L.M. Choosey, who is the owner of a large airplane factory. A sign on his desk, center stage, says in big letters, "Boss." As the scene opens, Mr. Choosey is sitting at his desk smoking a cigar and writing something on a piece of paper. He hears someone knocking at the door.

Mr. Choosey: Come in!

(Miss Cinder Rella enters, looking about the office timidly.)

Mr. Choosey: Well, don't just stand there! Who are you, and what do you want?

Cinder: (Frightened) I'm Miss Rella. Miss Cinder Rella. (She regains her composure and walks over to his desk.) Are you Mr. I.M. Choosey?

Mr. Choosey: Yes, I am. But my friends call me "Boss."

Cinder: Well, I'm from the ACME employment agency. I really need a job. Oh, Mr. Choosey, I need a job so badly.

348

Mr. Choosey: Hmmmmmmmmmmm. Well, what can you do?

Cinder: Oh, I'm a marvelous floor sweeper—and I wash windows beautifully. I'm also good at cleaning out chimneys and dusting rooms and washing walls...

Mr. Choosey: Is cleaning all you can do?

Cinder: Well, yes, sir. It's all I've ever learned to do.

Mr. Choosey: And what experience do you have?

Cinder: Oh, I've worked for years for my mean stepmother and my three stepsisters. They were all pretty hard to please, sir. My work had to be perfect.

Mr. Choosey: I'm sure you can clean very well, but didn't you ever think of planning any other career? There are hundreds of job openings for girls who are willing to learn and work toward them.

Cinder: But I never needed to—I mean, this whole thing is a terrible mistake, sir. You see, actually, the way it was planned, I was supposed to be a princess.

Mr. Choosey: A princess?

Cinder: Oh, yes, sir. I was to go to this big dance, meet the prince, and lose a glass slipper. I was supposed to end up marrying the prince, but it didn't work out. (She sobs into her handkerchief.)

Mr. Choosey: There, there, my dear. I'm sure you would have been an excellent princess. What went wrong?

Cinder: Well, my fairy godmother was supposed to help me out. She was supposed to turn mice into horses and a pumpkin into a coach to take me to the dance. But she got in a rush and lost her magic wand.

Mr. Choosey: Then what happened?

350

Cinder: When my mean stepmother came home from the dance, the mice and the pumpkin were all over the living room...and she kicked me out, Mr. Choosey. Oh, I'm desperate. Please give me a job.

Mr. Choosey: Well, I'd really like to help you, but we don't need a floor sweeper right now. We need engineers, secretaries, and mechanics, but not floor sweepers.

Cinder: Please! (Sob)

Mr. Choosey: All right...what did you say your salary was at your last place of employment?

Cinder: Three cups of water and two crusts of bread a day.

Mr. Choosey: Well, we'll try you out. And since you've had those years of experience working for your stepmother, we'll give you a raise. We'll give you four cups of water and three crusts of bread a day.

Cinder: Oh, thank you, sir!

Mr. Choosey: And if you work hard, in a year or so maybe we'll promote you to head floor sweeper.

Cinder: Oh, I will! I'll work hard, Mr. Choosey.

Mr. Choosey: Good! Now, let's fill out this job application. (He takes a pen and a piece of paper from his desk.)

Cinder: Okay, what do you need to know?

Mr. Choosey: Where do you live?

Cinder: Well, my fairy godmother let me move in with her. We live at 941 Forest Lane.

Mr. Choosey: Where did you graduate from high school?

Cinder: Oh! Is that important? I mean, I dropped out of school in the eighth grade.

Mr. Choosey: Well, Miss Rella, that's too bad. I'm sorry, really sorry. But these days no one hires anyone who doesn't have at least a high school diploma. I'm sorry but I can't give you the job.

Cinder: (She rises.) Oh! (Sob) If only I had thought ahead! I never realized how little I knew how to do. (Sob) Who would have ever thought I would end up like this? (She is crying as she leaves the office.)

Mr. Choosey: Too bad about that. She was a nice girl, too. Miss Rella. Miss Cinder Rella. That's funny. Seems like I've heard that name someplace before.

Announcer: (Reading epilogue) Well, you might be asking yourself, what did Cinder Rella end up doing? Years later she is still sweeping out chimneys in whatever household will hire her. She has never learned how to do anything else. Her pay did increase with the times—five crusts of bread four cups of water.

You might also be asking, "Whatever happened to the prince?" Right now the prince is out of work. His country became a republic and there was no longer any need for royalty. And the prince didn't know how to do anything but be a prince.

The moral of the story is clear. Those who do not sit on thrones and do not have reliable fairy godmothers must have a salable skill and an education if they are to support themselves in life.

CHECKING PROGRESS

1. State the moral or lesson of the play in your own words. Then compare what you said with the statement that was given in the epilogue.
2. Reread the prologue and the epilogue to the play, "Miss Cinder Rella." What is told in the prologue? What is told in the epilogue?
3. What do you think are some types of skills that might be especially salable in today's job market?
4. What are some skills that might have been salable in the job market one hundred years ago?
5. What are skills that might not be salable within the next one hundred years?

CHOOSING NEXT STEPS

1. Plan with one of your classmates to present the play, "Miss Cinder Rella," in one of the ways listed below.
   (1) Wear costumes and present the play on stage.
   (2) Read the play and record it on a tape recorder. Then play it for your classmates.
   (3) Make your own puppets and use them to present the play on a puppet stage.
2. Write your own play. Prepare a prologue and an epilogue and have the play teach a moral or lesson. You may make it a parody if you want.
3. Read some plays you have selected from the library.

FOREVER YOURS

THINKING THINGS THROUGH

Have you ever thought about something as being forever yours? What possessions do you have that you consider permanent? What opportunities do you consider to be available at all times? In this selection the author discusses something that is really yours forever. Read the selection and find out what it is that the author points out as something permanent or forever yours.

ABOUT WORDS

1. Look up the meanings of the following words which are used in this selection and add them to your vocabulary list.

   adjoining   visualize
   dramatic   customs
   nourishing   circumstances
   primitive   cultural
   flourishing   consultant
   antiques   artifacts

2. Write five sentences of your own using as many of the above listed words as you can.

3. On the first page of the selection, "Forever Yours," the author has used two similes. Find the sentences and explain what you think the author had in mind when he wrote them.

BEFORE YOU READ

355

INVESTIGATE

Forever Yours

In the mass of caps and gowns it was hard to pick the two of them out. Being side by side in Central's largest graduating class was a result of alphabetical order. She was Frances B. and he was Frank B. She would move across the stage one step ahead of him. Now they were as alone and as lost as threads in a carpet.

Everyone in the class knew about them. All of the parents knew about them. Soon everyone in the audience would know about them. Their names would be called.

Now they were as one in a sea of sameness. Their togetherness was strengthened by the words of the speaker. Others may have seen her admiring smile, but only the one to her left felt it—knew its real meaning. One or two others saw the salty tear slip down her cheek. Only the one on the left knew why it was there. No one saw him ease a strong hand over her fingers, for the sleeves of the gowns draped their hands.

The moment came. All in caps and gowns stood. The A's were already across the stage. Some B's had gone. Frances B. was stepping upon the stage, assisted by the young man who was standing by the steps to give all the ladies a hand. The principal arose and signaled Frank B. forward. He smiled a message to the president of the school board, who was giving out the diplomas. The president picked up another diploma. He had one in each hand.

"We delay a moment here," the president announced, "to give two diplomas at the same time."

The principal moved to the microphone. "Ladies and gentlemen, Frank Brace was to have been the last member of his family to graduate from Central. Two brothers and a sister have finished ahead of him. We are pleased to announce that another Brace will finish with him."

The president of the school board extended two diplomas and exclaimed: "Frank Brace and his mother, Frances Brace!"

Mrs. Brace held on to Frank's strong arm as they walked across the stage and down the steps. The audience rose and applauded.

When the Braces were back at their places and the audience was seated, the principal explained, "Mrs. Brace has been here each morning for years, helping to fix hot lunches for all of us. She has gone to school at night. Next year she will be our lunchroom manager."

More applause filled the auditorium. Not everyone may have the dramatic experience of Mrs. Frances Brace. Not everyone will graduate from school after raising a family. A chief reason for going to school is to *learn how to learn*.

The mind of the person needs nourishing just as the body does. In learning for today we learn also for the future—by using our senses, asking questions, giving answers, working with others, knowing how to find out things, using what we learn, and making it part of our thinking and doing. This helps us to keep up with changes, find new facts, and extend what we know.

In the classroom everybody is a teacher and a student. We teach each other many things in our own way. Learning can be fun.

We are never too old to learn. Consider Grandma Moses. At seventy-eight years of age she began learning to paint with oils. She had enjoyed doing simple pictures with her needle and thread. When her fingers became too stiff for needlework, she took up oil painting and became famous for her paintings of rural scenes. She enjoyed painting scenes from her childhood in the hills of New York State, and similar settings she had loved. She relived happy

357

the birds, the horses, the sleighs, the hills, the old houses, and much more she saw in the wide out-of-doors.

We keep on learning for many reasons. Sometimes we keep on learning just to satisfy ourselves and to live more fully. A *senora* from South America was teaching Spanish at the YMCA evening school. There were teachers, businessmen, lawyers, and others in the class. All wanted to learn to speak Spanish—some went for business reasons, some for cultural reasons, and some for personal reasons. Soon Spanish could be heard.

"*Muy bien*," (very well—fine!) the *senora* said to the oldest member of the class after he answered a question in Spanish.

"*Cuantos anos tiene vd.?*" (how old are you?) she asked with interest.

"*Tengo setenta y dos anos,*" (seventy-two) he replied at once.

Cheers were followed by remarks in English. A manager of a warehouse said, "Come sit in my stockroom so you can interpret for my

days of the past this way and stretched her mature days into new ways of seeing and feeling and new ways of communicating with others. She lived to the age of one hundred and one. Her paintings hang in museums throughout America. Because she kept on learning and doing, the world now can visualize the snows,

Spanish-speaking employees. I will pay well."

The old gentlemen shook his head in the way that means "no." "Not yet," he said. "See me after I get tired of retirement."

"See me now," a young typist in the class said. "I will be your *bilingual* (two-language) secretary — if the pay is good."

The seventy-two-year-old man spent two months vacationing in Mexico. The typist got the job as the bilingual secretary.

A hobby can lead to much learning. This, in turn, can lead to a new life. An oil company executive liked gardens and lawns. His company's need for beautiful lawns and his interest in lawns as a hobby led him to become a lawn specialist. He learned about different grasses, soils, fertilizers, pests, lawn care, and all that a person needs to know in order to keep a lawn growing and flourishing. This interest was outside his duties as an executive, but it made him more valuable to his company.

After retirement he made speeches about lawn care and his speeches were printed. A company invited him to be their consultant for a lawn development program. Homeowners asked him for advice. He finally set up a firm to advise people on the care of their lawns.

Another man who had produced films for a living became interested in developing phonetic spellings of the English language. With the help of his wife he developed a *Sensubul Speling Dikshuneri*. He learned so much about English words that he attracted the attention of scholars across the country. He has had fun learning and has influenced others to learn.

A school official and his wife who was a teacher became interested in antiques and artifacts. She studied cut glass; he studied arrowheads and other Indian artifacts. When they retired, they turned their hobby into a business and made a good living.

Learning is forever. It is forever yours.

CHECKING PROGRESS

1. State the main idea of "Forever Yours" in one sentence using your own words.
2. Explain what you think the author means by the statement: "A chief reason for going to school is to *learn how to learn.*" Rereading the first three paragraphs following the introductory story will help you decide what the author means.
3. What are some reasons why you think people need to keep on learning?

CHOOSING NEXT STEPS

1. Write a short selection about how you learned something such as:
   (1) how I learned to swim
   (2) how I learned to sew
   (3) how I learned to play baseball
   (4) how I learned to cook
   (5) how I learned to play the piano
2. Write or give an oral description about one of the following:
   (1) how to care for a pet
   (2) how to plant a garden
   (3) how to make a dress
   (4) how to play basketball
3. Interview a writer, a composer of music, or an inventor who lives in your area. Ask questions such as:
   (1) When did you decide you wanted to do the work you are now doing?
   (2) Why did you want to do it?
   (3) What are some of the ways you learned to do this?

HELP WANTED

THINKING THINGS THROUGH

How would you go about looking for a job? One place you might look is in the Want Ad section of a newspaper. But there are many ads printed every day. How do you choose which jobs might be right for you?

To start, you might want to consider what your qualifications are. You wouldn't want to apply for a job as a truck driver if you didn't have a chauffeur's licence. Your qualifications for a job might be based on courses you have taken in school or work experience you have had. You should match your qualifications with those requested in the ads.

Each page in this selection shows some want ads as they might appear in the newspaper. Each page also tells the educational background and work experience of a person who is looking for a job. Which jobs do you think each person should apply for? What are their qualifications? What qualifications are asked for in the ads?

ABOUT WORDS

These are some terms appearing in the ads which might not be familiar to you. Be sure to find their meanings before you begin reading this selection.

profit sharing
resume
references
fringe benefits

361

INVESTIGATE

HELP WANTED

X-Ray Technician

If you are a conscientious, qualified, registered technician interested in performing a dependable, professional job for which you were trained, we have openings for you. Our benefits are competitive, and we have a superior radiology dept. We have positions open full time, part time, and on call.

Call or apply to Personnel, 671-3100, Ext. 414.

General Hospital
8600 Logan   Woodlawn

PHARMACIST

Full-time. Excellent working conditions. No Sundays or holidays. Benefits include insurance plus bonus. Call Jack, 443-2170.

Ambulance Driver

Must be over 21 and desire opportunity for lifelong career. Steady work. No experience necessary. 644-2727.

Medical Assistant

Medical assistant or trainee for work in office of general practice. References needed. For interview, call Dr. Jackson at 758-1325.

Registered Nurses

Are you a nurse who loves children? Do you have lots of patience? Are you willing to work hard? If you can answer yes to all 3 questions, Mrs. Walters, our head nurse, and our 47 pediatrics patients need you now. Day or evening shift. Call 552-1222.

Nursing Director

We are seeking an individual with demonstrated managerial ability. Bachelor's degree required. Master's degree desirable. Salary open. Exceptional fringe benefits. Call for appointment, 287-1500, Ext. 11.
Mr. Sommers
Mitchell Memorial Hosp.
203 N. Central Ave.
Parkview

RN'S

Excellent opportunities available to work in modern suburban hospital. Positions available in medical-surgical and psychiatric units. For further information and confidential interview, contact Mrs. Nichols, 553-6200.

Educational Background

1971-74   School: Parkson School of Nursing

1974   Passed examination needed to become a registered nurse in this state.

Work Experience

1968-71   Hospital: Talcott Medical Center

Job Description: Volunteer work as candy striper. Duties included answering phones, bringing mail to patients, reading to patients, and assisting nurses with non-medical duties.

362

Educational Background

1962-67   School: Northern University
           Major: Business Administration   Minor: Finance
           Degree: Bachelor of Science

1967-70   Attended four classes at IBM school to learn programming languages, COBOL and BAL.

Work Experience

1967-70   Company: Mitchell Insurance Co.
           Job Description: Began working as a computer operator on an IBM 360/30 computer system. Began training for a programming position in 1968. Was promoted to manager of computer center in 1969. Supervised three programmers, two computer operators, and three keypunch operators.
           Reason for Leaving: Was offered a better position.

1970-   Company: York State Bank
           Job Description: Manage a computer center. Supervise twenty people. Design operations of banking procedures and do programming. Supervised the change from IBM 360 system to IBM 370 system.
           Reason for leaving: No advancement opportunities.

Educational Background

1968-72   School: Norton High School
1973   School: Viking College Night School
           Class: Beginning Typing—received 3 credit hours

Work Experience

1972-73   Company: Acme Electrical Co.
           Job Description: Did general office work, including filing and typing. Also did light bookkeeping.
           Reason for Leaving: Wanted higher salary.
1973-   Company: Wilson Business Machines
           Job Description: Do general office work. Duties include filing and some light typing.

364

Educational Background

1966-68 School: Trinton Community College
Degree: Associate in Applied Sciences
Major: Drafting Technology

Work Experience

1967- Company: Norris Oil Corporation
Job Description: Prepare preliminary layouts, location plans, and piping sketches. Prepare finished piping designs, flow sheets, layouts, piping drawings, bills of materials, and piping details. Review contractors piping drawings to see if they follow the specifications of the company.

CHECKING PROGRESS

1. How do you go about choosing a job which might be right for you?
2. Which jobs did you select for each person in this selection?
3. Tell why each of the following might be important to a company hiring someone for a job. What other things might the company want to consider?
   (a) education
   (b) work experience
   (c) age
4. Tell why each of these things might be important to you when applying for a job. What other things about a company might you want to consider?
   (a) location and size of company
   (b) fringe benefits
   (c) working conditions
5. What information is included in most want ads?
6. What are some of the ways in which a person might contact a company about applying for a job?

CHOOSING NEXT STEPS

1. Try to find a book in the library about writing resumes. What information is included in a resume?
2. Matching people with jobs, and jobs with people is one of the duties of an employment counselor. Try to arrange for an employment counselor to come and speak to your class. Each class member should prepare one or two questions to ask him about his job.
3. One of the people described in this selection has only had volunteer work experience. How do you think this kind of experience can help when applying for a job?

FOOTPRINTS

THINKING THINGS THROUGH

What makes a poem something special and enjoyable to read? It is the patterning and repetition of sounds. It is the meaning and feeling created by the poet's use and arrangement of words. When you read a poem:

1) listen for repetition of sounds.
2) observe rhythmic patterns.
3) give attention to the meaning.
4) catch the feeling and thought of the poem.

ABOUT WORDS

There is one kind of poem, called the *haiku*, which originated in Japan. It consists of only three short lines which express how the author sees or feels about something. Read the following haiku.

> Beyond the darkness,
> silent lights glimmer brightly,
> signaling the way.

Do you think the writer expresses himself well? Count the number of syllables in each line. The haiku should have five syllables in the first line, seven in the second, and five in the third. Does this haiku follow that pattern? Since a haiku only has seventeen syllables, each word becomes very important. Try writing one or more of your own haiku.

367

INVESTIGATE

footprints

There they lie
Ahead of me—
Footprints.

"The job I do has purpose and skill," says my father.
"Follow in my footprints."
"I am proud of the work I create," my mother smiles and says.
"Wouldn't you like to do it, too?"
"Come with me," my brother calls.
"Try my way of life."
"I am pleased with my job," my aunt tells me.
"It might be the one for you."

I look at the footprints.
They are not mine.
There are lessons I must learn,
Ideas I must explore,
People I must discover,
And places I must visit.
Then someday I will be able to make footprints, too.
And they will be my footprints—
Only mine—
Leaving a mark forever upon the earth.

CHECKING PROGRESS

1. In one sentence state what you think is the main idea of this poem.
2. How well do you think the poet expresses the main idea of this poem?
3. Does the poet's use and arrangement of words create the meaning and feeling of it? Give specific examples to support your answer.
4. What are four suggestions given in *Thinking Things Through* that you should follow when reading a poem?

CHOOSING NEXT STEPS

1. Read the poem, "Footprints," aloud to yourself several times, then read it to a classmate or friend.
2. Select a book of poems from the library and read for your own enjoyment.
3. Try writing a poem of your own. Decide on the main idea or thought of your poem. Either write it in your own style or follow the suggestions below for writing a *cinquain*, or five-line poem. There are other pattern variations that may be used, but this is a common one.

    first line—one word, expressing title
    second line—two words, describing title.
    third line—three words, expressing action
    fourth line—four words, expressing feeling
    fifth line—a synonym for title.

REFERENCE BOOKS: ENCYCLOPEDIAS, ALMANACS, AND ATLASES

At times we need to find out specific information about a subject. Finding the information may be a problem to us if we do not know where to look for it. Reference books found in the library can usually help us find what we need to know. Some types of reference books are encyclopedias, almanacs, and atlases. The copyright or publication date of these books is important to note because the date tells us how current the information is in the book.

ATLASES

An atlas is a book of maps. It may also include facts and figures about the places included in the maps. A geographical atlas usually contains charts, tables, and maps showing cities, towns, roads, countries, rivers, and mountains. It shows size and relationship of bodies of land and water and gives the names and location of special features and places of interest. The index lists the names of mountains, parks, and memorials. It tells where to find them on a map. Maps in the atlas may also show such things as the distribution of economic resources, population, types of climate, and plant life. Some atlases which you might find in the library are:

Goode's World Atlas
Rand McNally Cosmopolitan Atlas
Medallian World Atlas
American Heritage Pictorial History of the United States

1. What is the main content of an atlas?
2. If you want to locate a specific river or mountain, where would you look first in an atlas?
3. List several types of information which you might be able to find in an atlas.
4. Go to the library and locate at least one atlas. Find a specific river, park, or city.
5. What are some atlases that you have in your school library that are not included in the list above?
6. Why is the copyright or publication date an important thing to notice on any of the reference books that you are using?
7. How do you think *Goode's World Atlas* might differ from the *American Heritage Pictorial History of the United States*? What different kinds of information might be included in each?

Information found in encyclopedias is usually in alphabetical order. There are two types of encyclopedias, general encyclopedias and specific or special encyclopedias.

General encyclopedias deal with all subjects and give broad treatment to all sides of a subject. General encyclopedias usually have more than one volume. Some general encyclopedias which may be found in the school library are:

Colliers' Encyclopedia
Compton's Pictured Encyclopedia
Encyclopedia Americana
Britannica Junior
Encyclopedia International
World Book Encyclopedia

Most of these encyclopedias, besides being arranged alphabetically, have an index that gives a more specific breakdown of the subjects included in the encyclopedia. The index may be at the end of each volume or in a separate volume. This separate volume may also have a section which identifies the author of each of the articles or gives a list of contributing authors. This volume sometimes has an atlas in it, too.

Special encyclopedias usually are concerned with only one specific subject area. They may be complete in one volume, or there may be several volumes. Some special or specific encyclopedias which may be found in the library are:

Book of Popular Science
Encyclopedia of American History
Larousse Encyclopedia of Animal Life
Medical and Health Encyclopedia
Pictorial Encyclopedia of American History
The Reader's Encyclopedia
Van Nostrand's Scientific Encyclopedia

1. Name two types of encyclopedias which may be found in a school library. Explain the difference between the two.
2. In what order is material in an encyclopedia usually arranged?
3. How can you find out when the articles in an encyclopedia were written? Why is this information important?
4. Which of the two types of encyclopedias would be most likely to have only one volume?
5. Go to the library and locate one specific or special encyclopedia. Then locate one general encyclopedia.

An almanac or a yearbook is a book that is usually published annually and contains many kinds of information. It often includes calendars, outstanding dates and events, and facts about government, history, geography, weather, and the solar system. It may also give figures on population, industry, and natural resources.

The *World Almanac* is published every year. It contains general information—facts, statistics, and documents of that particular year. Some specifics included in the *World Almanac* are:

    Actors and Actresses
    Ambassadors
    Awards, Medals, Prizes
    Books, Best Sellers
    Cabinet, U.S.
    Ecology
    Flags
    Sports
    Heads of State
    Postal Information
    Memorable Dates
    Vital Statistics

Here are the names of some other almanacs that you might be able to find in the library:

    Information Please Almanac
    The Official Associated Press Almanac

Newspapers, such as the *New York Times*, or groups, such as the United Nations, sometimes publish almanacs. Also religious groups, business organizations, and professions with specialized information publish almanacs. Yearbooks are sometimes published to keep a series of books, such as encyclopedias, up to date.

1. How often are yearbooks and almanacs usually published?
2. Name some of the groups that publish yearbooks and almanacs.
3. For what reason would the publisher of an encyclopedia publish a yearbook?
4. List three or four types of information which may be found in the *World Almanac*.
5. Go to the library and locate the *World Almanac*.
6. What is the difference between a yearbook and an almanac?
7. Go to your school library and see if there are any yearbooks that have been published to keep encyclopedias up to date.

1. Would you look in an almanac, encyclopedia, or an atlas to find information on any one of these subjects? You may be able to find information on them in more than one kind of reference book.

   Fire

   Zebras

   The exact location of DeKalb, Illinois

   Benjamin Franklin

   Best selling books in 1973

   Mars

   Pearl Harbor

   Population of the United States in 1973

   Detailed map of the Battle of Gettysburg

   The Vice-President of the United States in 1900

2. Go to the library and use reference books to help you answer the following questions. You may be able to find the answers in more than one kind of reference book mentioned.

   (1) Who is the current mayor of Tulsa, Oklahoma?

   (2) What record album received the Grammy Award last year?

   (3) Name three players who are in Pro Football's Hall of Fame.

   (4) What is the zip code for Bluff Park, Alabama?

   (5) What is the population of Geneva, Switzerland? of Budapest, Hungary? of Barcelona, Spain?

   (6) How old is Lucille Ball? Where was she born?

   (7) How many miles is it from Chicago to New York? from Austin, Texas, to Tampa, Florida?

   (8) In what Canadian province is Lake Winnipeg?

   (9) Is Santa Barbara in the southern or northern half of the state of California?

   (10) What symbol is used to show a National Interstate Highway? a U.S. Highway?

   (11) What are some well-known beef breeds of cattle?

   (12) What was the circus like in days of ancient Rome?

   (13) What is the story of the mythological character Pegasus, the winged horse?

   (14) Who is Robert Peary, and what did he do that made him become so well known?

   (15) What is one national park found in Colorado? What is one mountain range found in Colorado?

   (16) What is the state flower of South Dakota? What is South Dakota's largest city? What is its capital city?

Pronunciation Symbols

The following guide is used by permission. From Webster's New Collegiate Dictionary, copyright 1973 by G. & C. Merriam Co., Publishers of the Merriam-Webster Dictionaries.

a as in map
ā as in day
ä as in cot
à as in father
aů as in out
b as in baby
ch as in chin
d as in did
e as in bed
ē as in easy
f as in cuff
g as in go
h as in hat

i as in tip
ī as in inside
j as in job
k as in kin
l as in pool
m as in dim
n as in no
ŋ as in sing
ō as in bone
ȯ as in saw
ȯi as in coin
p as in lip
r as in rarity

s as in less
sh as in shy
t as in tie
th as in thin
th̄ as in then
ü as in rule
ů as in pull
v as in give
w as in we
y as in yard
z as in zone
zh as in vision
ə as in banana, collect

Glossary

abstract reasoning /ab-'strakt 'rēz-niŋ/ Measures your ability to think without numbers or words to guide you. 319

achievement test /a-'chēv-mant test/ A test which measures a person's present knowledge and skills in a particular area or field. 146

acronym /'ak-rə-,nim/ A word formed from the initial letter or letters of several other words. 325

alliteration /a-,lit-a-'rā-shan/ Two or more words that begin with the same letter. 33

alphanumeric /al-fa-n(y)ü-'mer-ik/ Consisting of both letters and numbers. 97

alternative /ȯl-'tar-nat-iv/ Choice. 159

antonyms /'an-ta-,nim/ Words that have opposite meanings. 127

apprentice /ə-'prent-əs/ One who trains for a job in which special skills are learned from an experienced worker. 18

aptitude test /áp-ta-tüd test/ A test which predicts future success based on a person's knowledge and skills when he takes the test. 147

aquaculture /ák-wa-'kal-char/ The raising of aquatic plants and animals. 221

bilingual /(') bī-'liŋ-gwal/ expressed in two languages. 359

375

blinders /blīn-dərz/ Flaps put over the eyes so that they cannot see everything in sight. 145

campus /'kam-pəs/ School grounds. 172

caption /'kap-shən/ A comment that explains an illustration. 239

choice card /'chȯis 'kärd/ Card showing courses a student plans to take. 247

cinquain /siŋ-'kān/ A five-line stanza. 370

clerical and speed accuracy /'kler-i-kal an(d) 'spēd 'ak-ya-ra-sē/ Assesses your ability to accurately compare and mark lists of names and numbers. 319

climax /'klī-maks/ The time or part of anything that is of greatest interest, excitement, or importance. 63

cluster /'kləs-tər'/ A number of things that are alike and form a group. 174

connotations /kän-a-'tā-shan/ The meaning suggested by a word or thing. 141

context /'kän-tekst/ The words that surround a particular word and help explain its meaning. 17

cutaway diagram /'kat-a-'wā dī-a-gram/ A drawing which shows the outside surface cut away so that the inside may be shown easily. 93

data /'dāt-a/ Collected information. 100

diagram /'dī-a-gram/ A drawing with labels. 91

duals /'d(y)ü-al/ Double tires. 282

economic /ek-a-'näm-ik/ Having to do with wealth and its use. 239

elective /i-lek-tiv/ Something chosen based on preference. 247

empathy /'em-pa-thē/ The ability to understand another's feelings or ideas by putting oneself into their role. 136

epilogue /'ep-ə-ˌlog/ A conclusion at the end of a play or literary work. 347

flowchart /'flō-chärt/ A diagram or outline showing progress of material through a manufacturing process. 96

ford /'fo(a)rd/ A shallow part of a body of water that may be crossed by wading. 246

freedom /fred-am/ Independence; power to do as one likes. 239

376

free-lance /'frē-'lants/ One who works on his own without committing himself to any one employer. 132

futurologists /fyü-char-äl'-a-jasts/ People who predict the future from studying present day trends. 53

gauge /'gāj/ An instrument for measuring or testing. 282

growth /grōth/ Development; process of growing. 239

guidance /'gīd-ants/ The process of giving advice on careers and school problems to students. 145

haiku /'hī(,)kü/ An unrhymed Japanese poem which consists of three lines containing 5, 7, and 5 syllables respectively and which express the way the author feels about or sees something. 367

homophones /'häm-a-fōn/ Words that sound alike, but may be spelled differently or may have different meanings. 313

hypothesis /hī-'päth-a-sas/ A statement which seems to explain a scientific event. 100

impending /im-'pend-iŋ/ About to occur. 47

interest profile /'in-trast 'prō-fīl/ A graph on which a student's interest test scores are plotted. 161

interest test /'in-trast test/ A test which measures a person's tendency to like or dislike certain activities. 146

interstate /ˌint-ar-'stāt/ Connecting between two or more states. 281

justice /'jas-tas/ Rightfulness; fair dealing. 239

language usage /'laŋ-gwij 'yü-sij/ Tells how well you do in spelling, punctuation, and grammar. 319

legend /'lej-and/ Explanation of symbols. 96

manuscript /'man-ya-skript/ A handwritten or typed article. 131

mechanical reasoning /mi-'kan-i-kal 'rez-niŋ/ Measures your grasp of common laws of physics. 319

numerical ability /n(y)ù-'mer-i-kal ə-'bil-at-ē/ Indicates possible success in mathematics, physics, chemistry, and in engineering if scores are high. 319

outline /'aut-līn/ A brief summary of main points in a written work. 131

parody /'par-əd-ē/ An imitation done for comedy or ridicule. 347

personification /pər-ˌsän-ə-fə-'kā-shən/ Representing an object as human by giving it human qualities or characteristics. 79

persuasion /par-'swā-zhan/ The act of convincing others to believe in a certain cause or to respond in a certain way. 117

plot /'plät/ The plan or main story, as of a play or novel. 63

prologue /'prō-ˌlòg/ Preface; introduction. 347

regulations /ˌreg-ya-'la-shan/ A rule or order having the force of law issued by a government. 281

revving /rev-iŋ/ To operate at an increased speed. 47

rotor /'rōt-ar/ Revolving part of a rotary engine. 92

salary /'sal-a-rē/ An amount of money paid regularly for work done. 131

security /si-'kyūr-at-ē/ Certainty; a feeling of being safe. 239

seismographs /'sīz-mə-ˌgraf/ An instrument which measures and records earth vibrations. 266

sensory perception /'sen(t)s-(a)rē par-'sep-shan/ Making use of the five senses. 138

setting /'set-iŋ/ The time and place within which a scene of a play or motion picture is enacted. 63

skyline /'skī-līn/ Outline of tall building against the sky. 172

space relations /'spās ri-lā-shan/ Measures your ability to visualize the shape of surfaces from drawings to the real object. 319

stability /sta-'bil-at-e/ Unchangeableness; constancy. 239

standardized /'stan-dar-dīzd/ A test given to many people so that one can compare his results with the rest of the group. 145

stereotype /stér-ē-ə-tīp/ A general, often untrue, idea in a person's mind about what another person is like. 100

strategy /'strat-jē/ Plan of attack. 247

subtopics /səb-'täp-ikz/ Topics of lesser importance which relate to the main topics. 131

surge /'sərj/ A sudden rise in activity. 158

synonym /'sin-ə-ˌnim/ Words that have similar meanings. 127

technique /tek-'nēk/ A method used to accomplish an aim. 158

tiltmeter /'tilt-ˌmēt-ər/ An instrument to measure the tilting of the earth's surface. 267

traditional /tra-'dish-ən-l/ Subjects such as science, reading, and history which have always been taught in schools. 171

valid /val-əd/ Shown by experiments and testing to be true. 100

verbal reasoning /'vər-bəl 'rēz-niŋ/ Measures your comprehension and understanding of what is read. 319

verbal reasoning and numerical ability /'vər-bəl 'rēz-niŋ ən(d) n(y)u̇-'mer-ikəl ə-'bil-at-ē/ Indicates that a student should definitely expect to do well in college if scores are high. 319

vocational /vō-'kə-shən-l/ Subjects which give training in a skill or trade which may later become a person's career. 171

volcanologist /ˌväl-kə-'näl-ə-jəst/ A scientist who studies volcanoes. 264

Wankel /'wang-kəl/ An automobile engine which has rotors instead of pistons. 92

INDEX

380

ACKNOWLEDGMENTS

Illustrations

Jim Carleton — 42, 43, 44, 45, 88, 122, 124/125, 132, 187, 189, 205, 266, 267, 315, 317, 345, 368, 369

Roger Herrington — 25, 28, 31, 51, 53, 54, 55, 92, 93, 97, 147, 152, 163, 166, 168, 198, 200, 201, 232, 233, 237, 252, 253, 254, 256, 265, 271, 275, 284, 291, 292, 322, 323, 339, 341, 356, 358

Rudi Magnani — 10, 11, 12, 13, 52, 101, 157, 158, 192, 194, 246, 249, 297

Jack Merryweather — 65, 66, 68, 69, 71

Carol Stutz — 34, 35, 38, 58, 59, 60, 61, 112, 114, 129, 210, 211, 212

Jim Teason — Cover, 7, 48, 49, 77, 81, 85, 119, 137, 153, 229, 303

Bert Tiedemann — 142, 162, 178, 179, 181, 183, 216, 217, 307, 308, 310, 333, 349, 350, 351, 352

Other

Allied Van Lines, Inc. — 283

Argonne National Laboratory — 220

The Bettmann Archive — 18, 20

Detroit News, "Passing Dad on The Moving Stairs," cartoon by Poinier, October, 5, 1973 — 241

By permission of Johnny Hart and Field Enterprises, Inc., cartoon — "Wizard of Id" — 242

King Features Syndicate, cartoons — "Dooley's World" and "Dagwood" — 242, 243

Harold M. Lambert Studios — 89

Loyola University Medical Center — 219

Meston Specialties — 268, 269

NASA — 261

H. Armstrong Roberts — 220

Science Research Associates, Inc. — 163

Scott, Foresman and Company — 151, 152

Trans World Airlines — 223

United Features Syndicate, Inc., cartoon — "Peanuts" — 240

UPI-Compix — 337